POIROT AND ME

POIROT AND ME

David Suchet

And Geoffrey Wansell

headline

First published in 2013 by HEADLINE PUBLISHING GROUP

2

Cataloguing in Publication Data is available from the British Library

ISBN 978 0 7553 6419 0

Typeset in Garamond by Avon DataSet Ltd, Bidford-on-Avon, Warwickshire

Plate sections designed by Fiona Andreanelli

Printed and bound in the UK by Clays Ltd, St Ives plc

All photographs © ITV plc, except where marked

DISCLAIMER
This is David Suchet's personal account of his life playing Poirot and has been written by him
independently (but with necessary permission) from ITV and the Agatha Christie estate.

HEADLINE PUBLISHING GROUP
An Hachette UK Company
338 Euston Road
London NW1 3BH

www.headline.co.uk
www.hachette.co.uk

For my wife Sheila

ABOUT THE AUTHORS

DAVID SUCHET is an award-winning English actor, best known around the world for his portrayal of Hercule Poirot. In a career that has spanned more than four decades David has appeared in many theatrical productions. He is also an Associate Artist of the Royal Shakespeare Company. He has won awards for his portrayals of the university teacher John in David Mamet's *Oleanna* and the composer Antonio Salieri in Peter Shaffer's *Amadeus* in the theatre, as well as for playing two disgraced tycoons, Augustus Melmotte in Anthony Trollope's *The Way We Live Now* and Robert Maxwell, on television. A keen photographer, he is married with two adult children and lives in London. David was awarded the CBE in 2011 for services to drama. This is his first book.

GEOFFREY WANSELL is the author of more than a dozen books, including biographies of the movie star Cary Grant, the billionaire Sir James Goldsmith and the playwright Sir Terence Rattigan. He was also the authorised biographer of the Gloucester serial killer Frederick West, appointed to the role by the Official Solicitor to the Supreme Court, and is now the official historian of the

Garrick Club in London. As a journalist, he has worked for *The Times*, the *Observer*, the *Sunday Telegraph* and the *Daily Mail*, among many other newspapers and magazines in Britain and around the world. He first met David Suchet when he appeared in the film *When the Whales Came* for Twentieth Century Fox, when Geoffrey was the executive producer, and the two have remained close friends.

CONTENTS

PROLOGUE

It is a damp, chill Friday morning in November and I am feeling old, very old; so old, indeed, that I am on the brink of death. I have lost two stone in weight, my face is the colour of aged parchment, and my hands are gnarled like human claws.

I am about to breathe my last as Agatha Christie's idiosyncratic Belgian detective, Hercule Poirot, who has been a part of my life as an actor for almost a quarter of a century. I have played him in no fewer than sixty-six television films, and I am about to bid him farewell.

It is, quite simply, one of the hardest things I have ever had to do, even though I am, of course, only an actor playing a part. Poirot's death is to take place on sound stage A at Pinewood Studios in Buckinghamshire, twenty miles or so north-west of London, at eleven o'clock in the morning on this November day, and I am in the middle of the great, echoing stage where Poirot is to meet his end in this, his last case *Curtain*.

All around me are the crew of ninety with their huge lights and the swinging sound booms: the make-up and hair ladies, the director of photography, the two cameras and their operators, the man with the clapper board, and, of course, the talented young director Hettie Macdonald.

Now in her late thirties, Hettie is one of Britain's most delicate yet forceful directors, with the capacity to surprise her audience and charm her cast. She directed 'Blink', which has been called the 'scariest ever' episode of the British television series *Doctor Who*, in 2007, but she is not here to terrify anyone today: she is here to preside over the death of a fictional icon, a detective as famous as his counterpart Sherlock Holmes and who has brought every bit as much pleasure to millions around the world.

That brings sadness to the air. There is none of the usual banter and laughter of a film unit in action. Our beloved Belgian is dying, and no one can really bear it. Everyone is caught up in the emotion of watching me – as Poirot – pass away in front of their eyes.

It does not happen at once, however. There are two scenes to be filmed before we get to the denouement, and both of them feature just two actors – Poirot and his old and trusted colleague Captain Hastings, played by my dear friend Hugh Fraser.

A loud bell echoes across the set to indicate that we are about to shoot. Hugh and I play out the melancholy scene, each knowing that we are nearing the end. Finally, my old friend walks quietly off the set and I sigh to myself.

When the great bell rings to indicate the end of the scene, hardly anyone moves. There is barely a sound. Every person there knows that we are nearing the end of a television era, one of the longest-running series ever starring a single actor as the main character. Each man and woman working with me is supporting me in every way they can – but we all know there is no avoiding the truth.

On the sound stage outside the set, my wife Sheila is sitting beside the sound man, watching the scene on the video playback. It is the first time she has come to this shoot, because she knows – better than anyone – just how difficult it will be for me to say goodbye to the little man who has inhabited our lives since 1988.

I step out of the small set perched in the middle of the sound stage. Sheila puts her arm around me. We walk away from the group clustered around the set preparing for the next scene – which will see Poirot bid his final farewell to Hastings. She hugs me, and I hug her back; there is nothing more we can really say.

The make-up ladies arrive to check the prosthetics on my hands which make them look old, and to make sure that I look 'pretty poorly', as Hettie likes to put it.

The truth is that I do feel pretty poorly; I have a cold. I always seem to get an infection when Poirot does – it is mysterious, but it has been happening for years. What would Dr Freud make of it, I wonder? I played him in a six-part BBC television series once – and even died for the screen on his own day bed, brought down to the set from his home in Hampstead – but that death was simple compared to this one. This is the death of a dear friend.

For years it has been Poirot and me, and to lose him is a pain almost beyond imagining.

Yet as I walk back on to the set, I know I have to clear my mind of everything, of every emotion. I must concentrate on what is about to happen to my old friend, and to me.

The script for Poirot's last case is written by the British playwright and screenwriter Kevin Elyot, and he has chosen a haunting piece of Chopin to accompany Poirot's last words to Hastings. And now

Hettie calls for this to be played in the studio. The gentle, poignant chords surround us all, only serving to intensify the grief in our hearts.

The music stops and I wait for the great bell to ring again, to mark the fact that we are about to shoot. Then I quietly ask if I may have silence for a few moments, just to allow Poirot and me a little peace to collect our thoughts. I will raise a single finger to indicate that the sound should start recording and the cameras roll before Hettie murmurs, 'Action.'

Lying there, I have decided to make my breathing more shallow, to underline the struggle that Poirot is having as he fights for life, but also to reveal that other things are troubling him as well. For he is also afraid: there is a part of this final story that has made him wonder whether God will truly ever forgive him for his actions, and, as any good Catholic, that thought troubles him deeply.

Poirot is aware that the end is coming, but he is not sure when. For once in his life, Poirot cannot control the events around him. He is rendered a mere mortal again.

In my mind, I have been exploring exactly how Poirot would feel in his last moments for weeks and weeks, but I did not fully understand what was happening until a month or so ago when I went for make-up and costume tests for this final film. That was the first time the old-age lines were painted onto my face and the prosthetics put on my hands; the first time that I sat in the wheelchair that I would be using in part of the story; the first time I fully understood emotionally that he was about to die. That brought home to me the reality that this was the end of the relationship between Poirot and me. Those thoughts come back to me as I ask for silence in order to clear my mind before I bid Hastings farewell. It is hard for both us. We have been as close as a pair of fictional friends could possibly be through nearly three decades of filming.

As I softly speak Poirot's final words to Hastings, I am looking at a man who I have worked with for so many years. As the music sweeps across the sound stage, the emotion overcomes even the strongest hearts. When Hastings leaves Poirot, the music swells – only to stop suddenly as the great bell rings to mark the end of the scene. Once again, silence falls across the set like a shroud.

Sitting beside the sound man, the lovely Andrew Sissons, who has worked with us so many times before, Sheila is crying quietly, and he says to her in his soft, kindly voice, 'I didn't realise how emotional it would be.'

My driver Sean O'Connor is watching the scene on the video playback in tears, and so is Peter Hale, who has been my stand-in for the past fourteen years, even though we do not look all that much alike. Sitting not far away, the make-up and continuity ladies are also wiping their eyes.

For me, it is quite extraordinary to see everyone so emotional. I have never, ever experienced anything like it in my entire career.

But Hettie and I dare not lose our focus. We know that there is a little way to go yet, and that we have to get there before we can allow ourselves to mourn. As an actor, I have always believed that I have to stand outside the role I am playing, aware of it, immersed in it, but still watchful. Otherwise what I am doing will not really be true, and I will never allow that.

Hettie calls for the crew to move on to the scene in which Poirot is about to take his final, breaths, and I know that I am so lucky to have her as the director. We worked together once before, on a two-hour version of Dame Agatha's *The Mystery of the Blue Train*, and I was very keen that she should be with me for Poirot's final case because she was so sympathetic to his character. I believed her sensibilities and skill would be good for his last story, while it also meant that I could give 100 per cent of my trust to her, which was enormously important for me.

As Hettie and the crew prepare, I leave the set. My dresser, Anne-Marie Digby, gives me my dressing gown and Sheila and I walk away into one of the far corners to talk.

The next scenes are important. We must get them right, because I don't want Poirot's death to be sentimental; I want to make it as real as I possibly can. I would like the audience to understand that he is fighting to keep himself together, so that when he reaches for his rosary to ask God's forgiveness, there is truth in every single frame of film.

All around me the crew are trying their best to help me. I realise that I am so lucky to have them too, and vow to tell them so when we finally wrap the filming the following Monday afternoon – after we've had the weekend to recover.

Sheila walks me back to the set, and I take my position. I am the only actor in this next scene, and the two cameras are set up to take different angles of these last moments of my life as Poirot.

The challenge is to make the scene moving but not too melodramatic. But at the same time I want to convince every single member of the audience, wherever they may be around the world, that dying is not easy, or comfortable. I do not want to sugar-coat the end of Poirot.

Once again, the bell rings to announce the start of the scene. Once again, I explain that I will lift my finger to announce when I'm ready to start. Then, and only then, will Hettie call for action.

Finally I'm ready, and she does. I do not want to have to do this scene more than once. So I concentrate every fibre of my being on getting it exactly right. I am there to serve the Hercule Poirot that

Dame Agatha Christie created, and nowhere can that be more important than in his last words.

Thankfully, it seems to work. Hettie calls, 'Cut,' and the great bell rings to mark the end of this one and only take.

Now there is just one scene left on this damp, grey Friday in November – the discovery of Poirot's body by Hastings. And, once again, I am determined that it should not be sugary. I discuss it with Hettie, and with Sheila, asking them what they think – but in my heart I know that I do not want his death to seem too chocolate-box.

It is a little after six in the evening now, and the crew are beginning to tire, as am I. This is the twenty-second day of shooting, with only one day off on some weekends, and the emotion of the day has made it all the more draining. I can see it in the faces of the people around me.

No matter how tired I am, one thing I am sure of: I want Sheila to join Hettie and me on the set, to see what they both feel about how Poirot should be found after his death. I want to make him look as though he has been struggling with the fear that there might be no redemption. Passing is not always as easy as it is portrayed on film.

It has to be real. For me, that is what every actor should aim to bring to any part he plays. You remain true to your character, no matter what happens. I do not want my Poirot to have a neat, sanitised death, filmed through soft gauze to give it a romantic haze. I want him to die as I hope I have helped him to live: as a real, extraordinary human being.

Hettie keeps the filming as brief as she possibly can, just getting Hugh's reaction in close-up as well as when he bursts into the room. Not a single person on that small set, including Hugh, Sheila and I, want it to go on for one moment longer than it absolutely has to. It has been a brutal day and we want it to end.

It does. Hettie calls, 'Cut,' the great bell rings and we have finished for the day.

As I walk back to my trailer, parked outside the sound stage, I feel completely lost. Sheila and I are going home for the weekend, but I do not know what to do with myself. I cannot sit or stand still, and so I pace about the trailer. When we finally get home, I still cannot settle. I am not sure if I want to eat or not; not sure whether to go out and see friends, or just stay at home.

In the end we stay at home together. But the hardest part is that we have to go back to Pinewood on Monday morning for the twenty-third and last day of filming, even though Poirot is already dead. The future hangs over us both like a dark cloud throughout the weekend, no matter how hard we try to put it out of our minds.

Another bleak, drizzly day dawns on Monday and I have to film the final moments of the story, which are vital because Poirot tells Hastings – in a letter delivered four months after his death – the solution to the mystery of the killings that surrounded them both in these last days at Styles.

I cannot allow myself to step back from the role, but, quite suddenly, sitting there at the writing desk in my stage bedroom, I recapture a little of the joy that has always been a part of Poirot and me.

I am writing a letter to Hastings to explain all that has happened, and what makes it all the extraordinary is that the art department have discovered a way to create my handwriting so that I do not have to write every word myself time after time. It is as though a ghost has taken over my life.

At the end of the scene Poirot gives one last look to the camera. I want to put across the twinkle in my eye that I have used so often when I have inhabited that little man. There has been enough gloom in this final story.

As I look across at the camera for the final time, I think back to Poirot's last words to Hastings on Friday.

'Cher ami,' I said softly, as he was leaving Poirot to rest.

That phrase meant an enormous amount to me, which is why I repeated it after he had shut the door behind him. But my second 'cher ami' in that scene was for someone other than Hastings. It was for my dear, dear friend Poirot. I was saying goodbye to him as well, and I felt it with all my heart.

CHAPTER 1

'I WOULDN'T TOUCH IT WITH A BARGE POLE'

When Hercule Poirot died on that late November afternoon in 2012, a part of me died with him.

Agatha Christie's fastidious little Belgian detective had been part of my life for almost a quarter of a century. I'd played him in more than a hundred hours of television over twenty-five years. And now here I was portraying his death.

Words really can't express how much that obsessive, kindly, gentle man with his mincing walk, his 'little grey cells' and his extraordinary accent had come to mean to me. To lose him now, after so long, was like losing the dearest of friends, even though I was only an actor playing a part.

But I knew, in my heart, that I had done him justice. I had brought him to life for millions of people around the world, and helped them to care about him as much as I did. That was my consolation as I breathed my last for him in the television studio that day, because I knew that I would never play him again: there were no more of his original stories to bring to the screen.

Hercule Poirot's death was the end of a long creative journey for me, made all the more emotional as I had only ever wanted to play Dame Agatha's true Poirot, the man she'd first created in *The Mysterious Affair at Styles* in 1920 and whose death she chronicled more than half a century later, in *Curtain* in 1975.

He was as real to me as he had been to her: a great detective, a remarkable man, if, perhaps, just now and then, a little irritating. He had inhabited my life every bit as much as he must have done hers as she wrote thirty-three novels, more than fifty short stories and a play about him, making Poirot one of the most famous fictional detectives in the world, alongside Sherlock Holmes.

But how had it come to this? How had I come to inhabit his morning jacket and pin-striped trousers, his black patent leather shoes and his elegantly brushed grey Homburg hat for so many years? What had brought us together? Was there something in me that found a particular echo in this short, tubby man in his sixties, given to pince-nez and saying 'chut' instead of 'ssh'?

Looking back now, these many years later, I suspect in my heart that there was.

To understand precisely what I mean we have to travel back in time – to an autumn evening in 1987 in an Indian restaurant in, of all places, Acton in west London – when I was first asked to play the role. But that also means that I must tell you something about me, as an actor, and how Poirot came to haunt my every step. For he and I are now inextricably linked, as I hope you will see.

Let's start at the beginning. Why on earth would anyone ask me to play the role? After all, I wasn't exactly the obvious choice.

I'd spent almost twenty years playing pretty menacing parts, rather than charming detectives. I'd played Shylock in *The Merchant of Venice* and Iago to Ben Kingsley's Othello for the Royal Shakespeare Company. I'd played Sigmund Freud in a six-hour drama documentary for BBC television, and won a radio drama award for a dramatisation of Tolstoy's horrifying portrayal of doomed love, *The Kreutzer Sonata*.

Yet, ironically, it was another dark role, my portrayal of Blott, the eccentric, malevolent gardener in Tom Sharpe's marvellous comic novel *Blott on the Landscape* – dramatised for the BBC in 1985 – that led to that Indian restaurant in Acton. It was my portrayal of that strange, haunted man intent on using every means at his disposal to save his aristocratic mistress and her country house from the developers that led to my becoming Poirot, the little man who was so much a part of the rest of my life.

I was forty-one years old when Poirot first appeared beside me. I'd been bitten by the acting bug when I was a member of the National Youth Theatre at eighteen and stood backstage at the Royal Court thinking, 'This is what I want to do with my life.'

My father didn't want me to follow in his footsteps and become a doctor. But he was horrified when I told him I wanted to be an actor. I'd acted at school, where the headmaster had told him that it was 'almost the only thing that David is really good at', which wasn't true at all because I was pretty good at rugby, tennis and cricket as well. But my father was still appalled at the idea of my becoming an actor and only very reluctantly accepted the inevitable.

Full of enthusiasm, I auditioned for the Central School of Music and Drama in London, but they turned me down flat because I couldn't sing, which upset me so much that I didn't even bother going to the audition for the Royal Academy of Dramatic Art. A few weeks later, however, I did pluck up the courage to audition for the London Academy of Music and Dramatic Art, and they offered me a place.

Not that I fitted in exactly. I was still living at home with my parents and I turned up for my first day at LAMDA in 1966 wearing a suit and tie, when everyone else was wearing Beatle caps and jeans. Then I arrived at my first movement class wearing my school rugby colours and was instantly sent out to buy a leotard and tights. One of the teachers even tried to persuade me to buy a pair of jeans, but I never managed to get into them because my thighs were too big – all those days of rugby at school.

In fact, I don't think LAMDA thought very much of me as an actor at first – at least until I was cast by the former child star Jeremy Spenser as the Mayor, Hebble Tyson, in Christopher Fry's 1948 comedy-drama *The Lady's Not for Burning*. It was my first character part, and it helped me find my metier. LAMDA thought so too because they awarded me a prize as their best student when I left.

From London, I went into rep as an assistant stage manager at the Gateway Theatre in Chester in 1969, working on a new play every two weeks. But that was only a start, and in the years that followed, there were some very lean times. I spent a good deal of time at the start of my career 'resting', as we actors like to call being out of work. To sustain myself in the early 1970s, I found myself unloading lorry loads of dog food, then working as a lift operator in a block of flats, and finally, selling and hiring formal wear at Moss Bros.

In fact, I was so terrified that I was never going to work as an actor again that when Moss Bros generously offered me an apprenticeship as a junior manager, I was all set to accept it. But fate intervened. On the very morning when I was going to say yes, I got a call offering me a part in a television show called *The Protectors*, starring Robert Vaughn and Nyree Dawn Porter, which was shooting at that very moment in Venice. I didn't hesitate – I took the plane to Venice. It was the end of my career in men's wear.

Since then, I've been lucky enough to work regularly in the theatre, in films and on radio and television. I joined the Royal Shakespeare Company in 1973, at the age of twenty-seven, and loved it, just as I loved appearing in films like *Song for Europe*, *Harry and the Hendersons*, with John Lithgow, and *The Falcon and the Snowman*, with Sean Penn and Tim Hutton, as well as *A World Apart*, where I played a distinctly frightening South African police interrogator.

But it was *Blott*, on television, that made me – Tom Sharpe rang me in tears to say that he'd never expected to see his character so beautifully portrayed. I was very touched.

That was why Brian Eastman, the Brighton-born film and television producer who'd produced *Blott* for the BBC, rang me up on that autumn evening in 1987 and asked if he could come round to see me and take me out to dinner. He's a tall, slim man who likes to work with people he knows and respects. As a result of *Blott*, we'd become friends – so I said yes.

Brian arrived at the house, had a chat with my wife Sheila and saw my son and daughter, Robert and Katherine, who were then six and four, before taking me out to the local Indian restaurant.

That's how we ended up sitting opposite each other over a chicken madras and a vegetable biryani when Brian said suddenly, 'Have you read much of Agatha Christie?'

I blanched. The honest truth was that I'd never read any at all, not so much as a single book. My father, a wonderful man and a leading gynaecologist in his day, had always encouraged my elder brother John, my younger brother Peter and me to read, but had also told us: 'Read the greats, never forget Shakespeare, challenge yourselves.' We'd all taken his advice, and it was one reason why I'd loved playing Tolstoy's poor Pozdnyshev in *The Kreutzer Sonata*.

'Well, to be honest, Brian, I haven't read any,' I said rather meekly. 'She's really not my style. But I know she has a great many fans.'

Brian seemed untroubled. 'Have you seen any of the Poirot films?' he asked, putting his spoon into the pilau rice.

I'd done more than that. I'd actually appeared in one.

'I appeared with Peter Ustinov in the CBS film *Thirteen at Dinner* in 1985, just before I did Iago,' I told him. 'I played Inspector Japp.'

In fact, I'd taken the job to make a little money before going up to Stratford, which I knew wouldn't make me a great deal. I had a young family to support. What I didn't tell Brian was that I thought Inspector Japp was probably the worst performance I'd ever given in my life. I didn't know what on earth to do with the part and so, for some unfathomable reason, I'd decided to play him like a kind of Jewish bookie and make him eat whenever he appeared on the screen. I even made him eat Poirot's breakfast in one scene, which amused Ustinov hugely.

Peter and I had talked about Poirot while we were filming. He liked the part because he could bring out what he saw as the comedy in the role, but he knew that he could never play the Poirot that Agatha Christie had actually written. Peter was too large, physically and as a character, for the true Poirot; his own personality got in the way, and he used the accent as part of his comic armoury.

But, during a break in the filming one day, Peter did say to me, 'You could play Poirot, you know, and you would be very good at it.' It was extremely flattering of him, but I did not take the idea very seriously. That conversation came back to me that October night, as Brian Eastman and I talked over our Indian meal.

'I've seen Albert Finney, of course,' I told him, as he pushed a plate of rice across the table, 'in *Murder on the Orient Express*, which I really enjoyed.'

I remember thinking privately that Albert's performance in the 1974 film had struck me as rather tense and stiff – he hardly ever seemed to move his neck – while his accent had been very gruff, almost angry. But that didn't detract from his excellent performance, nor the superb cast, which included Lauren Bacall, Ingrid Bergman, John Gielgud and Sean Connery, who used to live not that far away from me in Acton when he was still married to the achingly beautiful Diane Cilento.

Brian took another mouthful of curry and then said, 'Well, I've taken the idea of a new series of television films based on Poirot to ITV in London, and they're very keen on making ten one-hour films from the short stories next year.'

He paused, then dropped his bombshell.

'And we are very keen that you should play Poirot.'

My spoonful of curry stopped halfway to my mouth. I was, quite literally, astounded. I can remember the shock to this day.

Me, the serious Shakespearean actor, portrayer of men with haunted souls whose dark deeds forever surround them, playing a fastidious, balding detective; I couldn't quite grasp the idea, but I didn't say no. I was too astonished.

As we left the restaurant, Brian said, 'I'll send you some of the books. Have a look at them and see what you think.' Then he disappeared into the night, and I walked home to Sheila in a daze.

Two days later, a couple of the full-length Poirot novels arrived, and shortly afterwards, a copy of *Poirot's Casebook*, containing some of the short stories that Brian thought should make up the first series of ten television programmes. I was intrigued, but I also thought I'd better know what I might be getting myself into. So I started to read them.

And as I did so, it slowly dawned on me that I'd never actually seen the character I was reading about on the screen. He wasn't like Albert Finney, or Peter Ustinov, or Ian Holm in the 1986 BBC drama *Murder by the Book*. He was quite, quite different: more elusive, more pedantic and, most of all, more human than the person I'd seen on the screen.

But I still wasn't sure whether I should play him. So I decided to ask my elder brother John, who was then a newscaster at Independent Television News in London. He is two years older than I am, and I've always looked up to him, so I rang him.

'John,' I said, a little nervously, 'do you read Agatha Christie?'

There was a slight pause at the other end of the line. 'Not in recent years,' he said, 'but I've dipped into one or two in the past.'

'Do you know her character Hercule Poirot?' I asked.

'Of course, he's her most famous creation.'

'Well, they're thinking of making ten one-hour films of his stories, with me playing the role. Only I don't know the character. What do you think of him?'

There was a distinct hush.

'I wouldn't touch it with a barge pole,' John said firmly.

'Seriously?' I blurted out.

'Yes. I mean, Poirot's a bit of a joke, a buffoon. It's not you at all.'

I gulped.

'Well, what I'm reading isn't a buffoon,' I told him. 'It's a character that I've never seen portrayed.'

There was another silence.

'It would be a wonderful challenge to see if I could bring that character to the screen,' I said, stumbling on.

There was a slight sigh. John is an enormously kind and gentle man, and would never want to upset me.

'Of course, you must do it if you want to,' he said quietly. 'Good luck. Only one word of warning: it may be difficult to get people to take him seriously.'

It turned out he was quite right.

But the more I thought about the man in Dame Agatha's books, the more convinced I became that I could bring the true Poirot to life on the screen, a man no audience had seen before. And so, a few days later, I rang Brian Eastman.

'I think I'd like to do it, Brian,' I said, with my heart in my mouth. It was just after the New Year of 1988.

'That's wonderful news,' he said quickly. 'I'll be in touch with your agent. No one else was approached, you know. You were our first choice – and I'm absolutely delighted you'd like to play him.'

So began the long journey to bring Poirot to life for millions, and to do that, I knew I had to discover every single thing I could about the detective with the small waxed moustache and those ever-present 'little grey cells'.

I started by collecting copies of all the novels and short stories featuring him and piled them up beside my bed. I wanted to get to the very heart of what Dame Agatha thought of him and what he was really like, and to do that, I had to read every word his creator had ever written about him. I didn't want my Poirot to be a caricature, something made up in a film or television studio, I wanted him to be real, as real as he was in the books, as real as I could possibly make him.

The first thing I realised was that I was a slightly too young to play him. He was a retired police detective in his sixties when he first appeared in *The Mysterious Affair at Styles*, while I was in my early forties. Not only that, he was also described as a good deal fatter than I was. There was going to have to be some considerable padding, not to mention very careful make-up and costume, if I was going to convince the world that I was the great Hercule Poirot.

Even more important, the more I read about him, the more convinced I became that he was a character that demanded to be taken seriously. He wasn't a silly little man with a funny accent, any more than Sherlock Holmes was just a morphine addict with a taste for playing the violin. There was a depth and quality to the Poirot that Dame Agatha had created – and that was what I desperately wanted to bring to the screen.

I took the role of Poirot because it precisely symbolised everything I believed about being an actor, which I hadn't truly discovered until well after I'd started out in Chester, at the age of twenty-three, back in 1969.

In my first years in the profession, I struggled to find my identity, to understand why I was actually doing it. What was it that I wanted to be as an actor exactly? Was it just about dressing up and becoming someone else? Was I desperate to become some kind of star?

I was confused. I'd achieved part of my dream – I'd become a professional actor – but what did that mean? What did I want?

I was so uncertain that I looked up the dictionary definition of what an actor was. It defined it as a thespian, a theatre player – but that was really no help to me at all. It didn't strike any kind of chord. If my only objective was to strut around the stage or the film studio pretending to be someone else, I didn't feel comfortable.

There was no real purpose in that for me; it just didn't fit the man I knew I was: the serious, slightly reserved son of a South African-born gynaecologist and an English actress who was the daughter of a music-hall artist from Kent, and who'd gone on to become a dancer on the West End stage herself.

Deep down I knew that I didn't want to *pretend* to be someone else; I wanted to inhabit them, to bring them to life. The longer I thought about it, the more I realised that what I really wanted to do was to become different people, to transform myself into them. I wanted to be a character actor, not a star. That was what I enjoyed, that was what acting really meant to me.

It was at that moment that I also realised that the playwright or screenwriter of any piece I appeared in depended on me as an actor to give his or her character a personality and voice. That was what excited me, because without character and personality, there can be no drama. I was convinced that my purpose as an actor was to become the writer's voice.

That understanding came like a thunderclap. I realised – suddenly – that it wasn't about me. It was about the character I was lucky enough to play, and my job was to bring out the truth in the character – and what the writer wanted. Ultimately, that was what really lay behind my decision to play Poirot.

That's one of the reasons why I wanted to write this book. I wanted to try to explain what being a character actor means for me, and how it can sustain you even if you play a single part for more than a quarter of a century. I don't think any actors have ever really attempted that before – not Basil Rathbone or Jeremy Brett, who both played Sherlock Holmes; nor John Thaw, who played Inspector Morse; nor Raymond Burr, who brought us both Perry Mason and Ironside; nor even Richard Chamberlain, who was Doctor Kildare for all those years.

I wanted to try to explain what my craft and profession mean to me personally, especially when I've had the good fortune to be asked to play a man who is known, and loved, by so many millions of people around the world.

And so it was that 'inhabiting' Dame Agatha's Poirot preoccupied me in those first months of 1988. I wanted to understand everything about him, to become him, and to make him as real to the world as he was becoming to me. He gave my work a purpose, and I hoped that I would repay my debt to his creator by bringing him truly to life – in all his dimensions – for the first time.

Just as I was beginning to immerse myself in him, however, I was offered a part in a small British film based on a Michael Morpurgo children's story called *When the Whales Came*. It was a charming piece set in the Scilly Isles, thirty miles out from Land's End in the north Atlantic, about two children who set out to save a beached narwhal that had landed on their shores, and in doing so saved their island from a curse.

The stars were to be my old National Youth Theatre friend Helen Mirren and the unforgettable but distinctly shy Paul Scofield, Oscar-winner for his performance in the film of Robert Bolt's *A Man for All Seasons* in 1966, as well as receiving a Tony for playing Salieri in Peter Shaffer's *Amadeus* on Broadway in 1979. His portrayal of King Lear has been described as 'the greatest ever

Shakespearean performance', and he was undoubtedly one of the finest actors of his generation. Filming would take ten weeks on the Scillies between April and June, and I was to play the third lead, a local fisherman called Will.

It wasn't an enormous part, but it was a beautiful place to be, and I thought it would give me a chance to read even more Poirot, away from the demands of London and the telephone. Besides, Sheila and the children could visit me on the islands, which would give us all a week together during the half-term holiday.

So it was that I spent the beautiful spring of 1988 on the smallest of the Scilly Isles, Bryher, where the film was being shot, spending my spare time reading Poirot stories.

The more I did so, the more the little man entranced me. There were so many foibles, so many little habits that some people found hard to understand, so many mannerisms – his need for order, his dislike of the country, his determination to carry a silver 'Turnip' pocket watch wherever he went. Each was as idiosyncratic as the next, and each as fascinating.

Then, as the warm winds of May turned into an even warmer June, I started to write my private list of Poirot's habits and character. I called it my 'dossier of characteristics'. It ended up five pages long and detailed ninety-three different aspects of his life. I have the list to this day – in fact, I carried it around on the set with me throughout all my years as Poirot, just as I gave a copy to every director I worked with on a Poirot film.

The first note I made read simply: 'Belgian! NOT French.'

The second said: 'Drinks tisane – hardly ever tea, which he calls "the English Poison". Will drink coffee – black only.'

The third echoed the same theme: 'Has four lumps of sugar in tea and coffee – sometimes three. Once or twice, five!'

'Wears pointed, tight, very shiny patent leather shoes,' said the fourth, while the fifth added, 'Bows a great deal – even when shaking hands.'

Very gradually, from reading the books and keeping a note of every single item that illuminated his character, I was building a picture of the man I was about to play.

'Hates to fly. Makes him feel sick,' my list went on, but then also: 'Hates travelling by water. Uses the "so excellent Laverguier method" to prevent sea-sickness.'

'Regards his moustaches as a thing of perfect beauty,' said my eighth note to myself. 'Uses scented pomade.'

'Order and method are his "GODS",' was my ninth commandment, and the next: 'A man of faith and morals. Regards himself as "un bon Catholique". Reads his Bible every night before he goes to sleep.' The more I read about Poirot, the greater the respect I found for his creator. I had not realised that the woman born Agatha Mary Clarissa Miller on 15 September 1890, in my own father's favourite seaside resort of Torquay in Devon, was the best-selling novelist of all time.

Nor did I know that her books had sold some two billion copies around the world, that she was the most translated individual author ever – appearing in 103 languages – and that hers are ranked the third most widely published books in history, after the works of Shakespeare and the Bible.

Perhaps if I'd known all those things when I started out on the project, I might have been even more terrified at the prospect of playing Poirot and satisfying her millions of fans.

After all, they had a lot of experience of him: all those novels and short stories over fifty-five years. Indeed, even though Dame Agatha had professed to become 'tired' of him in the late 1940s, she nevertheless continued to write about him until 1972, when Collins published *Elephants Can Remember*. They went on to publish *Curtain: Poirot's Final Case*, which she had written many years earlier, just a few months before her death at the age of eighty-five in January 1976.

So, utterly determined to get Poirot as right as Dame Agatha would have wanted him, I sat in my room in the Hell Bay Hotel on Bryher, steadily compiling my ever-expanding list of his characteristics.

Number eleven read: 'A great thinker who says he has "undoubtedly the finest brain in Europe",' while number thirteen added: 'Conceited professionally – but not as a person.' Fourteen said: 'Loves his work and genuinely believes he is the best in the world and expects everyone to know him,' although fifteen conceded: 'Dislikes publicity.'

Every day Poirot's complexities and contradictions, his vanities and idiosyncrasies, became ever clearer in my mind, but as they did so, I began to worry about his voice.

In fact, in the ten weeks I spent on Bryher, it was Poirot's voice that worried me the most. I would walk round that beautiful, unspoilt little island, with its population of under a hundred and where there isn't a single tarmac road, thinking about how he would truly sound. Perhaps the quietness of the island helped me do so.

'Everybody thinks he's French,' I said to myself as I walked across the great stones that littered the beach at Rushy Bay, or stomped over the tussocky grass of Heathy Hill, with its famous dwarf pansies.

'The only reason people think Poirot is French is because of his accent,' I muttered. 'But he's Belgian, and I know that French-speaking Belgians don't sound French, not a bit of it.'

I started experimenting by talking to myself in a whole range of voices, some of them coming from my head – all nasal and clipped

– others coming from my chest, lower and a little slower, even a little gruff. Nothing sounded quite like the man I had been reading about in bed every night. They all sounded a little false, and that was the very last thing that I wanted.

I also was well aware of Brian Eastman's advice to me before I left for Bryher: 'Don't forget, he may have an accent, but the audience must be able to understand exactly what he's saying.' There was my problem in a nutshell.

It certainly wasn't the only one. I wanted to discover everything I could about the great detective, and as I read, I realised that there were some clues at hand. In the midst of compiling my list of Poirot's characteristics, I came across a letter the great man had apparently written himself in April 1936, to his American publisher. It appeared in an American omnibus of his stories, including *The Murder of Roger Ackroyd* and *Thirteen at Dinner* – or *Lord Edgware Dies*, as it is known in England – and it answered at least some of the questions in my mind.

'What was my first case?' Poirot wrote to 'Monsieur Dodd'.

> I began work as a member of the detective force in Brussels on the Abercrombie Forgery Case in 1904, and for many years was proud to be a member of the detective service in my native Belgium. Since the closing of the war, I have, as you know, been in London, having rooms for some time with *mon vieux ami* Hastings, at 14, Farraway Street, under the motherly supervision of Mrs Pearson.

As I read it, I remember being struck at how similar it all seemed to Sherlock Holmes, with Dr Watson and Mrs Hudson in 221B Baker

Street. What I didn't know, as I read, was exactly how much his creator had been influenced by the exploits of Sir Arthur Conan Doyle's master detective. Dame Agatha had been an avid reader of Holmes as a young woman and although she'd decided to make her detective as different in personality from Holmes as she possibly could, she'd liked the idea of having a Dr Watson-like friend and helper who could be the narrator of the story – enter Captain Hastings. And she'd liked the notion of a kindly housekeeper to look after them.

Keeping Poirot as different as she could from Holmes was absolutely vital, because his books were still appearing when she began to write her first Poirot story. Sir Arthur Conan Doyle's *The Valley of Fear* was published in 1915, when she was planning Poirot, and his next story, *His Last Bow*, in 1917, appeared after Dame Agatha had finished her first draft of *The Mysterious Affair at Styles*, her first book and Poirot's first appearance.

It was inevitable that Dame Agatha's detective would set himself quite apart from Holmes. 'How, you ask, would I be recognised in a crowd?' she had him write to his American publisher. 'What is there distinctive about my appearance? Alas, I have none of those theatrical peculiarities which distinguish the detectives in story books.'

Not quite true, I remember thinking, but I saw her point.

True, I have my little prejudices. Anything in the least crooked or disorderly is a torment to me. In my bookcase, I arrange the tallest books at the end; then the next tallest; and so on. My medicine bottles are placed in a neatly graduated row. If your necktie were not correct, I should find it irresistible not to make it straight for you. Should there be a morsel of omelette on your coat, a speck of dust on your collar, I must correct these . . . For my breakfast, I have only toast which is cut into neat little squares. The eggs – there must be two – they must be identical in size. I confess to you that I will stoop to pick up a burnt match from a flower bed and bury it neatly.

But Poirot denies that he's a little man, insisting fiercely:

I am five feet four inches high. My head, it is egg-shaped and I carry it a little to one side, the left. My eyes, I am told, shine green when I am excited. My boots are patent leather, smart and shiny. My stick is embossed with a gold band. My watch is large and keeps the time exactly. My moustache is the finest in all London. You see, *mon ami*? You comprehend? Hercule Poirot stands before you.

Well yes, he did, there was no doubt of that, and he certainly was not Sherlock Holmes. Yet the more I read, the more uncertain I was about his voice. I could hear the accent – but what was it? Seeing Poirot was one thing – I was sure that Brian Eastman and I could settle that – but hearing him, that was quite another matter.

There was also the matter of what playing him might mean to my career. Was I in danger of losing myself in a single character? Would that overwhelm me? Would I fall into that actor's trap of being typecast? I was determined not to, but I could sense a danger.

One evening in early June, shortly before the filming of *When the Whales Came* came to an end on Bryher, and just weeks before I was due to start shooting the first of the Poirot films, I had a conversation with the film's executive producer, Geoffrey Wansell, who was to become a dear friend and who is writing this book with me. We talked about my playing Poirot and what it might mean.

'Well, I'll tell you one thing,' Geoffrey said. 'It will change your life forever. You will go through a door and never be able to go back through it again.'

'Don't be so silly,' I told him. 'I'll still be exactly the same person I am now: an actor. That's all I ever want to be.'

'Believe me, you won't stay the same,' he replied. 'Everything will change, whether you want it to or not, and you won't be able to go back. But that doesn't mean for a moment that you'll be typecast. Poirot may consume part of you while you're playing him, but not every part of you.'

That was what I wanted: to play the character of Poirot as I had played the characters of Blott or Freud. I was a character actor. And that's exactly what I did. That was what I was doing now. I was going to become Poirot, not a 'star' personality performer.

Shortly afterwards, I started the long trip home from Bryher – a boat to St Mary's, the largest of the Scilly Isles, where the former Prime Minister Harold Wilson still had his bungalow, then a helicopter to Penzance, and then the long train ride back to Paddington and my house in Acton. As the journey progressed, I began to wonder exactly what I had let myself in for.

It didn't take long for me to find out.

CHAPTER 2

'WE MUST NEVER, EVER, LAUGH AT HIM'

Back in London, the one thing that was preoccupying me was still Poirot's voice. I had to get it right. It wasn't a joke, it wasn't there for anyone to laugh at; it was at the very heart of the man. But how could I find it?

To help me, I managed to get hold of a set of Belgian Walloon and French radio recordings from the BBC. Poirot came from Liège in Belgium and would have spoken Belgian French, the language of 30 per cent of the country's population, rather than Walloon, which is very much closer to the ordinary French language. To these I added recordings of English-language stations broadcasting from Belgium, as well as English-language programmes from Paris. My principal concern was to give my Poirot a voice that would ring true, and which would also be the voice of the man I heard in my head when I read his stories.

I listened for hours, and then gradually started mixing Walloon Belgian with French, while at the same time slowly relocating the sound of his voice in my body, moving it from my chest to my head, making it sound a little more high-pitched, and yes, a little more fastidious.

After several weeks, I finally began to believe that I'd captured it: this was what Poirot would have sounded like if I'd met him in the flesh. This was how he would have spoken to me – with that characteristic little bow as we shook hands, and that little nod of the head to the left as he removed his perfectly brushed grey Homburg hat.

The more I heard his voice in my head, and added to my own list of his personal characteristics, the more determined I became never to compromise in my portrayal of Poirot. I vowed to myself that I would never allow him to be a figure of fun. He may have been vain, but he was a serious man, just as I was, and I wanted to bring that out.

That was when I started to realise that perhaps he and I had more things in common than I'd suspected. We were both outsiders to some extent – he a Belgian living in England, me a Londoner who was born in Paddington but nevertheless had always somehow felt something of an outsider. That was not the only quality we shared, however. I had exactly the same appetite for order, method and symmetry that he did. And, like Poirot, I was not prepared to compromise what I believed in. That certainly applied to his clothes.

After I got back from Bryher, I was shown some of the proposed costumes for the television series. But they weren't quite right. In my eyes, they didn't represent the image of the man that I had formed after reading the books and making my own notes. They were too loud, too garish. They had more to do with a comedy programme than the character I wanted to play, and I didn't want that. I didn't want my Poirot to look foolish.

Sadly, the moustaches I was offered were almost as wrong: far too big, drowning my face, so that I looked like a walrus – quite horrible. I hardly knew what to say. I was terribly disappointed, but it made me all the more determined. I was not going to be put off. Everything I'd been shown had nothing to do with the Poirot I wanted to portray, and I was not going to allow him to be made a fool of.

With Brian Eastman's help, it was agreed that I would be 'permitted' to wear the clothes that Agatha Christie herself had dictated that Poirot should wear – a three-piece suit, a wing collar, shiny patent leather shoes and spats. There were one or two people working on preparing the series that weren't too keen. 'They will look so dull on television; they aren't interesting enough,' they said. But I dug my heels in.

If Agatha Christie said that Poirot would wear a morning jacket, striped trousers and a grey waistcoat at certain times of the day, then that was exactly what I wanted him to wear on television – not a jot more, nor a jot less. After all number twenty-two in my list of characteristics said: 'Very particular over his appearance,' while number twenty-four added: 'Always wears a separate collar – wing collar,' and number thirty-three explained: 'His appearance (including hair) is always immaculate. His nails groomed and shined.'

My Poirot would always be dressed like that or I wouldn't play him.

I felt exactly the same way about his moustache. I didn't want it to look like something stuck on, a silly afterthought. It was central to the man he was, a reflection of his fastidious attitude to life. There was never a single moment when Poirot wasn't enormously particular about it. As my note number twenty-one said firmly: 'Will always take his solid-silver moustache-grooming set with him when travelling.'

That was why Brian Eastman and I, together with a make-up artist, decided to design the moustache that I would wear for the television series ourselves, rather than to accept the suggestions we'd had so far. And we based our moustache on the description that Agatha Christie herself gave in *Murder on the Orient Express*, the full-length story that she wrote in 1933 and published the following year.

As she herself was to say, almost forty years later – when the film version starring Albert Finney appeared – 'I wrote that he had the finest moustache in England – and he didn't in the film. I thought that a pity. Why shouldn't he have the best moustache?' I was determined to serve my writer, and I certainly wasn't going to allow my Poirot not to have the finest moustache in England.

In the end, Brian and I came up with a moustache that we both thought exactly conveyed what Dame Agatha had in mind – a small, neat, carefully waxed one that curled upwards, and where the tip of each of end would be level with the tip of my nose. For us, it was the best-looking waxed moustache in England, and exactly what Hercule Poirot must have.

With those decisions behind me, I found myself at Twickenham Film Studios on the south-western outskirts of London, not far from the River Thames, in late June 1988, climbing carefully into the outfit that would define my portrait of Poirot. It was my first screen test.

First came the padding. I needed to wear a good deal on my stomach, chest, back and shoulders, to make sure I was the right shape. I'm actually fairly slim, but it was vital that Poirot shouldn't be. The padding helped me gain almost 40 pounds in appearance, transforming me into a man who weighed more than 200 pounds.

Even the separate wing collar that gripped my neck like a vice helped to make my face look a little fatter.

After the padding came the clothes, and I insisted that the striped trousers be immaculately creased, the black morning coat freshly pressed, the grey waistcoat a perfect fit and the white shirt sparkling for the screen test. Then my dresser added the little brooch of a vase containing a tiny posy of flowers for my buttonhole. All that was left was the moustache we'd taken such trouble with. It was put in place by the first of many make-up ladies I have had over the years. The moustache was always put on in the make-up truck or dressing room after I had put on my costume. There would always be two – when one wore out, we would have another one made, as a spare.

All that was necessary now was for the wardrobe mistress to brush Poirot's hat very carefully. I gently reminded her that number forty-six in my list of characteristics said that he would 'always brush his hat "tenderly" before leaving his flat'. Finally, I reminded myself of number forty-eight: 'Can't abide being or feeling untidy. A speck of dirt on his clothes is "as painful as a bullet wound".' There wasn't a speck to be seen anywhere.

Walking onto the sound stage for a set of still photographs and a full video screen test, I allowed myself to think – just for a moment – that Agatha Christie herself might just feel a touch of pride at the look of the man who was walking out to face the cameras that morning. Feeling quietly confident, I walked up and down, bowed, doffed my hat and smiled a little warily into the camera. I wasn't sure that I had quite mastered Poirot's distinctive, thin smile quite yet.

Pride cometh before a fall: there was something else that I most certainly hadn't mastered – Poirot's walk.

When Brian Eastman and I sat down to look at the screen test that afternoon, we realised that I simply didn't move as we both knew the great man would have done. My stride seemed too big and too certain. My Poirot should walk like a dancer – poised and graceful, always on the balls of his feet. Instead he was walking as though he were playing Iago – manly, dramatic and anything but fastidious.

Horrified, I left Twickenham in a panic and drove home on the verge of despair. How was I going to find his walk? I had no idea. I was absolutely at a loss. But then I remembered that Agatha Christie herself had once described it. The only question was where? I started going through her stories one by one, desperate to locate her description, and – quite by chance – I stumbled upon it.

These were his creator's words: 'Poirot crossed the lawn, with his rapid mincing steps, his feet painfully enclosed within his patent leather shoes.'

His feet hurt, that was part of the secret, and the other part was that he 'minced'. At last I understood, but the question was – how could I create that particular walk?

Then I remembered a famous Laurence Olivier story explaining how he'd managed to walk like a 'fop' in a Restoration comedy. 'I put a penny between the cheeks of my bum, old boy,' he'd said, 'and try to keep it there. If I can manage to do that, then I can produce the mincing walk I need to play the role.'

Without a moment's hesitation, I went out to walk round and round my garden with a penny between the cheeks of my bottom – except I used a small, modern, post-decimal penny. Larry had used a big old-fashioned one.

I practised walking for hours, stopping, turning and bowing – all with the penny clenched between my buttocks. It fell out a good many times at the start, but then, gradually, it began to stay in for longer and longer, so much so that I forgot it was there. My stride shortened, I came up on the balls of my feet, and all the time I kept imagining that my feet hurt, trapped in those painful patent leather shoes.

Finally, I rang Brian Eastman and suggested a second screen test. Back we went to Twickenham, where I got back into full costume and make-up – with the moustache, of course – and into those tight, shiny shoes. Then I went in front of the cameras.

It worked. At last we knew that we now had our Poirot, walk and all.

The only thing left for me to do was to go and find a book of Edwardian manners. After all, if one of Poirot's major cases when he was still in the Belgian police was the Abercrombie forgery case in 1904 – as Inspector Japp of Scotland Yard reveals in *The Mysterious Affair at Styles* – then he would most certainly have been aware of the delicacies of Edwardian Europe. He would have gradually confirmed his own manners at the end of the nineteenth century and the first years of the twentieth, as a man in his middle age. That's when they would have been formed, and they would have remained with him ever since.

I wanted to know the precise details of how an Edwardian gentleman would greet a lady; how to tip one's hat; how to walk with a cane; how to hold one's gloves; whether to take them off, and when; how to bow and to whom, and when; how to take a lady's hand and kiss it; how to sense a silence and not break it.

There aren't many men today who could cope with a Homburg hat, white gloves and a silver-topped cane without dropping one or all of them. I knew in my very soul that Poirot would never, ever, have allowed himself to make such a mistake.

And as the days passed in that summer of 1988, another thought struck me – I was beginning to see ever more clearly the parallels between Poirot and me.

As my list of characteristics pointed out, at number sixty-five, he 'will usually wear a morning suit when working at home – like a Harley Street specialist'. That struck a chord, for my own father had done the same in his rooms at Number 2, Harley Street, while treating his private patients as a gynaecologist and obstetrician.

I too liked things to be symmetrical around me. If I put two things on the mantelpiece, they have to be exactly evenly spaced, though I'm not quite as fanatical as Poirot. I also think people find it easy to talk to me, as they do to him. 'Women find him very sympathetic,' my note number seventy-five said. My brother John insists that I was always attracting the pretty girls when we were young men, while he wasn't, though I don't honestly remember that. But, like Poirot, I would admit that I have a 'twinkle' in my eye when it comes to ladies. I think my wife would agree with that, because I twinkled at her. As for my baldness, there was a similarity there too. I lost a great deal of my hair when I was just twenty-three, after a love affair collapsed. I was heartbroken, and so was my hair. Perhaps the same thing happened to Poirot – who, according to number sixty-seven of my notes: 'Once fell in love with an English girl who used to cook him fluffy omelettes.' He would have liked to have been married, and – as my note number eighty-nine reminded me – 'Genuinely believes that the happiness of one man and one woman is the greatest thing in all the world.'

It was almost as if Poirot and I had started to become one – though perhaps I had been a little luckier in love.

Quite by chance, Sheila and I were looking to buy a new house in the months before I started filming. The children were growing ever more active, and we wanted somewhere in the suburbs, rather than in the crowds of central London, for them to grow up in.

One house we looked at, Elmdene in Pinner, was owned by the late, great comic actor Ronnie Barker – and when we arrived, we both agreed that it looked exactly like a house in an Agatha Christie story. There were leaded lights in the windows, an Art Deco front door and reception rooms, even a garden large enough for all the suspects to assemble for Poirot's final revelation of the murder.

Even more extraordinary, when I went into the dining room to talk to Ronnie about the house and the possibility of buying it, above the mantelpiece, there was an oil painting of him dressed in character.

'Who's that?' I asked Ronnie.

'Oh, that's me as Hercule Poirot,' he said with a little smile. 'I played him in *Black Coffee* in rep. I wasn't very good.'

Perhaps inevitably, Sheila and I ended up buying the house – we knew that Poirot would have approved of it.

Poirot was suddenly everywhere I turned, peeking from the next room, reminding me – and challenging me – to bring him truthfully to life on the screen.

Then, just a couple of weeks before shooting was about to start, I was invited to lunch by Dame Agatha's daughter Rosalind Hicks and her lawyer husband Anthony, who I knew looked after the Christie affairs around the world.

We went to a small Italian restaurant just off Kensington High Street with glass-panelled walls and ferns, which made it all feel very light and airy. I sat down thinking that it was going to be a happy, congratulatory lunch, though I was also distinctly nervous, as this was the first time I'd met Dame Agatha's only child, who was then almost seventy.

What I didn't realise, as we sat down, was that I was about to be as grilled as the sole I ordered for lunch. The whole meal was taken up with Rosalind and Anthony asking me to clarify exactly what my intentions were towards Poirot. How was I going to play him? What did I have in mind for his voice and walk? How was I going to deal with his little idiosyncrasies?

The room may have been airy, but the atmosphere was rather less so. Then, towards the end of the meal, Anthony Hicks leant across the table towards me and looked me straight in the eye.

'I want you to remember', he said, a touch fiercely, 'that we, the audience, can and will smile with Poirot.'

Then he paused.

'But we must never, ever, laugh at him.'

There was another pause.

'And I am most certainly not joking.'

I gulped, before Rosalind said, equally forcefully, 'And that is why we want you to play him.'

With those words ringing in my ears, I knew that I had to be 100 per cent in character from the very first day of filming, and that I had to project Poirot's behaviour precisely as Dame Agatha had described it in her books from the first moment the cameras turned, because the character I was committing to celluloid would be fixed forever.

I also knew that this was one of the most important days of my life.

CHAPTER 3

'I'M SORRY, BUT I AM NOT GOING TO WEAR THAT SUIT'

It was just before 6.30 a.m. on a bright, sunny morning in late June 1988 when Sheila and I walked out of our new home on my first day of shooting for the first series of *Agatha Christie's Poirot* for ITV – the day that I knew could well be the most important in my life.

We'd finally bought Ronnie Barker's house in Pinner, Middlesex, not far from the church, and we'd moved in on Midsummer's Day, but we weren't quite settled – there were still boxes everywhere. Most frightening of all, neither of us knew whether we would actually be able to afford to stay there.

On the doorstep, Sheila and I turned to each other and said, almost in unison, 'We'll be very happy if we manage to stay here for a year.' It was such a special house for us, way beyond our dreams.

As I walked towards the car that the producers had arranged to collect me, I said, with a smile on my face, 'If we don't get another series, we sell.'

Sheila laughed as I climbed into the passenger seat and shut the door. Driving away, I looked back through the rear window to see her waving. My heart was in my mouth, and our house was on the line.

But there was some comfort on that summer Monday morning, because I was in good hands. The man driving me across London to Twickenham Studios was a friend, and, though I didn't know it then, a man that I was destined to spend the next twenty-five years sitting beside as we drove all over England.

How he came into my life is a rather lovely story. A couple of years earlier, just after I'd come back to England from filming *Harry and the Hendersons* in America, where I had played the 'Bigfoot' hunter Jacques Lafleur, who was determined to kill the giant animal that John Lithgow and his family wanted to save, I'd been offered a part in a play called *This Story of Yours* at the Hampstead Theatre Club.

It was a harrowing piece by John Hopkins – who had cut his teeth writing *Z Cars* for BBC Television – about a burned-out detective sergeant who kills a suspected paedophile in police custody. Written in 1968, it had been turned into a film called *The Offence* in 1972 by Sean Connery, who had bought the rights and played the detective, and was directed by Sidney Lumet.

Detective Sergeant Johnson was such an important part that I didn't want to miss any of the rehearsals, but about halfway through I caught the flu. Sheila and I were still living in Acton and it was a horrible battle to get across London to Hampstead by Tube, so we decided I should take a mini-cab – a rash decision really because we weren't sure we could really afford it. But there was no other way I was going to get there, so we called our local firm, and a nice Irish driver turned up.

As we set off, he looked in the rear-view mirror and said, in a cheery Irish brogue, 'You don't look too good.'

'I've got a bit of the flu,' I told him.

'Why are you going to work then?'

'There's no alternative. They can't go on without me. I've got to be there.'

As the 45-minute drive went on, the driver told me that his name was Sean O'Connor and that he'd been working for the firm for a few years. He was charming, and I ended up telling him, 'I wish I could afford to do this every day.'

Mightily relieved, I got to rehearsals and, at the end of the day – about 5.30 p.m. or so – I came out of the theatre, which is near Swiss Cottage Tube station in north London, bracing myself for what I knew would be a very unpleasant trip home on the Underground.

To my astonishment, Sean was outside waiting for me. He'd asked that morning what time I finished, but I hadn't paid much attention.

'I thought you'd need a ride home,' he said, as he got out of the car and opened the back door for me.

Sean took me back to Acton, and didn't charge me a penny. I couldn't believe it, and, from then on, whenever we wanted a mini-cab, Sheila and I would ring our local firm and always ask for Sean.

When I was offered the first Poirot series a couple of years later, my contract allowed me to have a car to and from the studio every day of shooting, and so I asked whether I could choose the driver. The production office said yes, and I asked for Sean.

Funnily enough, when I first told him, he was driving me to what was then still the Comedy Theatre in the West End, this time for Tom Kempinski's play *Separation*, because there was a bus and Tube strike in London that day.

'Do you want to change your life?' I said, as we struggled through the snarled traffic.

'What do you mean?'

So I told him about Poirot, and that it meant I was allowed a driver of my choice.

There was barely a moment's pause before he looked at me over his shoulder and said, 'Not half.'

Sean has been with me ever since, and has become a well-known driver in the film and television industry in this country.

But when he's driving me on Poirot, I always sit beside him in the front of the car – and there is a very specific reason why I do that. It goes to the heart of what I believe about being an actor. I always sit in the front because I never want to be perceived as a snob or a star. I don't feel comfortable with the idea of being chauffeured, and never have, although I have to admit that there's nothing that Poirot would have liked more. He would always sit in the back, quite happy at being chauffeured.

So it was Sean who ushered me across London on that June morning in 1988, the first day of filming. I sat there, feeling more nervous than I'd ever done in my entire career.

'Am I going to do this right?' I asked myself. 'Will it work?'

Things did not start well.

Shortly after Sean dropped me outside my dressing room at Twickenham, just down the road from the River Thames at Richmond, my rather nervous male dresser arrived with the suit I was supposed to wear for the first day's shooting.

It was for a scene in Poirot's flat in Whitehaven Mansions, as part of the opening to the short story *The Adventure of the Clapham Cook*, which told of a missing cook, a mysterious lodger and the disappearance of £90,000 pounds in foreign bank notes from a bank in the City of London.

I'd looked at the scene in the car with Sean on my way to the studio, and could see it clearly in my mind.

One of the things I could see was that Poirot would be dressed in his black patent leather shoes, his spats, striped trousers and waistcoat as part of his morning suit. But those were not the clothes that arrived with my dresser on that June morning. Instead, I was presented with a distinctly dull, ordinary grey suit. I was horrified. All the fears that had welled up inside during the first costume fittings a few weeks earlier came flooding back, and I sat down in my chair with a bump.

'I'm sorry, but I am *not* going to wear that suit,' I said quietly. 'It isn't what Poirot would wear. He would wear his morning suit.'

'But this is what I've been told to give you, David,' my dresser told me, the surprise – and the nervousness – only too obvious in his voice.

'Well, I won't be wearing it.'

I will never forget the look he gave me when I said that. There was despair in his eyes, as well as a little confusion. Who was he going to please – the director or me? He was caught in the middle.

There was a long pause, and then he backed quietly out of my dressing room, with the grey suit over his arm. But I was as determined as I'd ever been that I was going to be true to the Poirot I saw in my mind's eye and heard in my head.

In my heart, I knew that there was bound to be some reaction from the director, who had clearly decided that was what I should be wearing for the scene, but I wasn't going to be put off. So, after my dresser came back to help me on with the padding I needed to play Poirot, I waited for another costume.

I didn't have to wait long. Just a few minutes later, a costume lady arrived, this time carrying a morning suit, complete with striped trousers and waistcoat. My dresser took it from her. Hardly a word was said, but I was delighted that my views were being listened to.

Nevertheless, as I walked onto the set for my first scene, I was still trembling with nerves.

For the first shot, the camera was to track up from my feet, taking in my patent leather shoes, my spats and my striped trousers – I was to flick a speck of lint from them with my hand – and then rising to take in my waistcoat and bow tie, before arriving on my face, with my fingers stretched upwards in a steeple – the cathedral of hands, as I liked to call it.

Hastings was suggesting crimes that Poirot might be interested in from the newspaper, but Poirot carefully rejected all of them, before telling Hastings that he had to attend to his wardrobe. It was a little vignette of how very particular Poirot was about his clothes.

What was really terrifying me though was the simple fact that I knew that I had to be exactly right from the very first moment the camera caught sight of me, because once it did, I would never truly be able to change that first impression. I was still trembling when the director, the then 38-year-old Edward Bennett, who was to go on to work on many British television series, called, 'Action!'

But my years in the theatre had taught me one thing that helped enormously: the ability to block everything out and concentrate. I knew that if I focused entirely on my Poirot, he would help me conquer my nerves.

To my immense relief, the fastidious little detective did exactly that. He saw me through my first day, and my second, and my third, just as he has on every single day ever since. More than anyone, it was Hercule Poirot himself who helped me to bring him to life on that first day at Twickenham.

Mind you, I had a lot of help, especially from my fellow actors in the core of the cast, including the wonderful Hugh Fraser as Poirot's trusted friend and colleague Captain Hastings, Philip Jackson as Scotland Yard's Chief Inspector Japp, and Pauline Moran as Poirot's secretary, Miss Lemon. And then, of course, there were Clive Exton's superb scripts, adapted from Dame Agatha's stories.

Clive was a Londoner, born in Islington, who had started his career writing for *Armchair Theatre* on ITV in 1959 and had gone on to write for both television and film, spending ten years in Hollywood before returning in 1986. He would end up writing no fewer than twenty Poirot scripts.

Funnily enough, there also turned out to be a strange echo of my time on Bryher in the Isles of Scilly that year, because the music for my first Poirot series was written by Christopher Gunning, the exceptionally talented composer who had also written the score for *When the Whales Came*. His Poirot music, including the delightful theme, was to win him a British Academy Film Award in 1989 for the best original television music. People still tend to hum it whenever they think about the series, and even hum it to me when they meet me.

In the first scene of *The Adventure of the Clapham Cook*, Poirot is refusing to take an interest in any of the crimes Hastings suggests because they are not crimes of 'national importance', as he puts it, rather grandly.

Poirot is brought down to earth with a bump when Miss Lemon ushers in a banker's wife from Clapham, Mrs Todd, played by Brigit Forsyth, who wants him to find her missing cook, who disappeared just two days earlier. When Poirot tells her that this is too small a matter to concern him, Mrs Todd snaps back that he is just being 'high and mighty' and that a good cook is 'very hard to find' and 'most important'.

To Hastings' amazement, Poirot admits his error at once, and accepts the case, revealing two of his most endearing characteristics – his kindness and his ability not to take himself too seriously.

In fact, that first episode established a great deal about Poirot, not least the importance of his relationship with the ever-loyal Hastings. That was something that Hugh Fraser and I worked on throughout those first days of shooting.

Hugh had years of experience on the stage and on television, in everything from *Edward and Mrs Simpson*, in which he played Foreign Secretary Anthony Eden, and later to *Sharpe* where he was the Duke of Wellington. But though Hugh and I were almost exactly the same age, and he had studied at the Webber Douglas Academy of Dramatic Art, we had never actually worked together until that first day at Twickenham.

Yet we were destined to become forever intertwined in people's minds, just as Basil Rathbone and Nigel Bruce were after those twelve wonderful black and white Hollywood adventures of Sherlock Holmes between 1939 and 1946.

Hugh was born in London but brought up in the Midlands, and is married to the actress Belinda Lang. He became a tremendous support to me, someone I could rely on every bit as much as Poirot did on his Hastings, and I think I helped him too. But it was very difficult for us to work out exactly what our relationship should be on the screen. It meant that we had to be very aware about exactly where we stood or sat in relation to the camera. In the end, we decided that I should almost always be in the foreground and he slightly behind, unless the story dictated otherwise.

Quite rightly, Hugh didn't want Hastings to be a comedy character – a straight man, if you like – because he thought, as I did, that his character was there to represent the audience in the story. That meant we had to find a way of making sure that Hastings was never allowed to look like a complete fool.

To help him with this, Hugh developed a dead-pan expression to convey to the audience that Hastings was someone who may not have been hugely intelligent but nevertheless represented the ordinary man. As Hugh put it himself at the time, 'One of Hastings' functions is to elucidate what is going on in Poirot's mind.'

One way Hugh decided to do that was to use the phrases 'Good heavens' and 'Good Lord' regularly, as a gently ironic commentary on his attitude to Poirot. Was he truly amazed? Or was he actually making fun of the great detective? Whatever the truth, it was a wonderful device, and it worked.

The more upright and sensible Hastings became, the more it allowed me to accentuate Poirot's foibles, the little mannerisms that I knew lay at the heart of his character. Hastings also gave me things to react against – like his love of his dark-green, open-top Lagonda car, for example, as well as his delight in the English countryside and sport, especially golf.

Both the car and the countryside of the Lake District play their parts in *The Adventure of the Clapham Cook*, where Poirot amply displays his dislike of the 'wasteland' of the country on a trip to Keswick, by stepping in a cow pat and complaining that there is not one restaurant, theatre or art gallery in sight.

It was Hugh who pointed out to me how much money was being lavished on the sets, props, costumes and background to make the production look authentic. We were walking across the Albert Bridge in Chelsea, on our way back from Mrs Todd's house in

Clapham, in a night scene, when Hugh said to me, when the cameras weren't rolling, 'Look, they've even got a camera crane. And have you seen how many vintage cars and passers-by dressed in exactly the right period clothes we have? It's extraordinary.'

He was quite right, but it was the first time that I had really noticed it, because I'd been so caught up in my portrayal of Poirot. No sooner had he pointed it out, however, than I became even more nervous, as I knew that it meant that a very great deal of money and expectations were resting on my shoulders. Later on, I discovered that London Weekend Television, who financed that first series for Brian Eastman, spent almost £5 million on the filming of those first ten stories, an average of half a million pounds per episode, a fortune in 1988.

Our first story not only allowed me to introduce some of Poirot's idiosyncrasies, it also allowed me to show his finest qualities. His kindness to Mrs Todd's parlour maid, for example, which leads him to the Lake District and the missing cook's 'inheritance' of an isolated cottage, his elaborate politeness to everyone he meets, and his habit of reading the Bible in bed every night.

The Adventure of the Clapham Cook also introduced one of the other principal characters in Poirot's life, his friend and sometime foe, Chief Inspector Japp of Scotland Yard, played by the superb Philip Jackson. Strangely enough, like Hugh, I'd never worked with Philip before those first days of shooting. Only three years younger than Hugh and me, he was born in Nottinghamshire and had studied German and Drama at Bristol University before going to Liverpool rep for eighteen months. Astonishingly flexible as an actor, Philip had then played in everything from the BBC's *Last of the Summer Wine*, to Dennis Potter's acclaimed television drama *Pennies from Heaven*.

He had read Agatha Christie as a child, but he didn't go back and read the stories again after being asked to play Chief Inspector Japp.

'I chose to take the character from the scripts alone,' Philip said at the time. 'The challenge to an actor is to give the character a depth beyond what is printed on the page.'

What Philip did so well was to play what was essentially a comic policeman absolutely straight. There was no mugging for the camera from him, no raised eyebrows or comic winks. He just kept his trilby hat clasped to his chest and his eye on the man or woman he thought was guilty. Philip portrayed Japp as a down-to-earth, by-the-book copper who is unpretentious and almost child-like. He may have taken his cue from Inspector Lestrade of the Sherlock Holmes stories, but he never once allowed himself to be made to look like an imbecile. If he were a little slower than Poirot, so be it, but he would never allow Japp to be humiliated.

On the set, Philip quickly realised what I was trying to do as Poirot, and reacted to it by being more and more ordinary in the face of Poirot's idiosyncrasies, while all the time demonstrating his affection for the detective he spends so much time fencing with. As Philip puts it, 'He's sort of friends with Poirot in a strange kind of way, although he is certainly irritated by the fact that this Belgian detective keeps beating him.'

As Poirot's secretary, Miss Lemon, Pauline Moran also displayed the affection she felt for Poirot, even if he did infuriate her at times. Though she'd trained at RADA and worked a lot on television, as well as appearing with the Royal Shakespeare Company, once again, we had never worked together before. But she grasped immediately that her character was almost a reflection of Poirot.

As Pauline explained about Miss Lemon, 'She has the same

fastidiousness and obsession with detail and precision as Poirot. I have a great aptitude for minute detail myself.'

Pauline also grasped that although Poirot was always respectful and charming towards women, he was also always reserved with them, and so she remained meticulously professional with him in every scene, never flirting for a moment, no matter how much she may have cared about him privately. She was 'a wonderful secretary and very, very proper with Poirot', as she puts it. 'If she was even thirty seconds late, both of them would be horrified.'

In fact, *The Adventure of the Clapham Cook* encapsulated much of what would develop in the years to come. Poirot's fussiness; his pride in his 'little grey cells' and in being Belgian not French; his capacity for generosity of spirit, especially towards servants; his respect for Miss Lemon; his delight in Hastings' loyalty; his fondness for Japp; and, perhaps most of all, his ability to laugh at himself – for example, by framing the cheque for one guinea that Mrs Todd sent him after dispensing with his services.

The spectacular sets, clothes, props and locations underlined the authenticity that everyone wanted to bring to every frame. The audience truly felt that they were being transported to 1935, 1936 or 1937. The only downside was that we were forced to film each of the one-hour stories in just eleven shooting days, one of the tightest production schedules it is possible to imagine.

That meant that the only real chance I had to learn my lines for the next day's shooting came when I got home at about 8.30 p.m. each night, which was incredibly taxing. I would then repeat them to myself in the car on the way to the studio the next morning, which meant that my driver Sean heard every line, as I used to speak them out loud.

As the weeks passed, he would gently make suggestions from time to time: 'Maybe it might be a little better, if you don't mind me saying so, if you dropped that last line. You don't need to say it.' Sean gradually became my filter, and he came to know the role almost as well as I did.

It was all the more exhausting when, not long after we started shooting, the old arguments about what Poirot should or should not do raised their head again.

When Poirot and Hastings go to visit Mrs Todd's house in Clapham, in pursuit of the missing cook, they go for a stroll on the common while they wait for Mr Todd to come home from the office. They want to talk to him about his cook, as well as speak to the couple's 'paying guest', a lodger, at the same time.

Clive Exton's script called for Poirot to sit down on a park bench to talk to Hastings, and so, when the moment came to rehearse the shot, I did exactly what Poirot would have done. I removed my handkerchief from my pocket, carefully wiped the seat, spread the handkerchief out, and then sat on it, so that there would no danger of Poirot getting a stain on his trousers.

Ed Bennett, the director, genuinely thought that looked ridiculous, and said so, which rather upset me. Once again, it was as if all the conversations I'd had with everyone connected with the series over the past weeks – focusing on my determination to play Dame Agatha's Poirot exactly as she had written him – had been sidelined. It felt as though I was suddenly right back where I'd started.

But I was not prepared to budge. I felt certain that wiping the seat and sitting on the handkerchief was exactly what Poirot would have done in those circumstances. I refused point blank to sit down without doing so.

'But it looks ridiculous,' I was told again and again. 'The audience will think he is quite mad.'

'Nonsense,' I replied. 'It is exactly what Poirot would do and exactly what Agatha Christie has him doing.'

The director would not allow me to do what he believed looked ridiculous, and I would not sacrifice the integrity of my Poirot. It was a stalemate. But I was fighting for what Dame Agatha wrote, and in doing so, serving Poirot's creator.

If I lost the argument, it would mean that my custodianship of Poirot's character was in severe jeopardy – so much so that I really thought that I might not be able to go on playing him. I had to play the character she'd created, I was certain of that. I would not compromise.

Now, I am not a confrontational man. Frankly, I don't like any kind of confrontation at all. It upsets me too much. But I've always found it easier to argue for someone else – in this case, Hercule Poirot – rather than for myself. That way, I'm defending the character, not being a sort of grand 'luvvie', a word which I hate.

Ed Bennett was adamant that it looked silly, and I was every bit as certain that it was precisely in character, and so the shoot came to a dead stop.

Brian Eastman was summoned to adjudicate. I had some distinctly anxious moments as I waited for him to decide how we should play this scene. I only knew what my instinct told me. I had to be true to Poirot.

Fortunately, Brian went with the handkerchief, and the shoot resumed, with me wiping the park bench before sitting down. I'm not exactly sure what would have happened if Brian's decision had gone the other way. Perhaps I would have accepted it, but in my heart, I very much doubt it. I think it would have made continuing to play Poirot much more difficult for me, as I would not have been true to the man I had come to know so well.

Yet the irony is that in the final cut of *The Adventure of the Clapham Cook*, the one that was eventually broadcast around the world, you only see Poirot, umbrella in hand, standing beside Hastings, who is sitting on the park bench. Poirot never actually sits down! The scene of Poirot wiping the park bench with his handkerchief ended up on the cutting-room floor. When I saw that, I allowed myself a wry little smile.

I am not sure that it made the slightest difference to the audience's enjoyment of the story and, if I am truly honest, I do not believe that it diluted my interpretation of Poirot, but, in spite of that, the 'affair of the handkerchief' mattered desperately to me at the time. Someone had to stand up for and protect Dame Agatha's Poirot, and that person was going to be me, no matter what the consequences might be.

I felt that responsibility more and more as the weeks passed on the first series, because I knew that by putting myself in that position, I was getting closer and closer to the character I was playing. The more that I knew about Poirot, the more I could protect him.

What began as my exploring Poirot and his character gradually developed into a relationship in which we began to merge into one – so much so that by the end of the series, I knew that I could have gone out into the real world, rather than a television studio, dressed in his costume, and lived his life *exactly* as he would have lived it, and still have beeen myself.

Poirot and I steadily became one and the same man. Suddenly it was Poirot and me.

CHAPTER 4

'I'M AFRAID THEY'RE GOING TO BE TOO TAME, OR TOO ECCENTRIC'

The second Poirot story we shot, though it was the third to be transmitted, started exactly two weeks after our first. It was *The Adventure of Johnnie Waverly* – the case of an attempt to foil a threatened kidnap of the son of a wealthy landowner, Marcus Waverly, played by my old friend Geoffrey Bateman.

Geoffrey and I had definitely worked together before – at the Connaught Theatre in Worthing in 1971 – when he played a Samurai warrior in a stage version of the classic 1950 Japanese film drama *Rashomon*. It was very early in my career, and I directed all the fight scenes, as well as playing the bandit. Now Geoffrey was playing the landowner whose huge country house seems to be falling down around his ears, while his son is in danger.

For this story we had a new director, Renny Rye, who was then only forty and would go on to direct five episodes of that first Poirot series. Renny started his television career producing the children's programme *Blue Peter*, before graduating to drama. He was to stay with Poirot until 1991. Since then, he has gone on to direct episodes of the British television series *Midsomer Murders* and *Silent Witness*, among many other things.

Because of the schedule, Ed Bennett, who'd directed *Clapham Cook*, disappeared into the cutting room to edit his film, while Renny worked on *Johnnie Waverly*. Then Ed would return to direct the third, while Renny went away to edit his. Alternating the two directors was the only way we could be sure to produce the films within the twenty weeks that we had been given by London Weekend, who were keen to transmit the series in January 1989, barely three weeks after we would finish shooting.

Johnnie Waverly again reminded everyone how much Poirot loathed the countryside, especially when he is forced to walk across the fields after Hastings' Lagonda breaks down just minutes before the threatened kidnap is about to take place. The resilient Chief Inspector Japp arrives with a team of constables in an effort to foil the crime, but to no avail, although Poirot realises that the kidnap must have been organised by someone who knew the family, and eventually retrieves young Johnnie.

The bond that was beginning to develop between Hugh, Philip and me seemed to grow as the weeks passed, and it was certainly clear for all to see at the start of the third film, *Murder in the Mews*, which opened with the three characters walking home after dinner past a November fireworks party and the mews where Hastings garages his Lagonda.

I also seemed to develop a rapport with the rest of the cast. David Yelland was one of the guest stars of *Murder in the Mews*. He'd played the Prince of Wales in the Oscar-winning film *Chariots of Fire*. Educated at Cambridge, where he read English, and only a year younger than I am, he was wonderful as the ambitious MP Charles Laverton-West.

No sooner had we finished *Mews* than we were on to the next, *Four and Twenty Blackbirds*. There was hardly a moment for me to do anything except go to Twickenham and work. That meant that I had to leave home every morning at 6.30 a.m. and I often didn't get back to Pinner until 8.30 or 9 p.m. I'm afraid that meant that Sheila and the children did not see a great deal of me in the months between July and Christmas 1988, because even when I did get home, I had to look at the script for the next day. I eventually got into the habit of making sure that I learnt my lines at least two weeks ahead, to overcome the panic of trying to learn them the night before.

One difficulty for me was that Poirot always had to explain exactly who did it – at the end of the story – to whichever group of people had been involved, including, of course, Hastings and Japp. So I found myself often having to learn quite long speeches after I'd finished filming for the day. I tried to prepare for them by making sure I looked at them throughout the filming, but, inevitably, when it came down to making sure I had them firmly in my mind, everything hinged on the night before we were due to shoot.

The denouement was the moment when I revealed the murderer to everyone, including, most important of all, the audience. I simply could not allow myself to get it even a fraction wrong; that would have been to let Poirot down, and I would never allow myself to do that.

There was another issue about the denouements, however, which involved being true to Poirot and to myself as an actor.

When Dame Agatha wrote those final scenes where the villain is revealed, she was allowing Poirot his 'theatrical' moment. He is well aware of who is guilty as he goes round the room explaining the nature of the case, but Dame Agatha and he often take great pleasure in picking on an innocent party and seeming to accuse them of the crime, before revealing their innocence. It was her way of building up suspense for the final 'reveal'.

In those scenes, Poirot is acting – teasing the characters, apparently accusing them and then changing his mind, making them an essential part of the final drama – and in that sense, he is treading on *my* territory as an actor.

Now, because I am an actor, I know precisely how to play those scenes, for they allow me to use my theatricality. I feel instinctively what I need to do, and how to do it. No one needs to direct me in those denouements because Poirot has strayed into my world as an actor, which means that – in a strange way – I feel more comfortable doing those scenes than almost any other.

In fact, it is in those scenes that Poirot and I completely merge, touching one another in a quite extraordinary way. There is the actor in Poirot which merges almost seamlessly into me the actor; the perfectionist in Poirot and the same perfectionist in me; the need for order in Poirot precisely matched by my own need for order, not least in the filming of his stories.

We are all but one person, so much so that I often feel the line between us blurring. If he feels pain, so do I; if I feel unsettled, it shows in him. Our symbiosis is all but complete. Interestingly, the fifth film in the first series, *The Third Floor Flat*, reflects exactly that, especially when it comes to Poirot's respect for women.

The story is almost entirely set in Poirot's Whitehaven Mansions, which is actually named Florin Court and lies in Charterhouse Square in London, not far from a fourteenth-century monastery which later became a Tudor mansion, an almshouse and a school in the seventeenth century.

Hidden away not far from Smithfield Market, Charterhouse is one of the most beautiful and secret of all London's squares. On the east side, Florin Court was built in 1936, and consisted of nine floors, a roof garden and an indoor swimming pool, all in the Art Deco style. It is one of the best-preserved of all the Art Deco blocks of apartments in London, which made it the perfect location for Poirot's flat, Number 56B, on the fifth floor.

Regalian Properties refurbished the building in the 1980s and kindly allowed us to film there, but it still looked exactly as it had done when it was built. The stories in the first series were all set precisely at a time when the block would have been new, between 1936 and 1938, even though Dame Agatha had, in fact, written most of them a few years earlier. From the very beginning, Brian Eastman had been very keen to set all the films within a certain period of time, to give them a particular look and feel.

The Third Floor Flat allows Poirot to reveal his dislike of being ill and bored. As the story opens, he has a terrible cold, and is complaining to Miss Lemon that he has had nothing interesting to do for three weeks – 'an eternity for a brain like mine'. To divert him, Hastings arranges a trip to the theatre, inevitably to see a murder mystery, which only further infuriates Poirot, as he insists the man who is finally revealed to be the murderer could not possibly have done it. The true culprit was, for Poirot, obviously the butler.

The irony of a detective not agreeing with a playwright's view of who might have been the killer is not lost on Hastings on their way back to the flat. But the mood quickly changes – and Poirot's cold disappears – when a body is found in the flat two floors below Poirot's, number 36B. The victim was played by the comedienne Josie Lawrence in one of her first straight television roles.

Most important of all, however, is the fact that the heroine of the story, played by Suzanne Burden, makes Poirot a 'fluffy omelette' during his investigation, which only serves to remind him, and me, of his repressed love for a young Englishwoman in his past who once also made him 'fluffy omelettes'.

But what did those omelettes mean for a man like Poirot? I think they were a sign that he could only love at a distance, at one remove, rather than as a red-blooded man. Dame Agatha could not and did not allow him to cross the barrier and release himself into a full relationship with a woman because it would have proved too great a threat to his personality. Poirot could admire, even 'love', a woman, but it would always be from a distance, and I understood that instinctively, although it is not a feeling I share.

Those omelettes were a symbol of his remoteness, underlining the fact that Poirot was well aware of the fact that Suzanne's character reminded him of the love he could never quite have, and that affected me deeply. Once again, it helped me to understand his deep regret at never having truly experienced love, even though Dame Agatha did allow him a relationship with the dramatic Russian Countess Rossakoff, but one which was also destined to disappear into the wind.

What was so charming was that Suzanne, and every other actor and actress who came into the series, were genuinely thrilled to be in a Poirot story. They all seemed to have known and read Poirot as a child, whereas I didn't know him at all to begin with, even though I was becoming him more completely every single day.

The sixth and seventh films in the first series underlined exactly how much money London Weekend was spending. *Triangle at Rhodes* was set on the Greek island, and the whole unit was transported there. For the next, *Problem at Sea*, everyone stayed in the Mediterranean, while Poirot took a cruise on a magnificent 1930s motor yacht, and we visited another group of beautiful, exotic locations.

In fact, those two stories reflected Dame Agatha's own fascination with travel and adventure, and helped to set the series far apart from some of the other British fiction of the time, most of which seemed landlocked in Britain.

In *Triangle at Rhodes* Poirot uses a little wooden doll that belonged to a child, who was one of the characters, while in *Problem at Sea* he reveals an interest in ventriloquism. Both only increased the pressure on me to make sure that I could carry those vital scenes at the end of the film to satisfy every single person in the television audience.

One thing I knew was that Dame Agatha always made sure that all the clues were there for everyone to see – if only they looked for them. If you did grasp them all, then you would know who did it; if not, you would have to wait for Poirot to tell you. It was one of her greatest qualities as a writer – she was always honest with her readers – and I wanted to be equally honest with her viewers. They had to feel that they might have reached the same conclusion as Poirot if they had put all the clues together; although they knew, in their hearts, that although they might have noticed one or two, Poirot saw them all – which was why he was a *great* detective.

The Incredible Theft, which was the eighth film, demonstrated yet again the extraordinary lengths that Brian Eastman and London Weekend went to in order to find exactly the right backgrounds and props. The story revolves around a maverick aircraft manufacturer and his designs for a new fighter in 1936, because there is 'so much at stake for England' as the possibility of a second European war looms.

The fact that the producers found so many vintage planes to illustrate the story was extraordinary enough, but the cast was every bit as special, with John Stride as the maverick millionaire and John Carson as the politician Sir George Carrington.

I found myself explaining the nature of the 'theft' of a critical page of the aircraft's design at the denouement, this time in a wonderful country house. In fact, the Poirot stories were most often set in the homes of the landed aristocracy or millionaires, although *The Adventure of the Clapham Cook* demonstrated that he both could and did work with the rather less affluent. Nonetheless, Poirot does not take the wealth of those around him too seriously. He takes some considerable pleasure in gently poking fun at the foibles of the English aristocracy, often ridiculing their insistence on respecting 'good chaps'.

This is one of the great charms of Poirot's investigations, for they reveal a world where manners and morals are quite different from today. There are no overt and unnecessary sex scenes, no alcoholic, haunted detectives in Poirot's world. He lives in a simpler, some would say more human, era: a lost England, seen through the admiring eyes of this foreigner, this little Belgian detective. For me, that makes the stories all the more appealing, for although the days he lives in seem far away, they are all the more enchanting because of it.

The last stories for the first series were *The King of Clubs*, about the death of a film producer, which starts with Poirot visiting a film set – which, of course, was created at Twickenham Studios, next to our own set – and *The Dream*, about a famous pie manu-facturer who is killed in a locked room in his flat above the factory. The cast were as tremendous as they had been throughout, including Niamh Cusack as a film actress in the story about the movie mogul, and my old colleague from the Royal Shakespeare Company Alan Howard as the pie manufacturer. His daughter was played by the delightful Joely Richardson, in one of her first television appearances.

The Dream was the last to be shot, and we finished just a few days before Christmas 1988. By then, I had discovered that London Weekend had scheduled the films to start on the Sunday night exactly two weeks after Christmas Day, on 8 January 1989. The ten we had shot that year were to go out every Sunday evening thereafter at 8.45 p.m., ending on 19 March.

I honestly had no idea how they were going to turn out. In fact, I was privately rather frightened that they might be boring. I remember thinking to myself that these films were not action-packed like *The Professionals* or *The Sweeney*, both hugely successful in their time, nor were they comparable to the more recent Morse and Wexford series. Were they going to be entertaining enough for an audience in 1989?

'I'm afraid they're going to be too tame, or too eccentric,' I thought to myself.

At that end of the final day of shooting in December 1988, we had a party for the crew and regular members of the cast at Twickenham. Brian Eastman made a little speech, and then so did I. What I said precisely reflected my private uncertainty.

'I really have no idea whether Poirot will work,' I told everyone that evening. 'Possibly it won't, and so there might never be another series, which is why I want to say thank you to everybody here for all you've done to make it such a wonderful experience.'

What I did know, however, was that I had never been more tired in my acting career. I walked off the set on that final night utterly exhausted. I was barely off the screen throughout almost 500 minutes of prime-time television – working fourteen- and fifteen-hour days, and I could hardly think.

Sean took me home to our new house in Pinner, and I all but collapsed. Christmas was not quite cancelled, but it was jolly close to it, though I made every effort not to show it for the sake of the children. But Sheila knew.

All we had to do now was to wait and see what the reaction would be.

Yet, in my heart, I was afraid that no more films were going to be made, and that meant that I was going to have to say goodbye to the little Belgian whom I had grown so incredibly fond of. We had become so close that the pain of losing him would be almost too much to bear.

CHAPTER 5

'IT WAS LIKE BEING HIT OVER THE HEAD WITH A MALLET'

We had a family Christmas. Robert and Katherine were still quite young, and both my parents, as well as Sheila's mother, were still alive, so there was plenty to keep us occupied. But in the back of my mind, I could not stop thinking about Poirot. I was gradually recovering from the strain of filming, but I still wondered what the audience would think.

The publicity for the series started immediately after the holiday, and I suddenly found myself doing interview after interview about playing the role, without really knowing whether it worked on the screen. I was fascinated to know what the audience were being told about the nature of my work, and what the journalists I was meeting thought about the films themselves, as they'd seen at least the first episode in a preview, as they usually do. Thankfully, many of them were kind enough to tell me how good they thought it was.

That came as something of a relief, as I had not seen any of the films in their entirety. Brian Eastman had shown me bits of the filming here and there, when there was something we specifically needed to discuss, but the schedule was so tight that there was no time for me to sit down and look at every film as it was completed.

Nevertheless, as the days passed, and the first showing came ever closer, I got my first clue about how *Agatha Christie's Poirot* had turned out.

On the Friday morning of 6 January 1989 a piece by the veteran entertainment writer David Lewin appeared in the *Daily Mail* which said, very flatteringly, 'David Suchet has become Britain's first character actor star on television.' He had been one of the first people I talked to during the run of publicity after Christmas.

David then went on to compare me to Sir Alec Guinness, who was more famous for the characters he played than for his own personality – not least in the great Ealing comedy *Kind Hearts and Coronets* and David Lean's *Bridge on the River Kwai*. It was a great compliment, as I had always been an admirer of Guinness and his work, but to be mentioned in the same breath was a little overwhelming.

But when Sheila and I sat down together to watch *The Adventure of the Clapham Cook* go out on that Sunday evening in January 1989, we still really did not know what I would be like, how the series would look, or what the reaction would be. Even after we watched it, I wasn't exactly sure whether the audience would like it.

'What do you think?' I asked Sheila.

'It's wonderful,' she said. 'And so were you. It will be a tremendous success.'

I'm not sure I believed her. After all, this was only my second outing in a high-profile television series after *Blott on the Landscape*. In my heart, I still thought of myself as a rather serious classical actor. Could I mix the two? Could I be both Poirot and Iago?

On Monday morning I realised that I could, or at least the critics thought I could. They loved the show, and so, apparently, did the audience. London Weekend rang to tell me that more than eight million people had watched it the night before, a huge proportion of the television audience in the country.

As I looked at some of the reviews in the papers, I said to Sheila, 'I cannot believe what I'm reading. It is quite extraordinary.' I think she was as surprised as I was.

In the *Daily Express*, for example, Antonia Swinson called my portrayal of Poirot 'definitive', and added that I'd 'stepped nimbly into the role, with a beautiful set of moustaches, and every tiny detail of his appearance and personality perfect. Poirot now lives.'

Jaci Stephen, in that afternoon's *London Evening Standard*, called me 'brilliant' and added, 'More than any of his predecessors, he brought to the Belgian detective's character an entertaining mix of humour, inquisitiveness and pedantry.'

My mind went back to the previous summer on the Isles of Scilly, when Geoffrey had told me that Poirot would change my life. Although I still did not quite realise how much, that Monday morning in January 1989 showed beyond doubt that it had. Nothing was ever to be quite the same again.

To prove it, on the Tuesday morning, I was scheduled to have breakfast at the Ritz Hotel in London with a man from the *Daily Telegraph* called Hugh Montgomery-Massingberd. Hugh could clearly see that I was in a state of shock. His interview with me appeared the following morning, and neatly captured the new world that I suddenly found myself inhabiting.

'With the fame that only the telly can bestow,' Hugh wrote, 'David Suchet, alias Hercule Poirot, woke up yesterday morning to find himself a household name.'

Though we had never met before, Hugh and I got on terribly well at that breakfast – even though we only had fruit and muesli, as we were both on a diet – and he kindly concluded by describing me as 'most sympathetic and unactorish' as well as a 'sensitive and unshowy artist' who was 'surely a major star of the future'.

I was stunned when I read that the following morning.

The good reviews kept on coming. The following Sunday, Alan Coren in the *Mail on Sunday* suggested that 'by homing in unerringly on the most telegenic of Poirot's quirks', I had succeeded in making the character entirely my own.

As the reviews flowed, so did the fan letters. Suddenly people I did not know were writing to me as though I were a long-lost friend, and that started a train of thought in my mind that has remained with me ever since – what was it that people liked about Poirot?

I am convinced that the reaction to my work in that first series was more to do with Poirot than me. The reason the reviews were so flattering was because it was Dame Agatha's Poirot that mattered to them, not me. It was she and her creation that won their hearts and minds.

The fact that he had a kind heart was her work, not mine. The fact that he was always polite and respectful towards women was her doing, not mine, as was his charm and gentleness towards servants and waiters. His tendency to choose the wrong words – and allow himself to be corrected by Hastings – was her idea, not mine, as was his acute awareness of his fellow characters' sadness from time to time.

What I was doing was communicating Poirot's character to the world, and that was my job – to serve my original creator and my script writer.

In those first days after the series had begun on ITV, I realised for the first time that Poirot touches people's hearts in a way that I had never anticipated when I started to play him. I cannot put my finger on precisely how he does it, but somehow he makes those who watch him feel secure. People see him and feel better. I don't know exactly why that is, but there is something about him. My performance had touched that nerve.

That showed only too clearly in the audience's reaction. My mail bag of fan letters exploded overnight. Within a few weeks of the series starting in 1989, I was getting a hundred letters a week. Many of them were deeply touching.

It was like being hit over the head with a mallet. I did not know what had happened.

The show's success was a joy, but I still was not sure whether there would ever be another series, and I was an actor with a family to support. The reviews and fan letters were wonderful, but I had to work.

In fact, I had agreed to do two pieces for television: a screen version of Tom Kempinski's *Separation*, the play I had done at Hampstead and at the Comedy Theatre not all that long before Poirot started, and a new production of Edward Bond's *Bingo*, in which I was to play William Shakespeare. I was to portray him as a manic-depressive genius who had retired to Stratford-upon-Avon as a rich and disillusioned man.

Both parts could hardly have been further from Poirot, but they proved to me that my peers in the profession saw me as a character actor who could transform himself. I hoped the British public did too.

Mind you, my new found 'fame' took me to some strange places. Not long after the first series started, Sheila and I found ourselves featured in *Hello!* magazine, hardly a place that we thought that we would ever appear. We were photographed in our new house in Pinner, rather as though we were some sort of minor foreign royalty, which was a decidedly surreal experience, not least because the magazine suggested I was in 'a heady haze of euphoria' over my 'worldwide success'.

Nothing could have been further from the truth. It would have been more accurate to say that, far from being euphoric, Sheila and I were desperately worried about whether we would be able to stay in our house. London Weekend, as a part of the ITV network, had an option for Brian Eastman to produce and me to play a second series of ten Poirot films, but they had not exercised their options yet, which meant our financial position was still not exactly secure.

Would there ever be any more work? Could we pay the mortgage and the bills? I should confess that in the nineteen years before my first series as Poirot, I had never earned very much. I may have been a character actor with what I think was a good reputation, but I certainly was not a rich one.

It was not until late in February 1989 that ITV confirmed that they actually wanted to do a second series – on an almost identical schedule to the first. They were anxious for me to film another ten stories between early July and Christmas 1989, which they would broadcast between January and March 1990.

This time, Nick Elliott at London Weekend, who had been the executive producer on the first series with his colleague Linda Agran, wanted Brian Eastman to deliver an opening two-hour film, to be broadcast in early January 1990, based on Dame Agatha's magnificent Cornish mystery *Peril at End House*, and then a one-hour story for the each of the following eight Sundays. My Poirot was to become the cornerstone of ITV's Sunday nights.

It wasn't the critics that had convinced London Weekend to commission another series – though they were as thrilled by their reviews as I was. It was down to the fact that the viewing figures for each Sunday evening had stayed in their millions, and had even edged up from time to time. The series had also begun to sell around the world. As well as Canada and the United States, it looked as though other countries, particularly in Europe, were interested. Belgium had already started transmitting the films.

As a result of that worldwide audience, in addition to *Peril at End House* and the eight stories, London Weekend wanted Brian to produce a full-length special at the end of the second series: the very first Poirot story, *The Mysterious Affair at Styles* – the first book that Dame Agatha ever published. It was to be broadcast later in 1990, to celebrate the centenary of her birth.

The decision to commission a second series was a great compliment, as it would firmly establish my Poirot in the public consciousness, but it was also a great relief. It meant we would be able to stay in our house – at least for another year. Elmdene, as it was called, was becoming the house that Poirot built.

Just as importantly, however, the second series meant that I was going to become 'that little man' again, which made me truly happy. No matter what my fears might have been as an actor, I certainly wasn't ready to say goodbye to Hercule Poirot. I'd come to care about him far, far too much for that.

CHAPTER 6

'I WANTED HIM TO BECOME EVEN MORE HUMAN'

It was another hot summer's day, this time in late June 1989, when I became Hercule Poirot for the second time, and climbed back into my padding and his immaculate clothes to resume my relationship with the little man who had swept into my life, knocked me off my feet and come to mean so much to me.

And, once again, I would be revealing his foibles alongside my own, and sharing his obsessions with mine. For I was sure that this time the closeness between us would be revealed even more than it had been just a few months earlier, during the first series.

The first of the second series was to be the two-hour special, *Peril at End House*, shot partly on location, which opened with Poirot on an aeroplane on his way to a holiday in the west of England – and plainly not enjoying it at all. In fact, Poirot is feeling very uncomfortable indeed, because he does not like flying and makes no secret of the fact, while Hastings is sitting beside him looking serene and untroubled. In the character notes I had written about Poirot before the first series, I had at number six: 'Hates to fly. Makes him feel sick,' and so the scene was a perfect cameo of one of his little idiosyncrasies.

Dame Agatha wrote the full-length novel on which the film was based in 1932, and many of her admirers regard it as one of her finest murder-mysteries, even though in her own autobiography, published more than forty years later, she confessed that it had made so little impression on her that she could not even remember having written it. That led some commentators to mistakenly undervalue what is, to me, one of her most ingenious stories.

Poirot and Hastings are taking a holiday at 'the Queen of Watering Places' on the south-west coast of England, the fictional St Loo in Cornwall, where they are staying at the Majestic Hotel, which reminds Hastings of the French Riviera. A good proportion of the film was actually shot on location in Salcombe in Devon, rather than the studio, but the interesting thing for me was that Dame Agatha almost certainly used her own experience of the Imperial Hotel in Torquay, her birthplace, as part of its inspiration.

Here was another strange echo of my life intertwining with Poirot's. My father had a serviced apartment in the Imperial Hotel, which he and my mother visited regularly. So the world that Poirot was walking into in *Peril at End House* was one that I recognised immediately, having been there myself with them in the early 1980s.

At the Majestic, Poirot and Hastings meet a charming, if slightly anxious, young woman called 'Nick' Buckley, who lives at End House, high on the cliffs at the edge of town. Intriguingly for Poirot, she seems to have survived no fewer than three escapes from death in the past week, which convinces him that someone is trying to kill her. She laughs his theory off as a joke, until her cousin Maggie is actually killed – perhaps having been mistaken for her.

Directed by Renny Rye from the first series, and featuring another of Clive Exton's scripts, *End House* portrays a world of women in evening dresses and men in white tie and tails every night, with exotic cocktails before dinner, and obligatory ballroom dancing after it. It also features two of Dame Agatha's familiar, unlikely subsidiary characters, this time a slightly mysterious Australian couple who help to look after End House – a wheelchair-bound wife and a caring husband – whom Poirot describes as 'almost too good to be true'.

In the wake of the uncomfortable aeroplane flight, another of Poirot's foibles emerges immediately after he arrives in St Loo, when a waiter at breakfast serves him two boiled eggs of different sizes, which he refuses to touch as they offend his very particular sense of order. I had already put that down as number forty-two in my list of character notes: 'Will often have boiled eggs for breakfast. If more than one, they *must* be the same size or he really can't eat them.'

Poirot waves them away, but I made sure that he did so without looking petulant or silly, for I had made up my mind firmly that on this second series I would use every opportunity to make him as human as I could, no matter how odd his obsessions, and to reveal him as a warmer man than perhaps he had appeared in our first ten films.

Clive Exton's script certainly helped me. For he too wanted a little more humour in the new series, to make Poirot a bit more moving. It was an excellent idea, even if I sometimes had to restrain him from going too far towards making the little Belgian a comic character, for that certainly was not the Poirot I knew and wanted to portray. But at the same time, Clive also brightened both Hastings and Japp, making them a little less stiff. All this helped to make the films feel more affectionate towards Poirot than some of the first series.

I wanted him to become even more human. My aim was to draw the audience even more into his character, so that they could understand that this idiosyncratic little man, who may have had his eccentric ways, was also enormously compassionate and capable of eliciting information from every single person he met. He had the great gift of making people feel flattered by the simple fact that he was politely talking to them and took pains to listen to what they had to say with great intensity.

I believe that if you listen well, you are a sympathetic person, and this was very much what I wanted to show in my Poirot. There is nothing better, to me, than someone who has the patience to listen carefully, and give what I call 'good ear'. As my character note number twenty-seven said of him, 'An *excellent* listener. Often *disconcertingly* silent. Lets other people do the talking.'

Taking infinite care to listen and talk to everyone, regardless of their class or status, Poirot represents everyman – and he shows it time after time throughout Dame Agatha's stories. He is not Sherlock Holmes, dismissively lecturing a policeman or a wealthy landowner about their foolishness. Poirot cares about people too much for that. He sympathises with them, and shows that he does so, in story after story.

The more Poirot welcomes his fellow characters, the more the audience sympathise with him, and the more he extends his gentle control over everything around him, as if wrapping it all in his own personal glow. I believe he is unique in fictional detectives in that respect, because he carefully welcomes everyone – be they reader, viewer, or participant character – into his drama. He then quietly explains what it all means and, in doing so, he becomes what one critic called 'our dearest friend'.

That was exactly what I was trying to do, and so it was very satisfying when the critic in question, Dany Margolies, put it into words: 'In large part it's the contradictions Suchet has given the character that make him so appealing. Poirot dislikes so many things, so craves perfection in his own life, yet Suchet's interpretation feels such deep caring and empathy for humanity. He is brilliant, yet can communicate with everyone.'

That was my aim for the second series – to make my Poirot a man you would welcome to tea, who would not judge you, but who would listen to you and help you if you needed it. I think that began to emerge in *Peril at End House*.

End House demonstrates Dame Agatha's skill as a storyteller, for she always does something that neither the reader nor the television audience ever quite expect. Like an expert magician – a character she frequently puts into her stories – she knows how to compel her audience to concentrate on one thing while she is working her spell on something else that perhaps they ignore or miss. She always knows her ending well before the denouement – and it would usually never have entered the audience's head.

I have to confess at once that, even though I have become Poirot for millions of people around the world, even I cannot always work out the resolution to her mysteries before she tells me. Dame Agatha is too clever for me.

That is certainly true of *Peril at End House*, which ends in a séance after the reading of the fragile Miss Buckley's will. Poirot reveals the identity of the murderer with a real *coup de théâtre*, but only after inviting Miss Lemon to summon the spirit world. The true identity of the killer is certainly not obvious to the audience. They need Poirot to reveal it. Then they can see the truth, but only after they have been gently led towards it.

That makes the ending of the story all the more powerful, when the killer describes Poirot as a 'silly little man' before adding, 'You don't know anything,' when it is only too clear that he knows everything.

Peril at End House is such a fine mystery that the actor and playwright Arnold Ridley, author of *The Ghost Train* and star of BBC Television's *Dad's Army,* adapted it for the stage in 1940 with Francis L. Sullivan as Poirot. It opened at the Vaudeville Theatre in May 1940. Sadly it lasted for just twenty-three performances, in spite of receiving some positive reviews from the critics. Perhaps the theatre audience were looking for somewhat different fare as British troops were encircled on the French coast near Dunkirk.

Dame Agatha practises one of her 'little deceptions' on her readers and audience in *Peril at End House* – in which a character comes back to life after apparently dying – which was to reappear later. There is no doubt that she would, from time to time, repeat parts of her plots. That is hardly surprising, because I don't believe any writer could possibly complete more than seventy stories without repeating themselves. But that does not dilute for one moment their capacity to intrigue, for Poirot is always left to explain the 'how dunnit' of the murder and, even more important, to reveal the motive – and how the killer's mind truly works.

To me, it is precisely this quality that so appeals to the public's imagination when they see Poirot. Dame Agatha challenges her readers and viewers to exercise their own 'little grey cells' over her mysteries. She plays entirely fair, leaving clues in plain sight, if only the audience are clever enough to spot them, but she never, ever, patronises them.

As the filming of the second series went on in that summer of

1989, I came to realise the honesty and truthfulness in Dame Agatha's approach more and more. And as a result, I became ever more determined that my Poirot should become a man with an infinite reservoir of empathy for his fellow human beings, and who wanted the world to know it. So I worked harder and harder to humanise him, and as I did so, I think I became closer and closer to Poirot himself.

Yet even so, we are not totally alike, I assure you. My strain of perfectionism certainly matches Poirot's. In fact, we seemed to grow more alike in that respect the more I played him. But I have to admit that I had a problem with his egotism and vanity, qualities which I really don't share with him. I may be an actor, but I am most certainly not, I hope, a vain one.

If anything, I suffer from what Sheila and I both call 'repertory actor syndrome'. We both started in rep in the English provinces and have never forgotten the experience. Rep for us meant that we were never exactly sure where the next job – or the next penny – was coming from, and it made us very aware of exactly how precarious an actor's life can be. As a result, neither Sheila nor I ever take anything for granted.

It was that worry which paralysed us when we didn't know if there was going to be a second Poirot series. Could we afford to stay in our new house in Pinner?

But *Peril at End House* convinced me that there might just be a future for the little Belgian detective and me on television, for here we were making one of Dame Agatha's full-length novels, in a stunning set of locations, with no expense spared – the vintage aeroplane at the opening was just one example of that. As the series got underway, I suddenly found myself thinking, 'Perhaps we have a future, after all. Here is London Weekend making an episode that lasts longer than an hour, and they are clearly committed to it.'

In fact, Poirot also worries about money. In *The Lost Mine*, which was the third in the new series, the little man insists, 'No one makes Poirot look a fool where money is concerned' when he is confronted in his bank by the fact that he has an overdraft, rather than the precise sum of forty-four pounds four shillings and four pence which he always keeps in his current account. Then, in *Double Sin*, Poirot announces that he is 'finished' and 'in retirement' because no one has consulted him 'for weeks'.

I knew exactly how he felt. When the telephone stops ringing and an actor doesn't get any offers, he immediately starts to think of 'retirement'. 'No one wants me, so I will disappear,' I would say to myself in the dark days when there were no parts. 'I can't bear to appear to be desperate. I should never have left Moss Bros.'

Money worries and fears about retirement were two things that Poirot and I had in common, but there was another. We both like disguises. Every character actor loves his costume, which helps him to become someone else, and Poirot liked not only his own clothes, which helped to define his character, but also – from time to time – to use a disguise to help him achieve his end.

The Veiled Lady, the second film in the second series, demonstrates that perfectly. Poirot is asked to meet a mysterious woman – in a veil – in a London hotel. She turns out to be Lady Millicent Castle-Vaughan, played by Frances Barber, who is about to be married to the Duke of Southshire. The difficulty is that she is also being blackmailed over an indiscreet letter she wrote to a former lover some years earlier, which has fallen into the hands of an unscrupulous man called Lavingham, whom Hastings calls a 'dirty swine'.

Ever anxious to help a lady in distress, Poirot decides to disguise himself as a locksmith – complete with elderly bicycle and black beret – to get into Lavingham's Wimbledon home to find the offending letter and retrieve it, thereby bringing the blackmail to an end and saving Lady Millicent's reputation. All does not go well, however, and Poirot ends up in the cells, only to be rescued by Chief Inspector Japp. The spirited chase involving Poirot, Hastings and Japp in the spectacular setting of the Natural History Museum in London, as part of the story's denouement, was enormous fun to do.

The next film to be broadcast, *The Lost Mine*, opens with Hastings and Poirot playing Monopoly in Whitehaven Mansions, with Hastings winning comprehensively. The question of money, and in particular Poirot's skill with it, is at the heart of the story. Indeed, their game of Monopoly lasts all the way through it, until, inevitably, it ends with Hastings bankrupt and Poirot triumphant. Along the way, however, Poirot finds his current account is overdrawn – something which he would never allow to happen, and neither would I incidentally – and the chairman of the bank, played by Anthony Bate, asks for Poirot's help.

Once again, there was a rather spectacular setting, this time including the creation of Chinatown and a Chinese nightclub in the studio at Twickenham, which reminded me again of just how much London Weekend were spending on this series – certainly no less than the £500,000 per hour that they had spent on the first. With a Chinese victim, Wu Ling, and hints pointing to the opium trade in the East End of London, there are also echoes of the Charlie Chan mysteries, which were hugely popular at the time.

Dame Agatha's story, with its Chinatown background, had first appeared in the American edition of her short stories called *Poirot Investigates* in 1925, and the first full-length Chan novel, *The House*

Without a Key, appeared in the same year, although the American author Earl Derr Biggers had been working on him for almost six years. Like Poirot, Chan is an intelligent, honourable and benevolent detective, with a trace of eccentricity. He was to become a staple of American novels and films for the next three decades, often played by the Swedish actor Warner Oland. There are many similarities between the two detectives. Chan is always intensely polite and unthreatening, while often revealing the solution to his mysteries in a lengthy speech at the climax.

In sharp contrast to the exotic locale of Chinatown, the next film in the series, *The Cornish Mystery*, sees Poirot back in England, returning to the middle-class world of *Clapham Cook*. He is visited by Alice Pengelly, a distinctly nervous, not to say retiring, lady from Cornwall, who tells him that she gets stomach pains after every meal that she eats with her dentist husband Edward, but none when he goes away. Indeed, she is very afraid that she is being poisoned with weed killer, as she has found a half-empty jar in the house and the gardener insists that he has never used it.

'We have here a very poignant human drama,' Poirot confides to Hastings when Mrs Pengelly also tells him that she believes her husband is having an affair with his attractive blonde assistant. Hastings and Poirot travel down to Polgarwith in Cornwall the next day, only to discover that tragedy has already struck. Even though the good Chief Inspector Japp makes an appearance, and appears to have caught the murderer, things are not quite what they seem, as Poirot reveals.

The next three stories to be broadcast in the second series – though they were not shot in the order they were broadcast – were all comparatively slight, and I'm afraid the truth is that I was never really happy with *Double Sin*, *The Adventure of the Cheap Flat* and

The Adventure of the Western Star. They all seemed a little flat to me, a little too one-dimensional compared to the others.

Poirot announces his 'retirement' at the beginning of *Double Sin*, and decides to take Hastings on holiday to the seaside at Charlock Bay, where they meet a young woman, Mary Durrant, who is going to show a client a case of valuable antique miniatures.

When they are stolen, Mary asks Poirot to investigate, but – because of his 'retirement' – he instructs Hastings to take over the case, although he also asks him to 'tell me everything'. The lovely Elspet Gray, wife of Lord 'Brian' Rix, played Mary's wheelchair-bound mother, and there is rather a fine denouement in the hotel dining room, but somehow the film did not quite 'sing' in the way that I wanted it to, in spite of Clive Exton's fine script.

Sadly the same was true for *The Adventure of the Cheap Flat*, which starred Samantha Bond in one of her early television roles, six years before she became Miss Moneypenny to Pierce Brosnan's James Bond. The plot revolves around two of Hastings' friends, the Robinsons, who cannot believe their good luck in renting an expensive flat in a fashionable block for a tiny sum per month. Poirot is so intrigued that he decides to rent a flat in the same block himself – only to encounter an undercover FBI agent in pursuit of some secret plans for a submarine that may have been stolen by the Mafia. The FBI man pushes Chief Inspector Japp from his office at Scotland Yard, but it is Poirot who solves the mystery.

The Adventure of the Western Star is another of Dame Agatha's trifles. The beautiful Belgian actress Marie Marvelle – whom Poirot much admires – has received threatening letters demanding the return of a spectacular diamond known as the Western Star, which is reputed to have once been the left eye of a Chinese god. Meanwhile, the wife of an English aristocrat, Lord Yardley, who owns a similar diamond, known as the Eastern Star, has also received threatening letters demanding the return of their stone.

Poirot travels to meet Lord and Lady Yardley, but fails to prevent a daring robbery, and then races back to London, only to find that the Western Star has also been stolen. Engaging enough, and with a delightful portrait of Poirot becoming ever more excited about meeting Marie Marvelle, it depends on another of Dame Agatha's magical subterfuges. Poirot may have enjoyed the chase to find the diamonds, but I cannot say I was very happy with my own performance.

Western Star did, however, give me an opportunity to demonstrate Poirot's passion for cooking, when he serves Hastings supper and watches him eat with ill-concealed delight, all the while explaining the importance of exactly the right ingredients. It was my one opportunity in the story to bring out his humanity. For the rest, however, I felt uncomfortable and rather too near a parody in my desire to do Poirot's passion for Miss Marvelle justice.

Some people tend to see Poirot as one- or two-dimensional, but those who do so are almost always the ones who have never read the books. If you do read them, you realise at once that there are certainly three dimensions to his character. And every time I played him, I tried to bring those extra elements of Poirot's character to the surface, reflecting the different dimensions revealed in Dame Agatha's own stories about him.

Andrew Grieve, who directed the two remaining one-hour films in the second series, *The Disappearance of Mr Davenheim* and *The Kidnapped Prime Minister*, and who would go on to become a stalwart, positively revelled in Poirot's complexities, and has always been a delight to work with. It made *Prime Minister* one of my favourite Poirots of all, because the little man proves that no matter how idiosyncratic he may appear, he is exactly right, proving every-one else – particularly the British political establishment – wrong. Andrew had clearly read both stories, and wanted to talk to me at length about Poirot. He allowed me to explore the nuances in his character. There is no denying that *Mr Davenheim* is a quite delicious mystery, which opens with Hastings, Japp and Poirot at a theatre on location, watching an illusionist (another of Dame Agatha's magic-ians) – and the theme of illusions remains throughout the story. Banker Matthew Davenheim disappears one afternoon on his way to post a letter, after he gets home from his office, and Poirot tells Japp that he will solve the mystery before the police – without even leaving his flat.

In the story, Poirot delights in teaching himself magic tricks, as well as building a spectacular house of cards, while comfort-ably ensconced at Whitehaven Mansions. As he explains to Hastings, '*Non, mon ami*, I am not in my second childhood. I steady my nerves – that is all. This employment requires precision of the fingers. With precision of the fingers goes precision of the brain.' An expert was brought in to help me hone my skills in manipulating cards, which was rather fun, though I don't think I would make a good magician.

The only irritation on the horizon is that he is also looking after a rather talkative parrot, a bird that Poirot hates. Hastings, mean-while, is indulging his appetite for driving fast cars at Brooklands race track in Surrey. The delicious script was written by David Renwick, who would go on shortly afterwards to write the hugely successful BBC television comedy *One Foot in the Grave*.

In *The Kidnapped Prime Minister* Andrew allowed me to expand on Poirot's supreme confidence in himself. The story first appeared in a London illustrated weekly, the *Sketch*, in April 1923, as part of a series of twelve, but was quickly included in the collection of Dame Agatha's stories, *Poirot Investigates*, which was originally published in the United States.

Set against the background of the Versailles Peace Conference in the wake of the ending of the First World War, it opens with the kidnap of the British Prime Minister, who is on his way to address a League of Nations disarmament conference near Paris and is intent on stopping any possibility of German re-armament. Alone with his chauffeur, the Prime Minister boards a ferry to Boulogne, but disappears in France. The British government ask for Poirot's help and put a destroyer at his disposal to transport him to France immediately.

That only contrives to reveal Poirot's fear of sea-sickness. As he tells Hastings in the original story, 'It is the villainous sea that troubles me! The *mal de mer* – it is horrible suffering!' He is in no hurry to climb aboard the warship, and insists that he will start his search for the Prime Minister in England. Hastings and the Leader of the House of Commons cannot understand it, but the little Belgian is unmoved.

Poirot then outlines one of the central tenets of his attitude to solving a case, one which he returns to time and again.

'It is not so that the good detective should act, eh?' Dame Agatha had him say in her original story. 'I perceive your thought. He must be full of energy. He must rush to and fro. He should prostrate himself on the dusty road and seek the marks of tyres through a little glass. He must gather up the cigarette-end, the fallen match? That is your idea, is it not?'

Poirot fundamentally disagrees, and Dame Agatha has him say so firmly.

'But I – Hercule Poirot – tell you that it is not so! The true clues are within – *here*!' He tapped his forehead. 'All that matters is the little grey cells within. Secretly and silently they do their part, until suddenly I call for a map, and I lay my finger on a spot – so – and I say: the Prime Minister is *there*! And it is so.'

It is precisely the technique that Poirot depends on time after time.

There is another element in *The Kidnapped Prime Minister* that reveals another of the similarities between Poirot and me: the question of the English class system.

Throughout her stories, Dame Agatha was never afraid to criticise, and sometimes make fun of, the British upper class and their habits. As my character note number sixty-two about him puts it: 'HATES the English class system.' It is not just that Poirot calls tea 'the English poison', it is also that he is wary of accepting what might be called the British habit of respecting people of their own class, regardless of what the reality about them might be, and I must say I agree with him.

Although he is a Belgian, a refugee who arrived during the First World War, he emulates the British in his clothes and his manners, considering himself like an English doctor in Harley Street, and is content to observe what he regards as their strange customs. But he does not care, and neither do I, for the British respect for class, and what are so often called 'good chaps'. Time after time throughout his stories, Poirot rails against the British tendency to accept anything someone regarded as a 'good chap' says without a moment of hesitation.

I agree with him. It is another area in which Poirot and I are as one. I don't know exactly why that is, but it is absolutely true.

Perhaps it has something to do with my parents, or my own sense of being an outsider, even though I was born in London, but it is there anyway, one more thing that links Poirot and me.

In fact, it is Poirot's dislike of the restrained attitude of the English upper class that lies at the heart of the last, and most important, film of my second series as Poirot – a story that reveals, as my character note number fifty-five says, 'Doesn't like the English "reserve". Thinks the English are mad.'

CHAPTER 7

'I FELT THAT I HAD BECOME THE CUSTODIAN OF DAME AGATHA'S CREATION'

*T*he *Mysterious Affair at Styles* became our second two-hour television special at the end of the second series, and was scheduled to be broadcast to mark the centenary of Dame Agatha's birth. Indeed, it premiered in England on 16 September 1990, exactly one day after the centenary of her birth in 1890, and almost fifteen years after her death in Oxfordshire in January 1976.

What made it so significant for me, however, was that it was a television version of the very first crime novel Dame Agatha ever wrote, and the one that introduced the character of Hercule Poirot. It was a prequel to everything that I had done before in the nineteen stories we had already filmed.

There was no doubt that London Weekend were intent on making it as fine a film as they possibly could. The script, once again by Clive Exton, felt like the screenplay for a feature film rather than a television special, not least in using a huge number of extras and vintage vehicles, which were needed to give a feeling of London in the First World War. The director was the talented fifty-year-old South African Ross Devenish, whose 1980 film *Marigolds in August* had won a prize at the Berlin Film Festival that year.

Most of all, however, it gave me an opportunity to establish my Poirot from the very beginning of his career. The television audience may have seen the later Poirot, but they had never seen him as a younger man, shortly after he arrived in this country as a refugee from the German invasion of his native Belgium, forced to come to England to escape the carnage in his homeland.

But this was not an especially cheerful Poirot story. This was a serious crime and a complex mystery, which was downbeat from the very beginning. One of the early scenes features a younger Lieutenant Hastings recovering from his war wounds in a 'rather depressing' convalescent home in England. In fact, when we first encounter him, Hastings and his fellow patients are watching a black and white newsreel about the latest battles on the Western Front, which is then followed by a brief item about the Belgian refugees that are flooding into England.

It is just one of the many echoes in *The Mysterious Affair at Styles* of Dame Agatha's own life as a young woman, as she had seen Belgian refugees billeted near her home town as the war began to take its toll.

The story makes it worth recalling just a little about her upbringing. Born in the English seaside town of Torquay in September 1890, Agatha Miller started to write stories as a girl, during a bout of influenza, when her mother suggested that instead of telling stories – which she enjoyed doing – she should write them down. She did, and never lost the habit.

Then, when Agatha Miller was a teenager, she and her elder sister Madge were discussing a murder-mystery they were both reading when Agatha announced that she'd like to try her hand at writing a detective story. Madge challenged her to do it, while suspecting privately that she would never be able to. It was a challenge that the teenager never forgot.

By the time she was in her very early twenties, however, the young Miss Miller had one or two other things on her mind, not least the fact that she was being pursued by a number of young men with offers of marriage. Indeed, she even became engaged to one in 1912, at the age of twenty-two, only to break it off when she fell in love with the dashing Lieutenant Archibald Christie, the son of a judge in the Indian Civil Service and then serving with the Royal Field Artillery.

Less than eighteen months later, Agatha Miller married Archie, now Captain Christie, who had joined the newly formed Royal Flying Corps. The ceremony took place on Christmas Eve 1914, and war with Germany had begun just four months earlier. Captain Christie went back to the Western Front just two days later, while his new wife went to work in Torbay Hospital in Torquay, nursing some of the first casualties to come back from Flanders.

After eighteen months, she transferred to the hospital's dispensary, where she would acquire the extensive knowledge of poisons that would eventually appear in her novels – not least in *The Mysterious Affair at Styles*. It was during the quieter periods in the dispensary, in 1916, that the new Mrs Agatha Christie started writing what would be her first detective story, about that affair at Styles.

To do so, she drew on her new husband's experiences of the war, and on her own, as a nurse on the home front, treating the wounded, while also being well aware that England had provided a new home for some Belgian refugees – a colony had been billeted near her home in the parish of Tor in Torbay.

Why not make one of them her fictional detective, the young Mrs Christie thought to herself. Perhaps he could be a retired police officer from the Belgian force, not too young.

So Hercule Poirot was born, and the new Mrs Christie allowed the then still thirty-year-old Hastings to encounter Poirot – whom he had met before the war in Belgium, while working in insurance – during a trip away from his convalescent home. Hastings is invited to stay at a country house belonging to the family of his boyhood friend John Cavendish, Styles Court, a mile or so outside the fictional village of Styles St Mary in Essex.

The house is owned by John Cavendish's stepmother, who, although she is over seventy, has recently re-married the distinctly shady Alfred Inglethorpe, twenty years her junior. He is an 'absolute bounder', according to John Cavendish, because he has 'a great black beard and wears patent leather shoes in all weathers'. So the mystery begins.

Written and set during the 'war to end wars', *The Mysterious Affair at Styles* was eventually published in London in 1920, to quite extraordinary success, launching its author's career as the 'Queen of English crime fiction' in the twentieth century. More important for me, it also launched Hercule Poirot as a fictional detective who would come to rival the great Sherlock Holmes in the public's affection around the world.

To my mind, the story and the screenplay of *The Mysterious Affair at Styles* are both Dame Agatha and Clive Exton at their very best. It was no accident that the book was a huge best-seller, because it contains an extraordinary number of ingenious puzzles and a remarkable set of characters who live on in the memory.

But, as I said, *The Mysterious Affair at Styles* is not exactly a conventional Poirot. There is rather less of a twinkle in his eye than in some of the other stories. The background of the war makes it sombre in tone, and Poirot's attempt to settle into a new land is no laughing matter. He and his fellow Belgian refugees are struggling to understand the ways of their adopted homeland.

In television terms, it is even more unusual, because Poirot does not appear until eleven minutes of the film have passed. The old movie adage of 'putting the money on the screen' by making sure the leading actor appears as close to the opening as possible was completely ignored. Indeed, to establish it as something quite different from the rest of the series, *The Mysterious Affair at Styles* does not even begin with the series titles and Christopher Gunning's unmistakable theme music. Instead, it opens like a feature film, with wounded soldiers near Parliament Square in London, nurses ushering them to and fro, and a military band marching past.

It is only after that establishing scene that the action shifts to Hastings' convalescent home, where he is watching the news-reel. There too London Weekend took a risk. The black and white footage he and his fellow patients are watching was controversial at the time because it showed their fellow soldiers dying in the trenches, not something a prime-time television programme would normally air, as it would be deemed too distressing for an audience before the nine o'clock watershed, which could well include children.

After the newsreel, Hastings encounters his old friend John Cavendish, who invites him down to Styles – located in Wiltshire, rather than Essex, in Clive Exton's screenplay, though I was never quite sure why. When Hastings arrives, he meets John Cavendish's wife Mary and his younger brother Lawrence; a girl called Cynthia, a protégé of Mrs Inglethorp, who works in the dispensary of the local hospital (another parallel with Dame Agatha's life); and Evelyn

Howard, a lady in her forties who works for the mistress of the house as a general assistant.

When Mrs Inglethorp suddenly dies an agonising death in bed – another risk for ITV, as her death is incredibly graphic in the film – it is first thought that she has had a heart attack, but the local doctor quickly spots that it is murder by poisoning. The police are called, and, inevitably, suspicion falls on Mrs Inglethorp's new husband, Alfred, who is suspected by the family of being a bounty hunter, only interested in Mrs Inglethorp's considerable fortune.

By the time of the murder, however, Poirot has only appeared briefly. In my first scene Poirot is encountered leading a string of his fellow Belgian refugees through a local wood, instructing them on the wonders of the English countryside. The first glimpse of Poirot is of his spats treading careful through the leaves – and it is the very first time the audience hears his theme music gently rising in the background.

When Poirot first appears in full view, he is telling his fellow Belgians about one local plant, the 'Scarlet Pimpernel', which, he says, only opens during a lengthy period of good weather. Poirot then pauses, and gives a wry smile. 'It is seldom seen open in this country.'

We then see Poirot leading his troop of Belgians across a river bridge, while attempting to sing the famous First World War song 'It's a Long Way to Tipperary', even though their voices are clearly not up to it – and Poirot is patently tone deaf. Nevertheless, it instantly conveys the group's attempt to show loyalty to their new homeland. It is the only time that Poirot sings in the entire canon of his stories, which was a great relief, as I would not describe myself as a singer.

Just two minutes later, Hastings meets Poirot in the local post office, where the little man is attempting to persuade the postmistress to arrange the spices in the shop to reflect their countries of origin – those from India to the east, those from Africa to the south, and so on – only for her to tell him that she knows exactly where all the spice jars are, and, besides, they all come 'from the wholesaler'.

The postmistress's reaction pains Poirot deeply, because not having the jars and tins lined up in order of their size and placed in relation to their country of origin offends his sense of order and method, but there is nothing he can do. The story reveals that Hastings and Poirot have met before, when Hastings worked for Lloyd's of London, and while Poirot was still serving with the Belgian police. Now in his sixties, he has since retired and is living in exile, because 'the *Boche* have rendered my homeland uninhabitable'.

It is not long after their encounter in the post office that Mrs Inglethorp dies and Hastings suggests recruiting Poirot to help in the investigation into her death. He goes to the cottage where he and his countrymen are staying and knocks on the door early in the morning. Poirot is in bed, but gets up and opens the window to talk to Hastings.

It is to my eternal regret that this is one occasion when I totally let down the man I had become so close to. In the film, I open the window and look out without brushing my hair before doing so. Now, Poirot, the man I knew and loved, would never, ever, have done that. He would have brushed his hair carefully, no matter how urgent the knocking on his front door. To this day, I regret that I didn't brush my hair before opening the window. Every time I see that scene, I feel I've let him down.

Not surprisingly, the film's costume designer was very anxious that I should look younger for my introduction in the story – after all, the action is taking place twenty years before most of the stories that I had already filmed – and so I wore a little less padding, and a bowler hat rather than a Homburg. I also wore a tie held in place by a silver ring at the throat, rather than a bow tie.

But I kept every one of the mannerisms I had refined during the other films in the series, including his mincing walk and his tendency to keep his left hand firmly behind his back when he moves. 'That is him,' I told myself. 'It is part of who he is, and has been throughout his life'.

Privately, I was very glad I'd already filmed so many Poirots, for they gave me the confidence I needed to bring him alive in his first story. Had I filmed *Styles* first, I wonder if I would have had that same certainty about his character and his mannerisms. But my remaining true to the little man was made all the easier by Ross Devenish's direction. He was a delight because he took an enormous interest in Poirot. He would come to my caravan on the set after we'd finished filming and sit for hours, talking to me about him.

'Tell me who he is,' Ross would say. 'How does he feel? How does he think? How can we best bring him to life?'

Now, I fully accept that it was becoming difficult for some of the directors who had come to work on the second series to deal with me. There is no denying it; I had become an actor who was desperate to hang on to what he believed was the only correct view of his character. I felt, by then, that I had become the custodian of Dame Agatha's creation, and I was not going to allow anyone to dilute or alter anything that I felt strongly about. That made it difficult for some directors to deal with me – but that wasn't the case with Ross, who only ever wanted to help me serve Poirot and his creator.

I think that makes our version of *The Mysterious Affair at Styles* very special, for although it reveals Poirot's eccentricity, his egotism, his extraordinary knowledge and his ironic sense of humour, it never once allows him to topple over and become a caricature. Ross and I wanted him to be as human as we possibly could make him.

In the wake of Mrs Inglethorp's death, Poirot accepts Hastings' invitation to participate in the investigation without a moment's pause, not least, he tells Hastings, because 'she had kindly extended hospitality to seven of my country people, who, alas, are refugees from their native land . . . We Belgians will always remember her with gratitude.'

It is at precisely this moment in the original story that Dame Agatha first describes Poirot, in some detail:

> 'He was hardly more than five feet, four inches, but
> carried himself with great dignity. His head was exactly
> the shape of an egg, and he always perched it a little on
> one side. His moustache was very stiff and military.
> The neatness of his attire was almost incredible; I
> believe a speck of dust would have caused him more
> pain than a bullet wound.'

It was a description that I knew almost by heart, just as I remembered that when he first goes to Styles Court to inspect Mrs Inglethorp's bedroom, the scene of her death, Dame Agatha describes him as having 'darted from one object to the other with the agility of a grasshopper'. That phrase too was forever in my mind.

Two other qualities that define him also appear in Dame Agatha's first novel – her reference to Poirot's 'little grey cells' and his assertion to Hastings: 'I am not keeping back facts. Every fact that I know is in your possession. You can draw your own deductions from them.'

It is left to the then just Inspector Japp, who appears from London to participate in the investigation, to give us a little of Poirot's background by introducing him to a local police super-intendent by saying that they had worked together on the 'Abercrombie forgery case' (in the novel, that is indentified as taking place in 1904) and adding that 'we nailed him in Antwerp – thanks to Monsieur Poirot here'. The superintendent looks distinctly unimpressed by this odd-looking little man with a strange accent and a rather peculiar walk.

Poirot is undeterred. He positively relishes what is a complicated investigation, capable of several different solutions, and which calls on him to examine the exact nature of strychnine poisoning. But it also contains many of the elements that Dame Agatha used time and again in her stories. There is a large country house, with the servants necessary to maintain it, complete with a tennis lawn and stables to allow the guests to ride in the mornings, while the grooms look after the horses.

There is a sense in the story, and in our film, that those days of British Edwardian grandeur are fading as the impact of war introduces a new and different world, one in which old traditions and habits are ever more difficult to maintain. Poirot catches this when he describes one of the older female servants, Dorcas, in the novel by saying: 'I thought what a fine specimen she was of the old-fashioned servant that is so fast dying out.'

There is also the hint – in the murder of Mrs Inglethorp – that the time has suddenly arrived when young men are becoming increasingly impatient for their inheritance, no longer prepared to wait their turn under what they see as the 'yoke' of their elders.

Dame Agatha is quietly drawing attention to the materialism that she sensed was creeping into the world around her when she wrote the novel in 1916.

Nevertheless, all the essential ingredients of an Agatha Christie Poirot mystery are there, including a typically expansive denouement in which he seems to suggest that almost every single resident of Styles Court could have been guilty of poisoning Mrs Inglethorp, before finally revealing the killer. Yet the more he weaves his magical spell and unravels the story's many puzzles, the more the story's characters and the audience comes to love him. As Cynthia, Mrs Inglethorp's protégé, puts it, 'He is such a dear little man!' Poirot may leave the fictional Cavendish family in tatters in the novel and the film, but that does not detract for a moment from his audience's delight in him.

It is a delight that remains to this day. I am constantly amazed by people's affection for him. When people meet me, or stop me in the street, or come to see me in a play, they always want to talk about Poirot. Some of them even send enormous letters explaining exactly how much he means to them.

It is humbling, and almost overwhelming, because everyone I talk to seems to love him, though I never set out to make him loved – only to make him true to Dame Agatha's creation.

Yet when we finished filming the second series of *Agatha Christie's Poirot* in December 1989, I wasn't sure whether there would ever be another. London Weekend had not written an option into my contract for a new series – as they had into my contract for the first. In fact, there was no guarantee whatsoever from any-one associated with the production that there would ever be a third series.

Once again, I was high and dry, not sure what might happen

next, and yet desperate to go on playing the little man that everyone seemed to love so much.

Sheila and I tried to organise my life so that I would be available to play him again if the chance presented itself, but in the meantime I still had a family to support, not to mention a house to maintain. In the second week of the first series being transmitted, part of the roof had fallen in on us, quite without warning.

But that wasn't the reason I wanted to play Poirot again. He had become a part of my life, almost like a best friend. I too had come to love him. The thought that I might never bring him to life again made me sad because I wanted nothing more than to make room for him in my career.

CHAPTER 8

'TELEVISION'S UNLIKELIEST HEARTTHROB . . . THE MANGO MAN'

Another Christmas, and that niggling anxiety remained: would I be reunited with the idiosyncratic detective? I did not know, and neither did Sheila. We just knew, as we celebrated with the family, that the fans loved him and the critics liked him. But would that last? Might the audience be getting bored with Poirot and me?

The answer came quickly, and I should not have worried. On 7 January 1990, a Sunday evening, ITV launched the second series of *Agatha Christie's Poirot* with our two-hour special of *Peril at End House,* and to my intense relief, the British press were every bit as generous as they had been a year earlier.

In fact, even before the reviews appeared, I knew they liked the series, because there was a string of enthusiastic previews. Astonishingly, it was becoming clear that the little Belgian was almost on the brink of becoming a national treasure. It was a far cry from the first days of filming, eighteen months earlier, when no one knew what the world would think.

The television highlights for 1990 all included charming remarks about the new Poirot series, and, remarkably, his effect on women viewers.

On the Sunday morning the series began, the *People* newspaper reported that I was receiving 'sacks of mail from adoring women who simper and sigh at his portrayal of the elderly, moustachioed hero'. It wasn't quite true, but I was certainly getting dozens of letters a week at the peak of the series, though not quite all of them from women.

That same morning, the *Sunday Mirror* reported: 'Poirot has become a great family favourite' and a 'hit with women viewers too'. For my part, I had told the paper, 'A lot of ladies want to look after him . . . For although he's very self-sufficient, he is also slightly vulnerable. They want to help him in any way possible . . . And yet he is irritating and objectionable in lots of ways. He's a typical bachelor.'

That vulnerability was something I had been striving for throughout the second series, as I told the *Today* newspaper. One of its writers, Ivan Waterman, did an interview with me and I explained to him what I had been aiming at. 'I like Poirot very much,' I said. 'He's a great humanitarian – he has this love of people. He is a very warm man and I like to think I care as well.' It was entirely true.

The day before, the *Sun* had shared with its readers twenty clues they had unearthed about Poirot and me, including the fact that I – like Poirot – was 'ultra-tidy' and paid 'particular attention to detail'; that I'd met Sheila when we were both appearing in a stage production of *Dracula* in Coventry in 1972; and that I had played in the junior finals at Wimbledon at the age of fourteen, but had given up tennis for acting. In fact, the truth was that I just could not find the time to keep playing tennis at the level that I wanted to.

If there was a sport that I did give up for acting, it was rugby, which I loved, but the need for training just did not leave me time for acting.

All these personal details felt slightly surreal; I am a character actor, not a star or a celebrity, and that sense of the unreal only increased when, a few weeks later, *Women's Realm* magazine called me 'TV's unlikeliest heart-throb' – even though they also described me as 'portly'.

Nevertheless, *Women's Realm* also gave me a chance to explain what I felt about the little man, especially when I told them that an 'actor has to fall in love with his character . . . You have to have a deep, intimate relationship with him, get under the surface. I'm very fortunate in that I really like Poirot.'

The British television critics had been very kind. The *Sunday Times,* in particular, welcomed the return of my 'definitive, understated portrayal of the Belgian detective', and the reviews certainly worked in the series' favour. As January turned into February, in 1990, we began to exceed the audiences of eight million or so every Sunday evening from last season, rising towards ten, eleven and even, briefly, twelve million people each week.

The most intuitive remarks about my work in the new series came from the novelist and journalist Celia Brayfield, who turned herself into a critic in one of her columns and described my Poirot as 'enthralling' and 'the most mesmeric figure on television'. Celia also pointed out, very shrewdly, that I was unafraid to portray Poirot's less attractive traits, whilst taking care not to turn him into a caricature.

My peers in the acting profession were equally generous, because just a few days after the new series began, I discovered that one of the episodes in the first series, *Triangle at Rhodes*, had won first prize in the drama category at the International Film and Television Festival in New York. That happened just days before the first series was to launch in the United States, on Thursday 18 January 1990, as part of the PBS *Mystery* series.

The American reviews of the first series were astonishing. The *Philadelphia Inquirer* was particularly kind. Their staff writer, Jonathan Storm, praised the subtlety and integrity of my perform-ance, which '. . . over the years, have eluded such fine actors as Peter Ustinov and Albert Finney . . . Suchet adds a benevolence that also makes Poirot a fine friend.'

The *Washington Post* said that I made 'a fine Poirot, with just the essential twirl of his absurd moustache of self-importance', while the *New York Times* observed carefully that my interpretation 'does justice to the portrait on the page', and *Broadcast Week* called my performance 'stunning', adding that, 'He's taken the Belgian sleuth and has made him his own.' The *Wall Street Journal* concluded firmly: 'All in all, this Poirot is a delight.'

In Canada, at the same time, the *Toronto Star*'s Greg Quill was every bit as enthusiastic, describing my performance as 'the definitive Poirot – an excitable, fastidious, arrogant and essentially egomaniacal sleuth . . . qualities that shine through in his wonderful performance.'

I simply could not have asked for more generous reviews. They made me feel that my work was somehow vindicated.

All this success was wonderful, but – with no guarantee that there would ever be another series – I needed to work. Then, suddenly, a chance presented itself when Trevor Nunn, the artistic director of the Royal Shakespeare Company when I worked there in the 70s and 80s, asked me if I would consider playing Shakespeare's *Timon of Athens* at the Young Vic for two months in April and May 1990.

No longer working full-time with the RSC, Trevor had by then established himself as one of the leading directors of the West End stage, with a string of hits, including the musicals *Cats* and *Les Miserables*. I had enjoyed working with him on the Moss Hart and George S. Kaufman comedy *Once in a Lifetime* in the West End in 1979, but that was some time ago, and I certainly wanted to work with him again – but what if they suddenly asked me to start a new series of Poirot? Would I be able to do both? What if they overlapped? I really didn't know what to do.

Finally, after a great deal of heart-searching and without any firm news about a third series, I took the plunge and agreed to do *Timon* with Trevor. There were to be five weeks of rehearsals and a two-month run, which would take me into the last weeks of May 1990. The only thought in the back of my mind was that if there was going to be another series of Poirot, I was going to be very stretched indeed.

But *Timon* was a wonderful challenge. One of Shakespeare's last plays – first performed in 1607 or 1608 – it is not revived all that often. People tend to think it is about children being baked in pies, because they confuse it with *Titus Andronicus*. In fact, *Timon* had last been performed by the RSC a decade earlier, in 1981, with Richard Pasco in the leading role, and a few years before that with Paul Scofield as Timon. One reason for the reluctance to perform the play is that it is unfinished. Some experts are even convinced that not all of the play was written by Shakespeare himself.

There were a lot of reasons why I wanted to play the part. Of course, I longed for the challenge – what character actor would not? But it would also be my first time playing Shakespeare with Trevor, something that I had always wanted to do. It would also be the first time I had appeared on the stage since *Separation* back in 1987, and *Timon* would give me the opportunity to re-establish myself as a classical stage actor, alongside my television work. I also hoped that I might bring some of the millions of people who watched me on television into the theatre, and thereby unite two parts of my career.

You see, I have always firmly believed that, as an actor, my staple place of work is the theatre, and that means that I must keep returning to it. I have never wanted to be just a television actor, or a movie actor, or a star, or a celebrity. I want to remain exactly what I had always longed to be – a character actor. That's why, when people ask me if I have a favourite medium, I always tell them that I don't. I will do anything that allows me to be the actor I always wanted to be.

Before *Timon* even opened, however, I was thrown into a state of confusion. London Weekend suddenly decided that they were indeed going to do a third series of Poirot, starting in late June, and asked me to play the role again.

For a moment, I was in turmoil. If only they could have asked me earlier! If I went straight on from *Timon* to *Poirot*, I was going to be in grave danger of driving myself too hard and weakening my ability to perform as well as I wanted to. But what could I do?

London Weekend made the offer just as the second Poirot series was coming to an end in England, in March 1990, and I was rehearsing Timon. The recent success of the first series in the United States and the fact that it had sold well in Europe (Germany had now taken it too) had more than a little to do with the decision to commission a new set of Poirot, I suspect. In the end, I felt that I had no choice. I decided to play the little man again – I wanted to very much, and the opportunity was too good to turn down. So I agreed to start filming a third series of Poirot immediately after I had finished *Timon of Athens* in the West End, even though it meant that I would have no time to rest before starting the pre-production of the series. It also meant that I would have been working virtually non-stop throughout the year.

On one level, it is a wonderful thing to be given the chance to work, but on another level, I knew it was going to be both mentally and physically exhausting. Would that hurt my performance as Poirot? I did not think it would, but I would have to wait and see.

In the meantime, there was *Timon of Athens* to be launched. Thankfully, my approach to the play seemed to work for the audience, because the reviews were excellent and the theatre was full – some of the audience no doubt tempted by the possibility of seeing Poirot on stage. But it was a long piece, of almost three hours, and the second act in particular was all consuming. I left the theatre at the end of eight performances each week absolutely drained – though very satisfied with what I had achieved.

In fact, though I did not realise it for a time, *Timon* helped to establish me as an actor who could bring an audience into the theatre, and I was enormously grateful to the part for that.

No sooner had the run at the Young Vic finished, than I was back at Twickenham Studios in pre-production for Poirot, though certainly not feeling quite as fresh as I had when I'd started two summers before.

By chance, just as we started work on the new series, another of my television performances – playing a tortured William Shakespeare in a production of Edward Bond's *Bingo* – was broadcast, confirming the fact that I was certainly not only playing my little Belgian friend.

Once again, a television magazine kindly described me as 'fast becoming the Alec Guinness of his generation – the man with a face for every character'. Again, I was very flattered, but I did not have time to bask in the glory. I was too busy getting back into my padding and spats, not to mention a new set of moustaches.

The first film in the new series, all of which were once again based on Dame Agatha's short stories, was *How Does Your Garden Grow?* Poirot is to have a rose named after him at the Chelsea Flower Show of 1935, and while there, he meets an elderly lady in a wheelchair who gives him a packet of seeds with the words, 'I'm sure you will find them quite a revelation.' Shortly afterwards, she dies in agony in front of the camera, another bold move by the producers, and – just like Mrs Inglethorp at Styles – it turns out that she has been poisoned. Suddenly Poirot finds himself investigating her death at a Surrey house filled with memorabilia from the Russian Orthodox Church, as one of the suspects is a Russian émigré.

Published in *Poirot's Early Cases* in both Britain and the United States in 1974, not long before Dame Agatha's death, it is one of her slighter stories, which needed to be expanded in the script to make it even better for a television audience. To be honest, not every single one of her short stories was easily adaptable to the small screen. Some needed one or two extra ingredients to help them along. It was all done with a little sleight of hand, in this case by the screenwriter Andrew Marshall, to make her stories even more enjoyable.

One of the extra ingredients in the first film is a little sub-plot about Poirot's new aftershave lotion, which contrives to give Hastings what seems like hay fever, but turns out to be an allergy to the lotion itself. The gentle depiction of Poirot's vanity and the confusion about what is causing Hastings to sneeze all the time is one of the film's most charming elements.

The Million Dollar Bond Robbery, the second film, was another of the slighter stories, although it does involve Poirot overcoming his fear of sea-sickness when he and Hastings are required to travel to New York on the maiden voyage of the new Cunard liner, *Queen Mary*. In the end, though, it is Hastings, not Poirot, who succumbs to *mal de mer*, much to the detective's delight.

Directed by Andrew Grieve, who would go on to become one of the regulars on the Poirot films, it focuses on the theft of one million dollars' worth of bonds from a locked box on the ship as it sails across the Atlantic. Andrew used a great deal of black and white newsreel footage of the original maiden voyage to give his film a firm period flavour and to flesh out the story a little more.

The third film, *The Plymouth Express*, was a revelation, because it underlined just how much the Poirot series could now attract some of the finest actors in the profession. The cast included the exceptional Kenneth Haigh, who was the original Jimmy Porter in John Osborne's ground-breaking drama *Look Back in Anger* in 1956. I had known him in the theatre, and was immensely pleased that he accepted the part of a deceiving 'fence' in the story. He was a great addition to the cast.

But it wasn't just established actors that were attracted to the new Poirot series; the films also featured great actors who would later go on to become stars. That was certainly true for *Wasps' Nest*, the fourth film, which featured a thirty-something Peter Capaldi, later to become rightly famous for his role as the malevolent spin doctor Malcolm Tucker in the political series *The Thick of It*, and has now become the latest Doctor Who. Scots-born and intensely charismatic, Peter played the artist Claude Langton, who is acting as a clown at a village fete near the beginning of the story, and he did it beautifully.

The other thing that sticks in my mind from that film is that I found myself, once again, standing up for Poirot's foibles against the wishes of the film's director, Brian Farnham. Brian had set up an enormous crane shot to look down on the fete and its fairground, and he wanted Poirot to walk into the scene, as the camera watches him from above, and then shout across the fairground to Hastings.

I just could not do it. I took Brian aside and told him, 'I'm so, so sorry, but Poirot just would not do that. It's not within his being. He would never shout across to people; he would walk all the way over to Hastings rather than yell at him.'

I felt really badly about it, because here I was taking a wonderful director's shot away from him, and the crew had spent so long getting it ready, but I simply could not let Poirot down – no matter how embarrassed I felt.

Brian was very understanding, and so were the crew, but it did mean everyone had to rework the scene to allow me to walk across and speak to Hastings, as Poirot would have done. The irony is that in the short story itself, written by Dame Agatha in 1929, Hastings never appears. He was one of the additions for the screenplay.

After our debate about that crane shot, I made a point of always going onto the set in advance and discussing the camera setup with Brian, to avoid it ever happening again. In fact, *Wasps' Nest* became one of my favourite films of the series, not least because Peter Capaldi turned in such an extraordinary performance.

In the fifth film, the director, Renny Rye, who had worked on the first series, allowed me to indulge Poirot's obsessions without a moment's hesitation. So there I was, once again, laying my handkerchief on the ground to allow Poirot to kneel down without staining his trousers to examine some bird's eggs that played their part in the story of a fictional 'great crime' which is, in fact, the creation of the owner of the local hotel, who has ambitions to be a crime novelist. Poirot helps him to find an ending to his story, while at the same time revealing the truth behind *The Tragedy at Marsdon Manor*.

'Hercule Poirot sees everything and forgets nothing,' as he says while solving the murder at the manor, which seems to have been caused by a ghost, but, of course, is not. Part of the delight of the film is that it sees Poirot discover a waxwork of himself, which both horrifies and enraptures him at the same time. I think I would feel rather the same way if I ever came across a waxwork of me.

If *Wasps' Nest* was one of my favourite films in the series, there is no doubt that *Double Clue* was the most poignant. First written in 1925, it introduces the one woman with whom Poirot truly falls in love, the flamboyant, exotic Countess Vera Rossakoff.

She was to appear in two later Poirot stories, but this was their first meeting and, for Poirot – and me – it was never to be forgotten.

Like Irene Adler for Sherlock Holmes in the 1891 Conan Doyle story *A Scandal in Bohemia*, the Countess will always be '*the* woman' for Poirot. Yet she does not outwit him, as Adler did Holmes. Instead, Poirot allows her to get away with her crimes of stealing jewels from some of the wealthiest families in England. He signally does not hand her over to Chief Inspector Japp, who has come to him in a state of some considerable anxiety, so worried is he about losing his job after failing to catch the thief at the centre of a string of such high-profile robberies.

The Countess was played by the striking actress Kika Markham, who had something of a reputation at that time for playing strong women, and she brought exactly the right amount of glamour and dignity that the role demanded. She certainly made the Countess all the more attractive to Poirot.

'You are the most remarkable, the most unique woman I have met,' Poirot tells her, as the story unfolds. 'It is crime which has brought us together.'

Yet Poirot also tells the Countess, with a deep sadness in his voice, 'Marriage is not for me.' The end of the film has him effectively saying goodbye to any chance of love, and – as he waves the Countess away to a new life in the United States – reveals that he is condemned to remain wrapped forever in his own loneliness.

As he helps her leave the country and escape justice, Poirot and the Countess re-enact one of the most romantic scenes in the history of British cinema: the lovers' parting in David Lean's *Brief Encounter*, although this time it is the woman who is leaving the country for a new life, while Poirot is left standing on the station platform, alone with his thoughts of what might have been.

In the next film in the series, Poirot confronts menace rather than love.

The Mystery of the Spanish Chest first appeared in Dame Agatha's collection of short stories *The Adventure of the Christmas Pudding* in 1960, which hardly sounds threatening at all. Yet it is one of the most frightening stories she wrote. It was actually an expanded version of one of her earlier stories, *The Mystery of the Baghdad Chest*, which first appeared in a collection called *The Regatta Mystery* in the United States in 1939, but was not published in Britain until 1960.

Chilling from the very start, it opens with a ferocious fencing match involving the mysterious Colonel Curtiss, who, it transpires, might just be a British spymaster. He was played by another extraordinary actor John McEnery, then in his late forties and capable of conveying malice in the most dramatic way. An old friend, he was a former member of the National Theatre and had made his name in Franco Zeffirelli's 1968 version of *Romeo and Juliet*.

When John held a sword to my throat during the filming of *The Spanish Chest*, it was one of the few times when both Poirot and

I felt truly frightened, for he made it so realistic that there was a moment when I almost convinced myself that he would actually plunge the blade into my throat. It shows on the screen.

Set once again among the English upper classes, Poirot is hired by Lady Abbie Chatterton because she is afraid that her friend Marguerita Clayton may be killed by her husband Edward, who has a violent temper. As a result, Poirot is invited to a party to meet Clayton, who – mysteriously – fails to appear. His body is found the following day, hidden in a chest. He has been stabbed through the eye.

With a terrific script from Anthony Horowitz, and directed by Andrew Grieve, it allowed another of those special moments when Poirot and I came together.

'I was lucky, that is all,' Poirot says near the end of the story, and then adds, with a slight twinkle in his eye, 'It is more English, yes, the humbleness.' There is a pause before he concludes, with his tongue in his cheek, 'No one shall match Hercule Poirot for his humility.'

Like Poirot, I too believe in humility, but there is a twinkle in both of us, for there is also an element of confidence, perhaps even vanity, which we both share. How could we do what we do if there were not?

John McEnery was not the only old friend to grace the new series. The eighth film, *The Adventure of the Royal Ruby*, featured both the late Freddie Treves and Stephanie Cole, both of whom I had known for a long time. Freddie served in the merchant navy during the Second World War, and was awarded the British Empire Medal for bravery, which somehow led him to play a series of military officers after training at RADA. Stephanie, on the other hand, seemed to have been playing elderly ladies from her late thirties, not least in the BBC television series *Tenko* and Alan Bennett's *Talking Heads*.

Both helped the story of *The Royal Ruby* a great deal, and I was delighted that such fine actors wanted to be in the series.

Originally called *The Adventure of the Christmas Pudding* when it was first published in Britain in 1960, *The Royal Ruby* opens with Poirot delighting in being able to spend Christmas alone with a specially selected box of his favourite Belgian chocolates. But his plans are upset when he is asked by the British government to investigate the theft of a priceless stone that belongs to Prince Farouk, a member of the Egyptian royal family. Poirot discovers the Prince has given it to a mysterious young woman, and follows her to the country home of a noted Egyptologist, played by Freddie, with Stephanie as his wife.

My very favourite moment comes when everyone sits down to dinner on Christmas Eve and Poirot demonstrates exactly how to prepare and eat a mango. In fact, I asked for the scene to be put into the film and I must explain why.

In April 1990, just a few weeks before we were to start filming Poirot again, I received a letter from Buckingham Palace inviting me to a 'private' lunch with Her Majesty on 2 May, which was my forty-fourth birthday. Both Sheila and I were astonished, and I even asked her, partly as a joke, whether she thought it might be a hoax. But when Sheila rang the number in the letter, it turned out to be absolutely true.

And so it was that I found myself having lunch with the Queen and the Duke of Edinburgh on my birthday that year. There were twelve guests in all, and I discovered that Her Majesty likes to invite people from all walks of life that she finds interesting.

During lunch, I was deep in discussion with Prince Philip, who was sitting three chairs along from me on my side of the table, opposite the Queen, when I heard someone whisper in my left ear, 'Would you care for some fruit, sir?'

Without looking round, I nodded and put my hand into the giant fruit bowl that was being offered and I picked up something and put it on the plate in front of me. Then I looked down in horror. Without knowing it, I had picked a mango. I was horrified – I did not have any idea at all about how to peel it, or eat it, in 'polite company'.

Suffering from an acute attack of nerves, I turned to the Duke and confessed, 'Sir, I find myself in a most embarrassing situation – I wonder if you could help me. I am most terribly sorry, but I'm afraid I don't have the slightest idea how to deal with this mango.'

That provoked an enormous laugh from Prince Philip, who replied immediately, 'Well, let me show you.'

The Duke proceeded to take another mango and show me exactly what I should do. He took a sharp knife and put the tip into the mango until he could feel the pip at its centre. Then he went round the fruit, with the tip of the knife still held against the pip, until the mango was effectively in two halves, though still attached to the pip.

He then removed the knife, and placed a dessert spoon through the cut until he could feel the pip. He then used the spoon to loosen the pip from one side, and then repeated this on the other.

'Once you've done this,' he told me with a smile, 'you will be able to twist the two parts of the fruit apart. You then remove the pip altogether and cut across the soft fruit in the centre of both parts with a sharp knife.

'Once you have done that, you can turn each half inside out with your thumbs, so that the skin of each half is on the plate with the fruit uppermost. Then you can eat the mango.'

I was tremendously relieved that I wasn't left floundering and was now able to eat the mango in front of me.

Sean was driving me that day, and when I got back into the car after lunch, I immediately rang Brian Eastman to tell him the story and say that we simply had to include it in the dinner that formed part of the story of *The Royal Ruby*.

There is even a little joke about it in the film itself. When one of the dinner guests asks how Poirot knows how to treat a mango, the screenwriter Anthony Horowitz wrote the line, 'A certain duke taught me.'

We sent a copy of the finished film to Buckingham Palace on DVD, and I'm thrilled to say that it became the late Queen Mother's favourite film. Indeed, whenever I've met the Duke of Edinburgh since that lunch, he always calls me 'the mango man'.

I remember being tremendously pleased by the production values on display in the penultimate film of the series. *The Affair at the Victory Ball*, for example, needed a lavish set for a fancy-dress extravaganza to which every guest is supposed to come 'dressed as someone famous'. Poirot insists that he is quite famous enough to go as himself, though, in a little joke, Hastings decides to go as the Scarlet Pimpernel. The opening shots of the film focus on a set of beautiful pottery figures of the characters from the Italian *Commedia dell'Arte*. When two of the guests, who are dressed as characters from the *Commedia*, are found dead, Poirot finds himself helping Japp to reveal the murderer. At the end of the shoot, I was given the mock porcelain figures as a present, which I still have.

Part of the story of *The Victory Ball* takes place in a radio studio – and includes a little joke when one character in Andrew Marshall's script insists, 'Actors never know when to stop.' In fact, the denouement is held in a studio and broadcast live to the listening audience, with Poirot reconstructing what happened at the ball. Yet, no matter what the script may have suggested, Poirot knows exactly when to stop, no matter the temptation of a studio and a microphone.

The last story broadcast in the third series, *The Mystery of Hunter's Lodge*, is set during a grouse shoot on a moor in Yorkshire. It originally appeared in Dame Agatha's first collection of short stories, *Poirot Investigates*, in 1923, a collection that came into existence after being commissioned by the editor of the London-based illustrated weekly the *Sketch*. The stories appeared weekly before they were published in book form, much as the Sherlock Holmes stories had done in the *Strand Magazine* nearly thirty years earlier.

The shoot itself was cold, very cold. The temperature on the Yorkshire moors was freezing, and I kept falling off the shooting stick Poirot was supposed to be sitting on, because the ground was so soft after a long period of rain that my stick would not stay in place. On one occasion, it took the production team twenty minutes to clean me up again, as Poirot must never appear to be dirty, of course. In the film, Poirot catches a cold – just as I inevitably did. That happened many times over the years that I played him. I always seemed to catch whatever it was Poirot was supposed to have, and this was one of those cases. I remember it as one of the coldest shoots I had ever been on – there was snow on the ground and I was shivering, in spite of taking the precaution of wearing thermal underwear under my padding.

In the end, Poirot retires to bed in his hotel to recover, leaving Hastings and Japp to track down the murderer of the wealthy landowner of Harrington Place, who is holding the shoot on his land. But Poirot and I recovered sufficiently to uncover the killer in a denouement in front of the family living at Hunter's Lodge.

The shoot for the third series came to an end shortly before Christmas 1990, and the first film was due to be broadcast by

London Weekend on Sunday, 6 January 1991. Yet again, it was an astonishingly quick turnaround for such complicated films – the last of the ten was to go out on 10 March – and the decision to televise them so quickly after we had finished filming meant that we always seemed to be rushing to finish one before immediately starting the next.

I remember thinking, as Sean and I drove back to Pinner, 'How many actors have had the life I've had – and the opportunity to play such an extraordinary part?'

By then I had played Poirot thirty times in thirty stories, including two two-hour specials, a total of thirty-two hours of prime-time television. What would happen next?

CHAPTER 9

'YOU HAVE TO MAKE SURE THAT NOTHING GOES TO YOUR HEAD'

As the last Poirot episode I had filmed was transmitted, all I knew for certain was that London Weekend had not taken out an option on me for another series. I looked forward to playing him again but I was also aware that my children were growing up and I had to keep working. I had to try to make sure I was available in case another Poirot series was commissioned, but there was also a life to be lived, and that meant working.

It was my uncertainty about the future, and my need to work, that encouraged me to accept what some of my friends thought was a rather unlikely role – that of the anarchist and spy Alfred Verloc in a new BBC adaptation of Joseph Conrad's dark Victorian masterpiece *The Secret Agent*, which was first published in 1907, but set in 1886.

The script was by the British playwright Dusty Hughes and the director, another Englishman, David Drury, had assembled a terrific cast, including Cheryl Campbell, to play my wife Winnie,

Patrick Malahide as the assistant commissioner of the Metropolitan Police, and Warren Clarke as Chief Inspector Heat, the detective bent on tracking down the agent provocateur Verloc in London's East End.

Verloc was a milestone for me because it was the first genuinely evil part that I had played on television, and it was in the starkest possible contrast to the endlessly charming, if sometimes irritating, Poirot. There was no disguising the fact that Verloc was an evil man, intent on destroying society, and that it would be hard for any audience to find much affection for him. But playing him provided me with a real challenge: to bring to life one of European literature's most malignant souls without turning him into a monster with a tail and horns. Indeed, in spite of the material, I never once allowed myself to be depressed by his character, no matter how despicable he might be. I knew that Verloc was an opportunity to show myself to the audience in a different light, and that meant a great deal to me.

By now I was forty-five years old, a time when most people are pretty settled in their lives and career. They have a house and children, as I did, and, if they are lucky, they also have a fairly predictable future. But no actor has that luxury – certainly not one determined to make a career out of being a character actor, as I was. I had known for a long time that I had to be more flexible than that, and take the chances I was offered. But I could not have managed that without Sheila's support, because she understood – having been an actress herself – exactly what an actor's lifestyle meant. It was always a rollercoaster, with neither of us knowing what was to come next.

That's the life you join as an actor, and it was one reason why Sheila and I trained ourselves never to look more than six months into the future – if things went badly, we were always ready to make a change to our lives. It was a thought that sustained us through the good times as well as the bad. If things went badly, we always told each other, we would sell the house and move into something smaller, or even move back into a narrow boat on the canals, which is where we started our life together. It was an attitude that meant we were always ready to drop everything at a moment's notice if the right chance came up, no matter where it took us.

I had decided, however, that there was one thing I really could not do while Poirot remained a possibility – and that was to go back to work with the Royal Shakespeare Company at Stratford. But the decision upset me for I loved the company. In fact, I was lucky enough to be asked to rejoin them almost every year, even for just one production, but I knew that making that commitment would demand a long period of my time, and it would also mean that I would not be available for another Poirot series if one was recommissioned. Not going to the RSC was the right thing to do, but it was very hard to refuse my friends there, especially the principal associate director Michael Attenborough, who was always trying, very gently, to persuade me to go back to a company I had always treasured.

But even though I turned down the RSC, the decision did not depress me, because I have always been a very positive person. I've always felt enormously fortunate to be an actor, but I have also realised that you need to keep your feet firmly on the ground if you are. You have to make sure that nothing goes to your head – not even the greatest reviews. And I also believe that the higher you go up the ladder of success, the more certain it is that one day it might just stop. My philosophy was to choose what I did very carefully, and always to do the best and most challenging work that I could, and see where that took me.

Yet beneath all that, I also knew that I wanted to go on playing Poirot. Some of my friends would ask, 'Haven't you had enough of him?'

But I would always tell them, 'The public love him, and the truth is, I do too.'

That made the uncertainty about whether I would play him again all the more testing, but there were consolations – not least the extraordinary fan letters that I had received since *Agatha Christie's Poirot* began. I had been used to one or two bits of fan mail in the past, but suddenly a tidal wave of letters overtook me, and they came as a considerable shock. They really did.

Those letters made me realise that I had a responsibility to the audience to keep up the quality of everything I did on the series, to surround myself with the very best people and the finest scripts. It was something I had tried to do throughout my career, but now it became even more important. I simply could not let the letter-writers down, and so I replied to them all, and found myself taking on a part-time secretary to help.

The letters came from all sorts of people, and each and every one of them was touching in its own way. Mind you, it did not entirely escape my attention that the majority of them came from women.

One elderly lady of almost ninety years of age, who lived alone, wrote to thank me for making her Sunday evenings a treat. She told me she drew her dining table up in front of her television set before each episode, so that she could have supper with me.

Then a young woman in her twenties wrote to ask me if I would come and meet her in a park one day, dressed as Poirot, so that she could know what it would be like to be treated like a lady. I am afraid I declined the invitation, but it revealed just how much Poirot meant to everyone that watched him.

One lady from Northern Ireland wrote to tell me that she had never before watched films that included Poirot because he had always seemed a little unbelievable to her, and a little repellent.

She told me that it was only because she had seen my Caliban for the RSC at Stratford that she had even turned on her television set to watch the Poirot series. To her amazement, she found him a credible character. She told me that she could see the person shining through, and asked me whether this was the fascination of acting.

Deeply moved, I replied to her letter, though I am far from certain whether I answered her question. In fact, I am not altogether sure if I could define exactly what the fascination of acting is, beyond that I love doing it.

Another lady, this time from Scotland, said she had felt compelled to write to congratulate me on my portrayal, and went into considerable detail about exactly why. She explained that she had always considered Poirot to be such a unique and complex character that it was impossible to bring him to life without turning him into some kind of music-hall turn. She was kind enough to tell me that, for her, my performance had come as a great surprise and a great relief. To know that these members of the audience had understood what I had been trying to do was tremendously heartening.

Not all the letters were from ladies.

One gentleman from Rhode Island in the United States confessed, 'I have not had much experience in writing fan letters, so please excuse the awkwardness of this letter. I just want you to know that you have many fans in America. I am happy to say I am one of them . . . but I am not an impressionable young girl, or a yuppie or some groupie. I am a sixty-four-year-old black American, a former postal worker now retired . . . a happily married man of thirty-nine years, to my first and only love. Father of three children – two boys and a girl – and last, but not least, a grandfather of ten.'

This delightful gentleman particularly liked Poirot's banter with Hastings – and especially over our game of Monopoly – just as he enjoyed his impatience with the other guests during the denouement in *Peril at End House*, which he called 'vintage Poirot'. But what he admired the most was the single fact that had preoccupied me the most: distilling the true humanity of the little man into my performance.

'No one has so captured the essence of Poirot as you have,' he wrote. 'Even though you reveal his vanity, his conceits, he is in some ways a ridiculous little man, you still, like no [other] actor convey his sweetness, his innate kindness and his tenacity. It is just wonderful.' He ended by wishing me 'much success in your future' and concluded with a sentence that touched my heart. 'I hope that my letter means something to you.' It most certainly did.

The letter that meant the most to me, however, did not come from a fan but from Rosalind Hicks, Dame Agatha's daughter, who had subjected me to that ordeal when we had met for lunch back in the summer of 1988, before the first series had even started filming, when she reminded me firmly that we must never laugh *at* Poirot – only *with* him.

'Dear "Poirot",' she was kind enough to write. 'Your appearance and mannerisms, the warmth and humour and occasional touches of impatience and fussiness – it is all just right . . . Agatha Christie's Poirot, you certainly are. I'm sure she would have been delighted.

'The order and method and the little grey cells are all there to see. The moustaches could have been a little more magnificent, but I do understand what you feel about this sensitive point!' She ended by saying simply, 'With many thanks and congratulations from us both.'

It brought back the memory of my terror that my Poirot might not match the ideal she had in mind. It was an enormous relief to hear that it did.

I think Rosalind Hicks' support for me may have been one of the factors – as well as the audience figures in this country and the show's success in the United States – that finally persuaded London Weekend to go on with a fourth series. After all, they were perfectly within their rights to stop, but – to their eternal credit – they did not. The decision came through while I was filming *The Secret Agent*, and I was thrilled.

The success of the two-hour versions of Dame Agatha's *Peril at End House* and *The Mysterious Affair at Styles* had apparently helped to convince executive producer Nick Elliott that there was an appetite for longer films, not least because the American audience seemed to like them. So he decided, in the first months of 1991, that they would film three two-hour specials later that year, and that, once again, he would ask Brian Eastman to produce them.

So, in the summer of 1991, three years after that lunch with Rosalind Hicks and her husband, I went back to Twickenham Studios to film three two-hour Poirot films. There were to be one or two changes, however. My old friend Hugh Fraser was only to appear in the first of the three stories as Hastings, though Inspector Japp was in them all. The indefatigable Miss Lemon, so neatly played by Pauline Moran in the first three series, was also missing from two of the new films.

The absence of two of my three allies made me a little sad, but the cast that Brian Eastman assembled for each of the three new films was so good that it almost made up for it, and the attention to period detail that he and London Weekend had been honing throughout the first three series was now on full display. The new films were going to look as good as British television could possibly make them – in our eyes, the equal of anything that the American networks might do.

The first of the three was Dame Agatha's classic *The ABC Murders*, called a masterpiece by many of her admirers, which features murders that are announced before they have even taken place, in letters to Poirot signed 'ABC'. The first murder is in Andover in Hampshire, the second in Bexhill in Kent, the third in the fictional town of Cherton, possibly in Devon, and the fourth is destined to happen in Doncaster in South Yorkshire, but Poirot is determined that it will never be allowed to happen. Beside the body of each of the victims lies a copy of the English *ABC Railway Guide*.

The original story began its life as a serialisation in the *Daily Express* in England, but the novel itself was published in both Britain and the United States in the first weeks of 1936. It was so strikingly good that it became an instant worldwide hit, and had even been made into a feature film in 1966, with the American Tony Randall as Poirot and the British actor Robert Morley as Hastings. There was even a rumour that the American comedian Zero Mostel was to have played the little Belgian in that production, but Dame Agatha, who took a great interest in any depiction of her character on the screen, objected strongly when the film's original screenplay called for Poirot not only to have a love interest, but also a love scene. In the end, it had neither.

Our new film had no such problems – there was not a trace of a love scene. The script was once again by the wonderful Clive Exton, and the director was Andrew Grieve, now both veterans of the series who exactly understood the character I was determined to portray.

In fact, *ABC* is a delight, perhaps even my favourite Poirot film.

It begins with Hastings returning from a trip to the Orinoco Delta in Venezuela, bearing a stuffed crocodile as a present for Poirot, which stands – decidedly uncomfortably – on the sideboard at Whitehaven Mansions when the first of the 'ABC' letters arrives. Poirot is very pleased to see his old friend, and insists he stay with him in the flat while Hastings finds himself somewhere to live, but the little man also confesses to him that he has not been very busy: 'The little grey cells, they have the rust.'

The cast was terrific, with Donald Sumpter particularly good as the travelling stockings salesman Alexander Bonaparte Cust, who becomes the prime suspect for the murders. For me, the scene that Donald and I played together in a jail cell is one of the highlights of all the Poirot films that I have made. When you have actors of his quality alongside you in a piece, it improves the work of everyone, and the better everyone one is, the happier I am, because it also makes me raise my own performance to match theirs. There is no competition between us as actors, just the pleasure of seeing one actor's performance bringing out the best in all of us. It certainly did on *ABC*.

The second film was *Death in the Clouds*, which Dame Agatha wrote in 1935, the year before *ABC*. Called *Death in the Air* in the United States, it is a prime example of one of her favourite plot devices: the victim and the potential murderers all isolated in a single location – be it in an English country house, on a train journey, on an isolated archaeological excavation in the Middle East, or – as in this case – on a flight from Le Bourget Airport in Paris to Croydon Airport to the south of London.

It was to be directed by the actor Stephen Whittaker, who had played alongside me in *Blott on the Landscape* for the BBC, but had now turned director. Stephen had never directed any of our films before, and indeed nothing on quite this scale, and I think he found it quite a challenge. He was also working with a script from another newcomer to the series, the experienced British screenwriter William Humble, who had started his career writing *Emmerdale*.

Nevertheless, Brian Eastman had surrounded them with another excellent cast, led by Sarah Woodward, daughter of the actor Edward Woodward, who was – effectively – my Hastings for the story. Nothing was lost by the transformation; in fact, it was a marvellous change for me to have a lady with a sharp mind as my companion rather than the ever-loyal Hastings.

At this stage, I had no say in who was to write or direct any of the films, but I had great faith in Brian Eastman's judgement as a producer. By now, he had a well-earned reputation for making high-quality television drama, which meant that not only did actors, writers and directors want to work with him, they also wanted to work on the Poirot series. It was his vision, and his ability to set the tone for what we were doing, that provided one of the cornerstones of the success of *Agatha Christie's Poirot*. I do not believe anyone else could have ensured the production quality that Brian did, especially when it came to the cast, locations and props – not least the vintage aeroplanes and cars – or matched his eye for an interesting background to add a little glamour to the story.

Set largely in France, which demanded a French crew alongside our English one, *Death in the Clouds* focuses on the death of Madame Giselle, a mysterious French moneylender, who is discovered dead during the plane's journey from Paris to London. Not surprisingly, it also features Poirot's fear of flying, which means that he is asleep, possibly from taking a sleeping draught, when the murder takes place. There is even a little Dame Agatha joke, as the plane's passengers include a 'mystery writer' called Daniel Clancy, who becomes one of the suspects, as well as being Inspector Japp's favourite author.

Filmed against the backdrop of the French Open tennis championship for men in Paris in 1935, which was won by the British amateur Fred Perry, the story makes a great deal of the appetite for gambling among the plane's occupants, particularly Lady Cicely Horbury, who is seen repeatedly losing in the casino, but it is the mystery of who killed Madame Giselle on the plane that brings the story its distinctive charm. How was she murdered, and by whom? It is one of Dame Agatha's most intricate plots. I like working on the longer films like this one because it gives me an opportunity to develop the character, but even more than that, I thought it was wonderful that a series like ours was now capable of going to Paris, even if only for a few days. I kept pinching myself to make sure it was true. This was also the first time that I ever visited the French sculptor Auguste Rodin's house in the Rue de Varenne, which helped me to understand the art of sculpture more completely. Ever since, I have always gone to Rodin's house whenever I am in Paris.

The last film in the fourth series was *One, Two, Buckle My Shoe*, which was, in some ways, the strongest of the three. It was the first of Dame Agatha's stories to use a nursery rhyme as its inspiration – an idea she was to return to time after time in the following thirty-five years. Written just after the outbreak of the Second World War in 1939, it reveals a changing world, where nothing is now quite as cosy and stable as it had been before the war intervened. There is revolution in the air, with references in the book itself both to the 'Reds' of the Soviet Union and 'our Blackshirted friends' of Oswald Mosley's British Union of Fascists. Both appear in Clive Exton's script for the film, which was directed by Ross Devenish, who had made such an excellent job of *The Mysterious Affair at Styles* two years before.

Once again the story displays one of Poirot's pet hates, this time of going to the dentist, as well as his suspicion of dentistry as a profession. It opens with a dentist's death in his Harley Street surgery, only a matter of minutes after Poirot has left the chair. At first, the death looks like suicide, but it quickly transpires that international politics could be involved as Poirot and Chief Inspector Japp begin to investigate. A second death follows shortly afterwards, and not long after that, the character of Frank Carter, who seems to support the Fascist movement, appears.

Carter was played by a new young actor called Christopher Eccleston, then just twenty-seven, who had made his reputation in the profession a few months earlier in the Peter Medak film *Let Him Have It*, about the 1953 hanging for murder of the illiterate teenager Derek Bentley, played by Eccleston. Formidably talented, Chris only had a small part in *One, Two*, but he was so good I could never forget him. I knew at once that here was a future star. So it proved, for he went on to confirm his reputation on television in *Cracker* and *Doctor Who*, in films with *Shallow Grave* and *28 Days Later*, and at the Donmar Warehouse and the National Theatre. It gives me great pleasure to think that Poirot was there at the beginning.

A shoe buckle certainly plays its part in Dame Agatha's story, which also serves to remind the audience just how excellent a detective Poirot can be, as well as being someone who is exceptionally considerate towards everyone he meets, be they the English aristocracy or their servants. That allowed Clive Exton to provide Japp with a little joke at Poirot's expense when he says, 'You always did move in exalted circles, Poirot.' Poirot brushes the remark off, even though he knows that it is true. Clive also allowed Poirot to confirm his principles as a detective, when he explains, 'I am methodical, orderly and logical,' before adding forcefully, 'and I do not like to distort facts to support a theory.' That was the Poirot I knew and loved, and it gave me enormous pleasure to say the line.

My daughter, Katherine, appeared in *One, Two*, as a schoolgirl in the park. She and Sheila happened to be on set one day, when we needed some extras. It was not the only time one or both of the children worked alongside me. A few years later, they were extras in a Tube train segment, only to find that, when the episode finally aired, they had been left on the cutting-room floor. They were very miffed.

After the filming was over, Sheila and I, as well as Robert and Katherine, who were then ten and eight, took off on holiday in our new narrow boat, called *Lark Rise*. It was our second boat, after *Prima Donna*, which had been our first home together and the one we lived on while we toured in rep. We paid all the proper charges for moorings, but even so, narrow boats make wonderful 'digs' for touring actors because they provide an economical place to live and you can usually find a mooring not too far from the theatre. This time, we toured our old haunts, the canals of the Midlands, hiding away from everyone and enjoying being a family together. I had been so busy, it was a relief to be alone with the people I cared most about in the world, away from the pressure.

I knew in my heart that we had done a good job with our latest three films – they felt right somehow. But that series also underlined something that was very important to me in the wake of all those letters: the fact that it contradicted the rule that seemed to say that even very good television series begin to fall off after a while, as their quality seems to dilute. I was delighted that our Poirot films had not done that.

The only shadow on the horizon, as we travelled the canals, was that my dear, dear mother Joan, who'd been a dancer alongside Evelyn Laye in the 1922 musical hit *Lilac Time*, before she married my father Jack, was not well again. There had been difficulties over the past few years, but as 1992 began, I was beginning to become very worried about her indeed. To be an actor is wonderful, but there is nothing more important than family.

CHAPTER 10

'I COULD BE SAYING GOODBYE TO HIM, PERHAPS FOR A YEAR, PERHAPS FOREVER'

What I feared might happen turned into a bleak reality not long after we came back from our family trip on *Lark Rise* along England's canals. My dear mum had gone into hospital for a hip operation just before Christmas, but some time after she came out of the anaesthetic, a blood embolism sent her into a deep coma, which began on New Year's Eve 1991. She came out of the coma in February, but the doctors told us that she would simply never be the same again, and on 5 May 1992 she died, at the age of just seventy-six, with her three sons, John, Peter and me, at her bedside.

It was a horrible and protracted death, which was very hard on her, and, of course, on all the rest of the family. Going to visit her was a dreadful ordeal, as we all knew she simply could not survive, and yet we all wanted her to. I do not think that John, Peter and I, her three sons, ever imagined living without her.

Yet, even then, at this dark point in my life, it was as if the ghost of Dame Agatha was looking over my shoulder. At the very moment we heard of my mother's descent into a coma, Sheila and I were staying at the Imperial Hotel in Torquay, the place that was one of the inspirations for some of Dame Agatha's stories. She was, of course, born in the town and her house, Greenway, was not far away, on the River Dart in south Devon.

I was devastated. My mother had meant so much to me. Without her support, I would never have become an actor. It was she who persuaded my father to let me go to drama school – very much against his will. In fact, she became a legend at LAMDA when I was a student there, turning up to watch me whenever there was a public performance. In one play I appeared in, my character had to call out for his mother at the start of the second act, which, of course, I did – only for my mother to call out 'Yes!' from the stalls. We had to start the second act again.

Mum also developed a technique for letting me know that she and my father were in the audience, by coughing loudly in my first dramatic pause in the production. Throughout every single day of my career, she was a wonderful source of encouragement, though she could be strange from time to time. When I was playing Petruchio in *The Taming of the Shrew* at Exeter on one occasion, I got a message to come to the telephone to speak to my mother while the production was going on.

My grandmother was ill at the time and I assumed it was about her, so I said, 'Is Nana all right?' There was a pause from my mother. 'I mean, I'm worried about her.'

Another pause, then my mother said, 'When you take your lovely feathered hat off, will you straighten your hair? You're looking bald.'

Mum always came to my dressing room after seeing one of my performances, and always worried about me, and that went on even after I was married to Sheila. I knew in my heart that I would not even have got my first job as an actor without her, let alone Poirot. The two of them made such a difference to me that I honestly do not think I could have survived in the profession without them.

My mother was so devoted to my career that she came to see every play that I performed on the stage. In fact, there was one occasion, when I was playing Bolingbroke in *Richard II* for the Royal Shakespeare Company in Stratford, when they even held up the rise of the curtain for her, so that she could get to her seat before we started the performance. That was how much she meant to me, and to my colleagues. She was so proud of everything I had done. My one consolation after her death was that at least she had seen my career blossom.

The moment my mother's funeral was over, I flew to Morocco to film the first of the eight films in the latest, fifth, Poirot series.

I cannot say that I was exactly ready to start filming. In fact, I found it very difficult indeed to climb back into my padding and my false moustaches as the little Belgian. My mother's death was in my mind at every moment, and I struggled to forget her as I put on the spats and picked up Poirot's silver-topped cane again. Looking back, I do not think that I was ever quite myself throughout this series, because of the long shadow cast by her death. But I did everything in my power to honour her memory and remain as professional as she had always wanted me to be.

My mother's death may have been the subconscious reason behind the fact that I collapsed during the filming of the first story in the new series, *The Adventure of the Egyptian Tomb*. It had never happened before. I was sitting in an open-topped car in the burning sun, without an umbrella to protect me, as we filmed a series of takes of Poirot arriving at a local police station. It was very hot, and getting hotter – and my padding was not helping.

To this day, I am not exactly sure what happened. All I know is that the car pulled up outside the police station on one of the takes, I went to climb out, and everything went black. I do not remember anything else at all until I woke up indoors, lying flat on my back, and found myself being given oxygen through a mask by the unit's nurse. Apparently, I had fallen down in a dead faint.

The only thing I remember clearly as I came round was the sight of one of the production team looking at his watch, worrying that we still had a lot to shoot that day and could not afford to waste any time. Such is an actor's destiny.

The story was clearly inspired by the discovery of the tomb of King Tutankhamun by the English Egyptologist Howard Carter in 1922. News of the find first appeared only a year or so before Dame Agatha's own story appeared in the *Daily Sketch*. It was later to be included in the collection *Poirot Investigates*, published in 1924. There could be no doubt about her inspiration. All the ingredients of King Tut's curse are there – right down to the discovery of a lost Egyptian tomb and the ancient curse that is destined to fall on anyone who dares open it.

Dame Agatha's version tells of a series of deaths following the discovery and opening of the tomb of King Men-her-Ra by British archaeologist Sir John Willard – who dies of what appears to be a heart attack at the very moment the tomb is opened. His widow is convinced that there has been foul play and consults Poirot, who finds himself, before long, on his way to the Valley of the Kings in Egypt – although, in our case, Morocco was standing in for the original.

Poirot appears to take the legend of the curse seriously, even saying to Hastings and Miss Lemon at one point, 'I also believe in the force of superstition – it is a power that is very great indeed.' He is, of course, talking about the power of the idea of superstition, rather than the curse itself, for Poirot always relies on logic.

Fortunately, the next story in the series was to be filmed in England, so I had a chance to recover in a rather more temperate climate. Dame Agatha wrote *The Underdog* in 1928, but it was not published in England until 1960, when it appeared as one of the stories in *The Adventure of the Christmas Pudding*. Our new version was written by a newcomer to the series, Bill Craig, who set it around a golf match, but, more significantly, it begins with Miss Lemon attempting to hypnotise Poirot using her new-found skill as a hypnotherapist. The therapy does not work with the little man, although it does play its part in the story.

The only thing I did not care for about the plot was the notion that Poirot might like to play golf. I simply did not agree. I can remember saying to the production team, 'Poirot does not play golf. He simply would not.' To my mind, he would always be perfectly happy to watch Hastings play – and indeed he takes some delight in the fact that his friend scores a hole in one, to the amazement of everyone, at the end of the story – but my Poirot would always prefer to watch.

The Underdog was one of Dame Agatha's slighter stories, but the next in the series, *The Yellow Iris* was one of her strongest. It had first appeared in the *Strand Magazine* in 1937 and was later published in a collection called *The Regatta Mystery* in 1939. But the screenwriter, Anthony Horowitz, expanded the story considerably, giving it a flashback sequence in Buenos Aires and adding the idea that this was a crime that Poirot had once failed to solve. Directed by Peter Barber-Fleming, it focuses on a restaurant called Le Jardin des Cygnes in Argentina and the intervention of a corrupt Argentinean general to prevent Poirot solving a murder there. Still smarting at the failure, Poirot seizes the chance two years later to reclaim his reputation when a new restaurant opens in London with exactly the same name, and where exactly the same group of characters that had been in Buenos Aires are reunited.

The story includes another of Dame Agatha's poisonings, and takes place almost entirely in the restaurant, which also features a cabaret with a singer, just as the original short story did, though she does not sing the lines written for her by Dame Agatha.

Thinking about *The Yellow Iris* now, it reminds me that her greatest fans sometimes object when we depart from her original story in the television films – and they write to tell me so. I always reply by telling them that I am terribly sorry, but not all of her stories adapt easily to the small screen, they are simply too slight, which is why we describe them as 'based on' her originals. I think her die-hard fans forgive us for the adaptations, but I do understand how they feel.

The next two films, *The Case of the Missing Will* and *The Adventure of the Italian Nobleman*, were both stories that originally appeared in the *Daily Sketch* and were later published in *Poirot Investigates*, in 1924. Neither were tremendously strong stories, and both needed more than a little adaptation to make the transition to television.

What was most interesting to me about these stories was that, at this point in Poirot's history, Dame Agatha was carefully developing his character, not only to allow her readers to discover his foibles, but also for them to grasp a sense of his beliefs. This is true of *The Case of the Missing Will* in particular, where one of the characters is a staunch feminist who believes that women should have the right to a university education, something Poirot wholeheartedly agrees with.

* * *

When I first started reading Poirot, I relied on these early stories to help me to understand him better, which was lucky for me, for as time went by and her audience grew to know him better, she reduced the amount of time she spent revealing his idiosyncrasies. By then, her audience had come to know them only too well.

The sixth film was one of my favourites, and remains so to this day. *The Chocolate Box*, which was originally known as *The Clue of the Chocolate Box*, first appeared in the *Daily Sketch* in 1923 and was then collected in *Poirot Investigates*. It is a simply wonderful story about Poirot's return to Brussels with Inspector Japp – the Scotland Yard detective is to receive a grand award – which reminds Poirot of a case when he was still an officer in the Belgian detective force. In the original story, Poirot's reminiscence is told in flashback, and the screenwriter, Douglas Watkinson again, had Philip Jackson and I travel to Brussels together to launch the story.

That made it very special for me. It was wonderful to go to Belgium, because I truly felt that I was returning to my homeland as Poirot. By then, I had discovered that he was born in the town of Spa in the principality of Liège, sometime between 1854 and 1856, and the film gave me the opportunity to unveil his character as a younger man and reveal something about his past. Just as exciting was the fact that I was to be dressed in a police uniform for the flashbacks in the 1890s, which allowed me to escape my padding, and even to renounce the walk I had used for so long playing him as an older man – remember, he was in his middle sixties when he was first discovered in *The Mysterious Affair at Styles*.

The story also gave me the chance to show Poirot's emotional side, for as part of the film, he loses his heart to a young woman, Mademoiselle Virginie Mesnard, who asks him to investigate a case of what may be murder, but is being called a natural death by the doctors. Virginie was played by the lovely Anna Chancellor, then still just twenty-seven, the year before she leapt to prominence as Henrietta, or 'Duckface', as she was known, in Richard Curtis's award-winning film *Four Weddings and a Funeral*. Then still in her bohemian period, Anna was quite superb in our film, bewitching the younger Poirot completely, and presenting him with the tiny silver vase for his lapel that he wore filled with wild flowers from that day onwards.

In fact, that never happened in Dame Agatha's original story, but was another example of the screenwriter allowing Poirot an opportunity to display rather more of himself to the audience on television than he did in the original story. Filming it made me truly happy, for there was Poirot as a younger man, pursuing the case against the wishes of his superiors, losing his heart to Virginie, even running through the streets of Brussels – not something the older Hercule Poirot would ever have allowed himself to do. It was a breath of fresh air, and a joy to do.

Anna's was not the only memorable performance in *The Chocolate Box*, for the director, Andrew Grieve, also had the incomparable Rosalie Crutchley playing an elderly matriarch. Then in her early seventies, Rosalie was a legend of both British films and television, having played Acte alongside Peter Ustinov's Nero in the 1951 epic *Quo Vadis* and Madame Defarge in the 1958 version of *A Tale of Two Cities*, alongside Dirk Bogarde. She had even played Henry VIII's sixth wife, Catherine Parr, in not one but two television series in the early 70s.

With her olive complexion and sad, dark eyes, Rosalie was capable of commanding the screen while doing almost nothing. As an actor, you simply could not ignore her strength, which communicated itself to the audience almost subliminally. She was superb in our film, though sadly she was to die only five years later, at the age of just seventy-seven. One of the delights of the filming was that I managed to photograph both Rosalie and Anna during breaks in the shooting, as I had begun to return to my old hobby of photography in what few spare moments I had.

Sadly, the last two films of our fifth series were not quite of the same exquisite quality as *The Chocolate Box*.

Dead Man's Mirror was a long short story that had first appeared in book form in a collection called *Murder in the Mews* in 1937, although it was, in fact, an expanded version of another of her stories, *The Second Gong*, which was first published in the magazines *Ladies' Home Journal* and the *Strand* in 1932. A locked room mystery – another of Dame Agatha's favourite plot devices – it centres on a rather pompous collector of Art Deco who outbids Poirot for a mirror at a London auction and then asks to consult him because he suspects that he is being defrauded by his architect. Poirot visits him – only for the collector to be found dead, in what looks like suicide, locked in his study. The striking of the gong which calls the house guests down to dinner plays a significant role in the denouement, but it is a gentle story rather than one to set the blood racing.

The same could also be said for *Jewel Robbery at the Grand Metropolitan*, another of the short stories from the *Daily Sketch* to be collected for *Poirot Investigates*. The original title was *The Curious Disappearance of the Opalsen Pearls*, which is a rather more accurate indication of the story, as it focuses on a theatre producer who purchases some expensive jewels at auction for his wife, who is an actress, to wear in his production of a new play called *Pearls Before Swine*. Poirot only gets involved because he has been forced to take a holiday due to overwork and finds himself in Brighton, staying at the Grand Metropolitan Hotel, together with the producer and his wife, at the time the play has its premiere. The jewels go missing, encouraging Poirot to overcome his illness to recover them.

In the original story, the pearls were purchased by a rich stockbroker 'who made a fortune in the recent oil boom', but the screenwriter, Anthony Horowitz, turned him into a theatrical producer, thereby allowing the denouement to take place in a theatre, a place that Dame Agatha used several times in her stories, although not in this one in its original version. Filmed in Brighton, it used another of her favourite devices – how the pearls could have disappeared from a locked box when the maid who was guarding them never let the box out of her sight. Another slight story, it lacked the energy and force of *The Yellow Iris* and *The Chocolate Box*.

Perhaps it had something to do with the death of my mother, I cannot be sure, but by the time we came to the end of the series, I was not entirely happy with what I had done. The stories worked, of course, especially *The Chocolate Box*, but I had a sinking feeling. I was not sure they were as quite as good as I could have made them. I was satisfied with my performances, but felt as though perhaps – like Poirot in the last film – I needed a break.

In this reflective mood, I went back to Pinner for a rest. I was not sure what to do next; nor, for that matter, exactly what I *wanted* to do. I certainly was not ready to give up Poirot, but there was something troubling me. Yet again, there was no indication from London Weekend about the future. My agent had given them a deadline in February 1993, by which they had to tell me their Poirot plans for the coming year, but they had not taken out an option for me to play the role again. That was familiar enough. The only option that they had ever taken out was for me to do a second series after the first.

Since then, I had been left in limbo every year. But this time I was restless, not completely happy with myself, and was waiting, waiting, waiting to discover what would happen to Poirot and me.

With nothing firm on my horizon, I accepted the role of the flamboyant Viennese business man Rudi Waltz in English director Jack Gold's film *The Lucona Affair*, a fictional account of a huge Austrian political scandal. It was based on the bombing of the cargo ship *Lucona* in the Indian Ocean in 1977, which had been chartered by my character, who then tried to claim £13 million in compensation for the loss from an insurance company. It set off one of the great financial and political dramas in modern Austrian history. In reality, the Austrian Minister of Defence committed suicide after it was discovered that he had allowed the bomb onto the ship, and several other ex-ministers were imprisoned for covering up the affair.

My co-star was the Italian Franco Nero, who had made his reputation in the 1970 version of D. H. Lawrence's novella *The Virgin and the Gypsy,* and had famously fallen in love with Britain's Vanessa Redgrave in the 1960s, in the wake of her divorce from director Tony Richardson. Franco's career had continued apace. In 1990 he had even appeared in the Hollywood blockbuster *Die Hard 2,* alongside Bruce Willis, although most of his work for the cinema was produced in Europe rather than in the United States. *The Lucona Affair* was a European production, with a large German and Austrian cast and crew, in spite of the presence of Jack Gold and me representing England.

Poirot was still there in the background, however. I simply could not ignore the little Belgian. Indeed, one of the nicest things that happened while I was filming in Austria was that the four two-hour Poirots that we had made finally emerged on American television, starting with *The ABC Murders* on 19 November 1992. The *New*

York Times's John J. O'Connor was particularly kind, noting that the Poirot series started immediately after my appearance in *The Secret Agent* on the same channel in the United States, and thereby gave the audience 'another opportunity to savour a gifted actor's versatility'.

'Mr Suchet's Poirot', he went on, 'is now a paragon of charming ego and unquestionable shrewdness . . . "Poirot" just keeps getting better. Much like Mr Suchet.' Mr O'Connor set the tone for most of the American reviews, which were almost all equally flattering. What those critics did not know, however, was that I had no idea whether I was ever to get the opportunity to make my Poirot any better.

The Americans liked the series so much that they even granted the show the accolade of a cartoon in the *New Yorker* magazine, with the title 'Hercule Parrot'. It featured a parrot with a Poirot-like moustache saying, 'A cracker, s'il vous plait.' I wondered what Dame Agatha would have made of it.

It was in early December 1992, when I was sitting in my hotel room in Vienna during the filming of *Lucona*, that the first indication of what the future might hold for me came in a telephone call from my agent in England at the time, Aude Powell – and it had nothing whatever to do with Poirot. Aude rang me to say that the playwright Harold Pinter was very interested in casting me in a new play by the American playwright David Mamet, called *Oleanna*, which he was going to direct.

'Harold would like you to read the script as soon as you can,' she said.

At that moment I knew nothing about the play, but I did know that no actor could refuse an opportunity to work with probably the most gifted English playwright of the second half of the twentieth century on a play written by one of the great talents of the American theatre in the same period. *Oleanna* represented a tremendously exciting opportunity, and I did not intend to let it slip away without exploring it carefully.

I read the play within a week and realised that mine was a wonderful role. I could not wait to tell Harold that I would love to play it. I was to play the college lecturer John in Mamet's ferocious examination of sexual harassment and exploitation in American universities. My character is accused by Carol, a female student, of attempted rape, abuse of power and 'classism', and his career is destroyed by the allegations.

The play had only been performed once before, in the United States, when Mamet had directed his wife, Rebecca Pidgeon, as Carol and William H. Macy as John. It had provoked an enormous response, not to say a controversy, with *Newsweek* magazine's famous theatre critic Jack Kroll describing it by saying, 'Mamet has sent a riveting report from the war zone between the genders and the classes, a war that will cause great havoc before it can create a new human order.'

The so-called 'Butcher of Broadway', the *New York Times* theatre critic Frank Rich, had enthused, 'John and Carol go to it with hand-to-hand combat that amounts to a primal struggle for power' with 'highly distilled dialogue unencumbered by literary frills or phony theatrical devices'. Mamet himself had asked Pinter to direct the play in London.

I was fascinated. It was a unique opportunity to appear in what could become one of the great new plays of the last quarter of the century, a work that had never been performed anywhere other than New York, and offered me the chance to return to the theatre in a part that would utterly confound the expectations of the television audience that had grown used to me in Poirot. Ironically, Harold's interest came just as the fifth series of *Agatha Christie's Poirot* started on ITV on Sunday, 17 January 1993, with *The Adventure of the Egyptian Tomb*. It was to air every Sunday until the first week of March, and was just as well-received as its predecessors had been. The audience clearly did not share my own slight sense of disappointment, one which Sheila, however, did share.

Still there was no word from London Weekend about what they intended for the future of Poirot, while now there was the tantalising prospect of *Oleanna*. I was torn in two directions, and did not know what to do, but a week or two after the original call from my agent Aude, and after I had finished the script, I got another telephone call from her.

'I'm terribly sorry to tell you, David,' she said, 'but Harold has decided to go in another direction for the part of John.'

My stomach did a somersault and my heart sank because this was a role that I desperately wanted to play.

'Please tell Harold that I quite understand,' I said to Aude, trying to conceal exactly how upset I was, 'but would you ask him if he would be prepared to have coffee with me, just to discuss his decision?'

Aude said she would, and came back later that day to say that Harold would be more than happy to see me.

So, in the early days of February, I found myself in Harold's office in his house in Camden Hill Square in Kensington, London. He was utterly charming. We talked about *The Lucona Affair*, and what else I was thinking of doing. In fact, we talked for almost half an hour before the subject of *Oleanna* came up.

What I did not realise was that Harold was using our conversation to audition me.

'Now look here,' he said finally. 'You are sitting here in front of me because – in essence – you require me to tell you why I am going another way in the casting of this role.'

He paused for what seemed like a very long time, while I kept absolutely silent.

'But you know, I have to admit something to you.'

There was another Pinteresque pause.

'I have been completely wrong, and I don't know whether you will take this as a compliment or not, but I think you are perfect casting.'

My jaw dropped, and I struggled to know what to say. Finally, I thanked him profusely for the compliment, but then confessed, 'But, Harold, I don't know whether or not I'm going to be offered another series of Poirot, though there is a time limit on London Weekend making an offer, which is very, very imminent.'

'Well, there you are, and there it is,' he said in his quiet, firm voice. 'It is for you to decide. It is yours if you want it, but I have to know very soon.' Rehearsals were due to begin in just a few weeks.

As I left his house, I realised that I had never been in a situation quite like this in my life before.

All I could think about was what London Weekend was going to do about Poirot, and exactly when the time limit on them having to make an offer to me ran out. I did not want to let them down, and would stand by our agreement to play him again if they wanted me to, even if that meant me turning my back on *Oleanna*, but I was still torn.

As it happened, Sheila and I had decided to go for a week's break to my parents' serviced flat in the Imperial Hotel in Torquay. There was no point in altering our plans. I simply asked my agent to re-check the date by which an offer for Poirot had to be made, and off we went.

The day of the deadline came, and I heard nothing at all. To me, that meant that I was now free of the obligation.

The next morning, I telephoned Aude and told her to ring Harold and accept the offer to play John. It was the first time ever in my five years with the little Belgian that I knew that I could be saying goodbye to him, perhaps for a year, perhaps forever.

As a courtesy, I also asked Aude to telephone Nick Elliott, the executive producer of the Poirot series since it began, to tell him my decision. Within minutes, Aude rang me back to say that Nick was desperate to speak to me.

A few moments later, Nick rang. He was as upset as I was. 'But you knew we were going to offer you another series,' he said, his voice all but breaking.

'But I didn't, Nick,' I told him. 'The deadline passed, and we'd heard nothing.'

'But we are. We want to shoot again this summer.'

I felt absolutely terrible. They had given me this wonderful opportunity to play the role of Poirot and here I was, letting them down.

'I hadn't heard, Nick. I thought nothing was going to happen, and so I said yes to Harold and *Oleanna*.'

'Can't you get out of it?'

'No,' I told him sadly. 'I don't want to go back to Harold, and besides, I really want to play in the theatre again. I haven't been on the stage since *Timon of Athens* in 1990, and this is a truly wonderful part.'

Nick was very upset, and I felt absolutely dreadful. I apologised profusely, but I also knew in my heart that I wanted to do this play.

It fulfilled my ambition to go back to the theatre and I knew I would be mad to turn it down. In the end, LWT postponed the new series for a year and waited for me, but I had no idea they would do that at the time. In fact, I wondered if I had lost Poirot altogether.

How an actor's life can change, I thought to myself, as I explained what had happened to Sheila. If I hadn't asked Aude to call Harold and see if I could have coffee with him in the wake of his decision 'to go in another direction', none of this would ever have happened.

Actors leap off into the unknown in their careers, without really ever knowing where their decisions are going to take them. It has always been my view that we, as human beings, go through our lives like spiders spinning our threads behind us, but only by looking backwards do we see how the past affects the present, and how those threads of our lives fit together.

What I certainly did not know then was that if I hadn't made the decision to say goodbye to Poirot at that moment, I would never have had the career in the theatre that I have been lucky enough to enjoy since then. Just as importantly, however, it also did not mean that it was the end for the little Belgian and me.

CHAPTER 11

'A VERY LONG WAY INDEED FROM POIROT'

Harold Pinter's rehearsals for *Oleanna* started just a few weeks after my decision to leave Poirot altogether, for a year at least, and they were particularly intense. As there were just two members of the cast, the talented young Lia Williams and me, there was nowhere to hide as Harold, looking as serious as ever in his habitual black sweater and thick glasses, took us through the battleground of the sexes that David Mamet had constructed in three lacerating acts.

These were some of the most difficult weeks I had ever spent in a rehearsal room, because the play is so consuming, so brutal about the true nature of the relationships between men and women, and so filled with poison that it was all but impossible to keep those emotions from spilling over into my own life. Sheila and the children had got used to the rather benign figure of Poirot returning from the studio each evening, but now I was this man struggling with exactly how he felt about women and himself, who in the end resorts to violence, even though he knows he should not.

The title comes from an American folk song which refers to a nineteenth-century version of utopia, but there is nothing utopian at all about the play itself. When it was first produced in 1992 in the United States, my character, John, was described as a 'smug, pompous, insufferable man whose power over academic lives he unconsciously abuses' – a very long way indeed from Poirot.

Curiously enough, I had experienced something of the problems that John faced in the play. In 1975 I was teaching drama at an American university when I found myself confronting the same issue of sexual politics that is examined in *Oleanna*. I was teaching on a very hot day. We were doing a drama exercise that involved passing a ball around, which made everyone very sweaty, so I suggested that my male students might take their shirts off.

The idea that my decision might infuriate the female students never occurred to me, but it most certainly did to them. My female students immediately complained to the head of the department, who told me that I had to write an apology, as I had discriminated against them because they could not take off their own shirts.

Rather than apologising, I asked to be sent back to London, as I honestly did not believe I could preserve any kind of relationship with my female students after their complaints. In the end, the storm blew over, and a few days later, a spokeswoman for the women in the group came to apologise, although she did point out that I obviously did not understand about rights for women at the university. I carried on teaching until the end of that academic year, although I have to confess that I kept a very careful eye on my relationship with my female students from then onwards. Perhaps my own experience may just have done something to illuminate my performance in Mamet's play.

What is not in doubt was that *Oleanna* provoked the most

extreme reactions from its audience. When it opened at New York's Orpheum Theatre, some of Carol's speeches elicited hisses and walk-outs from the audience. Couples left the theatre in a rage, so angry were they about the issues involved, while other members of the audience repeatedly shouted at the actors on the stage. There was even spontaneous clapping and cheering when John finally snaps and attacks Carol. William H. Macy, who created the role of John there, memorably remarked afterwards, 'It's not a good date-show.'

Neither Lia nor I knew, when we were rehearsing with Harold, what the reaction would be in England. I had never worked with Lia before, but I recognised her talent as soon as rehearsals began. Born in Cheshire, she was only twenty-nine when we started to work together. She had spent the year before working with the English director Michael Winner on the film *Dirty Weekend*. Her stage breakthrough had come in 1991, when she received the London Critics' Circle award for the most promising newcomer, for her performance in Alan Ayckbourn's play *The Revengers' Comedies*.

Slight, with long auburn hair, Lia sometimes looked as though she might be blown over by a puff of wind, but that concealed a very strong character beneath the surface, which certainly appeared as we rehearsed *Oleanna*.

We opened for previews at the Royal Court on London's Sloane Square on Thursday, 24 June, and the press reviews came out exactly a week later, on 1 July. They were quite extraordinary. Michael Billington, in the *Guardian*, commented that 'The first night . . . was greeted with rapt attentiveness which is a tribute to the power of the acting, the writing and, not least, to Harold Pinter's production.' Thankfully, every other West End critic was equally complimentary.

I was quietly delighted. It made my decision to put Poirot aside for a time worthwhile, and brought me back to my first love – the theatre – in a play that I was sure would become a classic, even though it had both fascinated and frightened me when I first read it.

Charles Spencer called *Oleanna* 'the most controversial hit in living memory', and it was hard to disagree with him. But he also recorded, in the *Telegraph*, that Lia and I made every effort not to allow our characters to overtake our lives completely. We always gave each other a hug in the wings at the end of each performance. 'We hold on to each other very tightly,' Lia told him, 'to remind ourselves that we actually like each other.'

The controversy, the reviews and the audience reaction helped to ensure that the play was a sell-out from September when it transferred to the Duke of York's in the West End until 8 January 1994, when we ended our run. The great English director Sir Peter Hall came to one of the last performances and sent me a postcard afterwards, which really made me feel my decision to forgo Poirot and do *Oleanna* was right. Peter was kind enough to say that my performance was one of the best pieces of acting he'd seen in years because I'd portrayed John's failings so well, and in doing so had truly challenged the audience.

It was a marvellous compliment, but it did not mean that I had become John. I was simply serving Mamet's text, serving him as the writer, as I had always wanted to do. In reality, as I told a lady from the *Daily Mail*, 'I am rather an old-fashioned man . . . I like what is called decent social behaviour. I was brought up like that, it's part of me. There is a way of opening a door so that the lady continues moving. There is nothing patronising about that. What's wrong with looking after someone?'

That is part of the reason why I always so enjoyed playing Poirot, and thankfully the little Belgian was waiting in the wings. I could never forget him, no matter what else was going on in my career, and now London Weekend had returned to my agent with an offer for me to film four two-hour Poirot specials at some point during 1994, which were to be broadcast at the very beginning of 1995, including one that was aimed specifically at the Christmas holidays, a new version of Dame Agatha's story *Hercule Poirot's Christmas*. I have to say that I was flattered, and mightily relieved, as the little man might just have disappeared altogether had LWT not been so generous.

But I could not start preparing right away, because I had agreed with my Poirot television producer Brian Eastman to appear in a brand-new play about the life of the famous Birmingham-born English comedian Sid Field, who died at the age of just forty-five in 1950, as one the greatest stars of the London stage, admired by everyone from Laurence Olivier to the American comedian Danny Kaye, from Charlie Chaplin to Noel Coward. Called *What a Performance*, after one of Field's best-known phrases, it had been written especially for me by William Humble – who, funnily enough, had written the two-hour film *Death in the Clouds* in the fourth series of *Agatha Christie's Poirot* – with a bit of advice from the legendary Jimmy Perry, one of the two creators of the BBC's dazzling sitcom *Dad's Army*.

Field was a mighty step away from *Oleanna*, and from Poirot. I had never sung before in front of an audience, never danced before, and I had hardly done a line of comedy in twenty-five years as a character actor. I remember telling one interviewer, only half joking, 'This is the new David Suchet.' It was a terrifying move to make, and yet the challenge of trying to recreate the gentle style of comedy sketch that Field specialised in during his London heyday in the 1940s was impossible to resist. It was a risk, of course it was, but I just could not say no to portraying the man I thought was probably the greatest English clown since Chaplin – and we were not going to try it out in the glare of the lights of Shaftesbury Avenue in London.

What A Performance was scheduled to open at the little Drum Theatre in Plymouth, just three weeks after the last night of *Oleanna* in London. In fact, I had been rehearsing it during the last weeks of Mamet's play, working partly with the great actor and comedian Jack Tripp, probably Britain's best-known pantomime dame at the time, who had once been Field's understudy and had performed for him on the small number of occasions when the great man was ill.

One of the things that attracted me to the role of Sid Field was that he had been such a complex, fragile man. He was so timid as a person that he could not stand up to anyone, and especially not his tyrannical, dressmaker mother Bertha. Sid was so terrified of her that he did not even tell her that he was married until the birth of his first child. He was also terrified that people would not laugh at his work, which I began to feel myself as I started turning myself into him. Field turned to drink to give him the courage to perform, but I had never done that. When I am working on a new project, I do not drink any alcohol at all; I need to focus on what I am doing so completely that I dare not risk it.

Slightly to my alarm, two of the London critics came down to Plymouth especially to see the premiere of the show. I was hoping for a little more time to hone my performance, but I need not have worried so much, because they were both kind. Jeremy Kingston, in *The Times*, even suggested that I played 'the buffoon as if he had never been away'. The local press were complimentary and we played to good houses during the three-week run in Plymouth.

Brian Eastman was keen to take the show on a tour before bringing it to London, but by the beginning of February 1994, we both knew that London Weekend were growing increasingly anxious to start the four new two-hour Poirot films, and neither of us wanted to keep them waiting. Besides, I had been away from the little Belgian for quite a long time, and his voice and manner was calling me back. The compromise was that I would tour with *What a Performance* as soon as the latest series of Poirot had finished filming, with a view to coming to the West End at the end of September.

I hardly had a moment to draw breath after I came back from Plymouth before Sean was back at our front door in Pinner to take me to Twickenham again – complete with its promise of Poirot's padding, silver-topped cane and Homburg. In fact, I was not needed for the first part of the first film in the new series, *Hercule Poirot's Christmas*, as it opens in South Africa in 1896, when a ruthless diamond prospector, Simeon Lee, betrays his fellow prospectors.

In fact, Dame Agatha's original story, which was published in 1938 in both Britain and the United States, where it was called *Murder for Christmas*, had no such beginning. Our new television version, written once more by Clive Exton, used the story of betrayal in South Africa to establish Lee's ruthless character, but then rapidly moved the events forward forty years, to 1936, when Lee is an old man and living in a grand country mansion in England. He has summoned his dysfunctional family to a reunion, while at the same time inviting Poirot to join them because he believes his life is in danger.

Lee's family are at each other's throats, and there is the scent of blood – even murder – in the air, which is not always the case in the build-up to Dame Agatha's mysteries. On Christmas Eve, Lee is found with his throat cut in the locked study of his house and Poirot begins an investigation in earnest, although he decides to do so with the help of Chief Inspector Japp, who is spending his Christmas not far away, across the border in Wales, with his wife's Welsh family. That is another of the elements that sets this story apart from some others of Dame Agatha's. Not only is there more blood – a brutal killing with a knife, rather than her more familiar poison – but Japp, rather than Hastings, plays Poirot's assistant, away from his formal job at Scotland Yard. Indeed, Hastings plays no part whatever in the story, which is not in the slightest bit 'Christmassy'.

Philip Jackson enjoyed himself hugely making the film, not least because Clive Exton had given him the opportunity to flesh out Japp's character, providing him with a set of hearty Welsh relations, who insist on celebrating Christmas by singing endlessly around the piano in the parlour, revealing Japp's sense of melancholy humour which is not always visible in the other stories.

Another joy for me was to appear alongside John Horsley, one of the great stalwarts among English character actors, who played Simeon Lee's faithful but elderly butler, Edward Tressilian, who plays a crucial role in unravelling the mystery. The denouement, which takes place on Christmas Day, slightly foreshadows her famous stage play, *The Mousetrap*, which began its life as a short story and radio play called *Three Blind Mice* in 1947, in that the least likely suspect is revealed to be the murderer.

The second film in the new series was one of Dame Agatha's better-known stories, and another with a nursery rhyme in its title, *Hickory, Dickory, Dock*, which had first appeared in England in 1955. The story opens with the usually faultless Miss Lemon making not one but three mistakes in a single letter she is typing for Poirot in Whitehaven Mansions, much to his annoyance and amazement.

It transpires that the good Miss Lemon's sister, Mrs Hubbard, who manages a hostel for London University students in Hickory Road, has been suffering a string of inexplicable petty thefts. Out of loyalty to the invaluable Miss Lemon, Poirot offers to help, only for the thefts rapidly to turn into not one but three murders.

When the novel itself was first published, it was not greeted with the universal acclaim that Dame Agatha usually garnered. Frances Iles, reviewing it for the *Sunday Times* in London, suggested, 'It reads like a tired effort. The usual sparkle is missing,' while the novelist Evelyn Waugh, one of Dame Agatha's greatest fans, recorded in his diary that one of 'the joys and sorrows of a simple life' was a new Agatha Christie story. This one, however, he recorded sadly, began well enough, which was a joy, only for sorrow to take its place as the novel 'deteriorated' one third of the way through into what he described – rather unfairly – as 'twaddle'.

Our film version was certainly not twaddle. The director, Andrew Grieve, who had worked with me so often in the series before, made a wonderful job of it, adding the visual theme of a mouse running beside a clock – a reference to the nursery rhyme itself – and recruiting a stunningly good cast that included the then twenty-three-year-old Damian Lewis, almost straight from the Guildhall School of Music and Drama, and long before his successes in *Band of Brothers*, *Life* and *Homeland* on international television. As so often, I was aware that here was a young actor who was going to have an extraordinary career. It was not just his performance – in a relatively small part – but the fact that the camera loved him. I could see that myself, and so could Poirot, who was never wrong. We could both always spot real talent when we saw it.

Andrew not only recruited a terrific cast, he was also fortunate enough to benefit from Brian Eastman and London Weekend's determination to provide our four new films with the best possible props and locations – which in this case included the regular use of a vintage London Underground train.

On top of that, Anthony Horowitz, who wrote the screenplay, decided to set Poirot's investigation against the background of the October 1936 march from Jarrow, six miles from Newcastle-upon-Tyne in the north-east of England, to London by 207 unemployed men and women to protest against unemployment in Britain and the extreme poverty that had seen their communities all but destroyed by the country's economic depression. The march meant that no policeman could take any kind of holiday, which leaves the redoubtable Chief Inspector Japp marooned in his office, only too eager to help Poirot.

I think our film revealed just how good Dame Agatha's original story really was and redeemed it from some of its original negative reviews. The adaptation was excellent and the locations stunning. The one strange thing was that I never actually saw our mouse on the set – all the scenes with it were shot by Andrew Grieve after my performance was over, which meant that the first time I saw it was in the final version. I thought it was beautifully done, and added something special to the story.

But I also felt the film demonstrated the confidence that we all now felt in the character of Poirot on the screen, which had been growing steadily since the series had begun five years earlier. By now, he no longer had to prove that he was interesting to the audience by displaying his foibles. He could just be himself, idiosyncratic, polite and a fully realised person that everyone – both behind and in front of the camera – could understand, and perhaps even love.

The third film was *Murder on the Links*, which is set principally in Deauville in France, where Poirot is being taken on holiday by

Hastings – the first story in the new series to feature Poirot's old friend. It too had a script by Anthony Horowitz and was directed by Andrew Grieve, but – just as important to me – it was also a story that gave me an opportunity to explore Poirot's inherent loneliness.

Significantly, this was Dame Agatha's second Poirot story, published in 1923, just three years after he was introduced in *The Mysterious Affair at Styles*, and, as she explained in her autobiography, in 1977, was influenced by Gaston Leroux's classic French detective story, *The Mystery of the Yellow Room*, which had appeared not long before she had started writing.

Just as importantly, it was also the novel that proved to her that she was 'stuck with Poirot' and how wrong she had been to create his character 'so old' at the very beginning. As she put it herself, 'I ought to have abandoned him after the first three or four books, and begun again with someone much younger.' I can only say that I am delighted that she never did.

Dame Agatha did, however, provide Hastings with a love interest in *Murder on the Links* – in fact, she was even thinking of marrying him off, as she was 'getting a little tired of him', as she put it. She also created what she called a 'human foxhound' for the story in the shape of Inspector Giraud of the French police, who regarded Poirot as 'old and passé', to use her own words. In the end, Poirot and Giraud face up to each other with a wager that means that the Frenchman will present Poirot with his beloved pipe if the Belgian solves the mystery before he does, while if the Frenchman succeeds in solving the case first, Poirot will be obliged to cut off his moustache.

I loved being in France, and Brian Eastman kindly brought Sheila and the children over to stay with me during the half-term holiday for a few days. We seldom spent much time filming out of the country because of the cost.

The film itself was not quite the success I had hoped, however, as I seemed to be struggling to keep Poirot human against the rather more caricatured portrait of Inspector Giraud. But it did give Poirot the opportunity to reveal his affection for his old friend, when he reunites Hastings and his love interest at the end of the story, while Poirot himself returns to England alone, and obviously rather lonely.

For me, the final two-hour film in this series was the most delightful. *Dumb Witness*, which was first published in 1937, is one of the best-loved of all Dame Agatha's stories, not least because it contains a wire-haired terrier called Bob, who is the dumb witness of the title. In fact, the original novel was dedicated to her own wire-haired terrier – 'To dear Peter,' it read, 'most faithful of friends and dearest of companions: A dog in a thousand.'

I felt exactly the same way about the terrier in our film. He captivated me from the moment I set eyes on him. The little dog, whose real name was actually Snubby, became my dear friend, and even managed to capture Poirot's heart, no easy task, as my little Belgian did not care for dogs, regarding them as rather smelly and dirty. Nevertheless, Bob allowed Poirot to show some affection for animals, without compromising his natural suspicions about dogs.

Directed by Edward Bennett, from a script by Douglas Watkinson, the film was set in the Lake District, which was another reason I found it so wonderful to do. The scenery was spectacular and the cast were excellent, especially the unforgettable Muriel Pavlow as one of two spiritualist sisters, an actress I had spent my childhood admiring in the cinema. The special effects were equally impressive, especially when showing, in a kind of haze, the death of Emily Arundell, the lady who has invited Poirot to investigate in the first place. And, of course, there was Bob, complete with his trick of sending a tennis ball bouncing down the stairs and running down past it to catch it in his mouth at the bottom.

The shoot was a joy from beginning to end – fresh air and wonderful locations, especially the cottage on Lake Windermere, which was so dear to me because of my own love of water and narrow boats. I simply could not have asked for anything nicer. I love the Lake District, and have done since I went on a hiking holiday with Sheila and the children, before Poirot. I can vividly remember carrying Robert around as a small boy and loving every minute of it. I think all this helped my performance, as I felt more relaxed and more at home than I had sometimes done in the past couple of series. Certainly, my now ever-expanding fan club wrote to tell me how much they enjoyed it, and, so they also told me, the sales of wire-haired terriers shot up exponentially after it was shown for the first time in March 1996.

I was lucky that I had enjoyed *Dumb Witness* so much, however, for no sooner were the four new films finished in the late summer of 1994, than I was back rehearsing for the tour and then London opening of *What a Performance*. Sadly, that proved to be a rather less joyful experience.

The show toured the country, including Bath and Richmond, and everywhere we went, the audiences seemed to like my portrayal of Sid Field in those golden days of comedy in the second half of the 1940s. One local paper insisted that it 'will run and run', while another called my performance 'stunning', even though, as I told one reporter who came to see me, the headline should have read, 'Suchet puts his head on the block.'

I knew the risk I was running in impersonating such a unique talent for a generation that had never seen him, but my fears disappeared on the opening night at the Queen's Theatre on

Shaftesbury Avenue in London's West End on Wednesday, 12 October 1994. The following morning, the *Daily Mail*'s theatre critic, Jack Tinker, was incredibly generous. 'Miraculously, that match-less actor Mr David Suchet conjures up the vaguely campish clowning which made the likes of the young Tony Hancock hold Field in such awe,' he wrote.

I received shoals of letters congratulating me on my tribute to Field, but the harsh reality of whether a modern audience actually wanted to pay to see the recreation of old comedy routines – with a script that did not seem quite strong enough – hung above the show like a dark cloud.

Just a few days after the show opened, Sheila rang the box office to book two tickets for the following Saturday week, only to be told over the phone that the show would not be running then.

Sheila telephoned me at once and said, 'Did you know you're not playing on Saturday week?'

I rang the box office myself immediately, and asked them if it was true.

There was a very long pause, before finally the box office manager said, 'I'm terribly sorry, sir, I thought you'd been told.'

What a Performance closed in the West End after just four weeks, in November 1994, even though we had been scheduled to run until at least the end of January. It was the shortest run I had ever had in the theatre in twenty-six years, and – even though I had known it was a risk – it shook my confidence.

Luckily, I was offered the role of a cold-blooded murderer in the BBC's adaptation of Emile Zola's 1890 novel *La Bête Humaine*, which had been renamed *Cruel Train* and set in 1940. I was to appear alongside Saskia Reeves, who had acted with me on stage in *Separation*, Adrian Dunbar and Minnie Driver, and the BBC's budget was £2 million. They had even built a vast set beneath a motorway in Birmingham, which included a recreation of London's Victoria Station and a real 1940s locomotive. It was a wonderful effort, but it did not really save the film, which was broadcast the following Easter to muted reviews.

So the year ended on a slightly sad note, in spite of the reviews for my Sid Field and the delights of the wire-haired terrier Bob and weeks in the Lake District. What I did not know was that far worse was to come – especially for Poirot and me.

CHAPTER 12

'THERE HASN'T BEEN ANY TROUBLE, HAS THERE?'

Hercule Poirot brought me so many happy memories over the years. There were times I will never, ever, forget, when the affection that the little man was held in by all kinds of ordinary people came to the surface wherever I was. Their pleasure in him was so disarming, so charming.

There was the time when we were shooting on location in the neat little seaside town of Hastings in East Sussex, and I wanted to just take a little time away from the hustle and bustle of the unit to collect my thoughts. In full costume, complete with my Homburg and cane, I walked just round the corner into a peaceful side street to stand on my own and think about what was to come.

Quite suddenly, out of the corner of my eye, I caught a glimpse of a little old lady walking slowly towards me on my side of the street, pushing one of those square shopping trolleys with four wheels, clearly on her way home. I did not say anything at all, but when she reached me, she stopped.

'Hello, Monsieur Poirot,' she said, with her head cocked to one side.

For a moment I was at a loss to know what to say. Should I respond as Poirot? Do I respond as David Suchet? What voice should I choose?

I made my decision.

'*Bonjour, madame*,' I said, sticking firmly to the little Belgian's voice and manners.

The little old lady smiled, and then a look of uncertainty spread slowly across her face.

'There hasn't been any trouble, has there?' she asked, her voice aquiver. 'I mean, there hasn't been a murder or anything?'

Now I really did not know what to say.

'*Non, non, madame. Rien.* Nothing at all,' I reassured her.

She smiled her tiny smile again, and started off past me. But she had only gone a yard or two when she stopped and turned back.

'If you don't mind my asking,' she said politely, 'what are you doing in Hastings?'

Once again, I did not know what on earth to say, but decided quickly: '*Mes vacances, madame.* I am here on holiday,' I said in my finest Poirot.

'Oh!' she said, apparently satisfied, and set off on her way again, only to stop once again moments later.

'Thank you for choosing Hastings,' she said, with a gentle wave, and she set off up the street away from me.

Even as I remember that day now, it brings a tear to my eye. It was so touching, and seemed to reflect exactly how much ordinary people really seemed to care about the little Belgian, even if he was entirely the product of Dame Agatha's imagination.

There was another wonderful moment when we were filming on location on the south coast of England, not far from Poole in Dorset, and – once again – I had slipped away from the unit to collect my thoughts.

This time, a middle-aged couple appeared, obviously on holiday and enjoying the spring sunshine. They were arm in arm, and had clearly been married for some considerable time, because theirs was one of those relationships in which the husband says something and the wife agrees almost at once.

Needless to say, it is the husband who spoke first.

'Oh,' he said, clearly recognising me as they passed and drawing them both to a stop. 'I hope you don't mind us interrupting you.'

I smiled, and nodded encouragingly in the most appropriate Poirot manner.

'Shall we tell him?' the husband asked the wife.

'Oh yes,' she said, smiling.

'Well,' the husband said, 'we love all your programmes. We really do. Don't we, darling?'

'Oh yes,' his wife agreed, still smiling.

'We always watch them when they come on. Don't we?'

'Oh yes.'

'We never miss one. Do we?'

'Oh no,' his wife replied.

'We see them all, we really do.'

His wife was now positively beaming with pleasure. I was transfixed.

'We even see the repeats. Don't we? Whenever they come on.'

'Oh yes.'

'And we've got all the box sets. Haven't we?'

'Oh yes.'

But then the husband paused for a moment, and a brief frown crossed his large, rather cheerful face. His wife's beam also faded slightly.

'The thing is . . .' he started to say, but then hesitated and turned to his wife. 'Shall I tell him what I said to you the other day?'

She nodded, taking the cue of seriousness from him.

'Well,' he went on in his warm, bluff voice, 'the thing is, you see, we love your programmes . . . but we can never understand a single word you say.'

I really did not know what to say. I was at a complete loss for words.

Then I smiled, as warmly as I could, before murmuring something as politely as I possibly could, before thinking to myself, 'Talk about a letdown!'

But then I thought about what a very long way Poirot and I had come from *The Adventure of the Clapham Cook* and *The Disappearance of Mr Davenheim* in those early days. People still loved him, even if they could not understand a single word he said.

These wonderful moments were in my mind as I came home after making *Cruel Train* in Birmingham for the BBC. There was no news from London Weekend about a new Poirot series, but that was nothing unusual. I was still struggling to reconcile the success of *Oleanna* with the failure of *What a Performance*, and was wondering exactly what the future would hold for me. I was going to be fifty in a year or so, the children were growing up, and I was beginning to question what would happen to the rest of my career.

I knew I had made the right decision to go back to the theatre, and that my television success with Poirot meant that I had developed a new theatre audience who would come and see me on the stage mainly because of the little Belgian. I also realised that he had helped me build an international reputation to go alongside my British one. Between them, Poirot and John in *Oleanna* had brought me offers from all sorts of different places around the world, including Hollywood.

One thing that underlined how much Poirot had come to be loved since the series began, and I had started to play him, was the steady expansion of what was to grow into my fan club. The whole process had begun gradually a couple of years before, but it was now growing at a pace that I found quite astonishing. This was before the internet, of course, which has seen an even more amazing expansion around the world, especially, believe it or not, in Russia.

To be honest, I was not quite sure how to react to it all, as I was a character actor playing a part, not a more conventional leading man, who would – to some extent at least – always play himself. But the amount of affection felt for Poirot was quite extraordinary.

So I was comparatively relaxed when, at nine o'clock in the evening of New Year's Day 1995, ITV broadcast our new version of *Hercule Poirot's Christmas*. It may not have been the best evening for the show, as people are generally exhausted after the exertions of New Year's Eve – audiences tend to dip that night – but it was received well, though there were rumours afterwards that the viewing figures were not quite up to their recent levels of about ten million.

Six weeks later, on Valentine's Day 1995, ITV went on to show *Hickory, Dickory, Dock*, which the critics seemed to like, though again the audience did not reach quite the dizzy heights they had done.

Perhaps I should have seen the writing on the wall because of those viewing figures. Perhaps I should have paid more attention to the rumours that started to circulate that the broadcast of *Murder on the Links* and *Dumb Witness* were to be delayed, but neither worried me unduly. In spite of my decision to play in *Oleanna*, everything appeared to have returned to normal with the filming of the four two-hour specials. In my heart, I expected LWT to come back to me before too long with a proposal for a seventh series.

That was a terrible mistake. One morning in the early spring of 1995, a friend rang out of the blue and said, 'Have you seen the paper this morning?'

'No,' I replied. 'Why?'

'There's a report that they aren't going to make any more Poirots.'

I was astonished. I had not heard anything about it, not a whisper, and I could hardly believe it. If they were going to cancel after more than fifty hours of television, forty-five films, nine of them two hours long, surely someone from London Weekend or ITV would have let me know – before anyone else.

More than a little upset, I rang my agent and asked her to find out what was going on. There was no direct answer, just all sorts of prevarications over the next week or two.

'A spokesman' for LWT told the *Daily Mail*, 'Talk of the sleuth's death is premature,' and then added, 'No decision has been made,' and 'A new series is being considered but we are waiting for the go-ahead from scheduling chiefs.' The two remaining unscreened films were left to hang in the air with no fixed transmission date.

The truth was, of course, that the decision not to make any more series of *Agatha Christie's Poirot* had been made. Maybe the drop in viewing figures was one cause; perhaps the fact that I had decided to do *Oleanna* had something to do with it; perhaps it was that someone at LWT felt that the series had run its course. I am not sure, and I have never been told.

To be honest, I never expected any great 'thank you' from anyone at ITV, but I did feel let down – badly. It was not so much the decision itself, but the way it had been handled. No one had bothered to talk to me, and the press had discovered the truth before I had. It was hurtful.

But I was professional enough to tell myself, and anyone who asked me about the decision, that 'That's show business . . . nothing lasts forever.' I had learnt from bitter experience over the years that the only thing you can possibly do as an actor is to close the door on what you have done in the past, no matter how proud you are of it, and move on. For the moment, however, I had to turn my back on Poirot and get on with the next part of my life and career – whatever that might mean. It would be five long years before I would encounter him again.

I ended up playing an Arab terrorist called Nagi Hassan in a £40 million Hollywood action-thriller called *Executive Decision*, alongside Kurt Russell, Steven Seagal and a gorgeous new young actress called Halle Berry. To be honest, the first script I saw was pretty dreadful, but, as always in Hollywood, it changed all the time, which meant that my character had at least two dimensions, even if he was not exactly a completely formed character by the time I got to play him on camera. This role meant I spent the summer of 1995 living in an extraordinary house just above Sunset Boulevard in Los Angeles, which belonged to a rock star, and which I paid for myself. Sheila and the children remember it because it had a swimming pool that was sculpted to look like a rock pool in Shangri-La. None of us had ever seen anything like it before – in fact, I am not sure that we ever have since then. I wondered what Poirot would have made of it.

The studio limo would arrive every morning to take me to the studio. It was an odd experience – there was none of the family feeling that there had been on our Poirot shoots. Everyone was very conscious of their status. Who had the biggest trailer, who got the special meals delivered, who was powerful enough to be late on the set – not like Poirot at all. *Executive Decision* was a decent-sized hit around the world, but as I was almost unrecognisable on the screen, in very dark make-up and with an Arab accent that you could cut with a knife (it was what the studio wanted). I can't honestly say that it made a great deal of an impact on my career.

Back home in Pinner, reality struck. There were no more Poirots, and that meant I had to look at all sorts of other opportunities. I was blessed, however, by my friends in the theatre. One in particular came to me with an offer I really could not turn down. Howard Davies, who had been an associate director of the Royal Shakespeare Company when I was there, asked if I would like to play the part of the henpecked academic George in Edward Albee's dramatic masterpiece *Who's Afraid of Virginia Woolf?*, which had been made into an international hit as a film directed by Mike Nichols and starring Richard Burton (as George) and Elizabeth Taylor as his viciously cruel wife, Martha. Howard had asked the incomparable Dame Diana Rigg, star of so many productions, most recently *Medea* in London and on Broadway, to play Martha in this new production for the Almeida Theatre in Islington, north London.

A brutal commentary on the scarred lives of a married couple in an American university who are unable to conceive a child and who invite an unknowing younger professor and his wife for dinner, *Who's Afraid of Virginia Woolf?* had premiered on Broadway in October 1962. At more than three hours in length, it has gone on to become one of the seminal works of the American theatre in the second half of the twentieth century. It won a Tony Award as best play in 1963, but was denied a Pulitzer Prize in that same year because of its use of swearing and overt sexuality.

I knew it would be a huge challenge to play George, as there is not a single moment to relax for an actor during the play's mesmerising and cathartic three acts. George is lacerated repeatedly for his weakness and stupidity by Martha, but now and again takes a bitter revenge on her. Albee's was not a play to be taken lightly, but it was a wonderful opportunity to play a tremendous part in a truly memorable portrait of marital savagery steeped in hatred, blood and alcohol. Not only could I not refuse, I jumped at the chance. The struggle was to bring this beautifully written part off the page of Albee's text and onto the stage.

Albee did not make that straightforward. A famously tight-lipped playwright, who never used more words than he absolutely had to, he had come over from the United States to see the rehearsals, and came up to me after one of the final run-throughs.

'Why are you playing George that way?' he said quietly.

'What way?' I asked.

'The way you're playing him.'

'Well, my interpretation is that I really do believe that you have written a love story rather than a play about two people hating each other.'

There was a silence from Albee.

'People think George is a drunk, but I think you only give him two drinks in the entire play. But it is he who pours everyone else drinks,' I went on. 'He is the puppet master, and he is doing what he does in order to save his marriage, to save his relationship with Martha.'

Another silence from Albee, before he finally murmured, 'That's what I wrote,' and walked out of the theatre.

I think, and hope, I had found the poignancy and humour that he had written into the play, but which had not always emerged before. Whatever the truth, the prospect of the first production of the play in London for more than two decades attracted an enormous amount of attention, and the run at the comparatively small Almeida was sold out before the first night. As a result, it had been decided to transfer it to the larger Aldwych Theatre in central London immediately after it closed in Islington at the end of October 1996. Thankfully, the reviews at the Almeida fully justified the move. They were incredibly supportive.

In the *Daily Telegraph*, Charles Spencer was kind enough to say that I matched Diana Rigg's volcanic performance 'every inch of the harrowing way', adding, 'The sense of buried pain and humiliation is palpable.' The *Times Literary Supplement* even added that the production 'must rank among the best'.

The wave of enthusiasm for *Who's Afraid of Virginia Woolf?* among theatregoers did not wane for one moment when we transferred to the Aldwych on 30 October 1996. With quotations on the advertising saying, 'One of the theatrical sensations of the year' and 'Masterpiece', we were to play there for almost five months, to incredibly receptive audiences.

Time magazine even came over from the United States in February 1997, to say that we brought out 'all the lacerating power and poignancy of Albee's depiction of the blasted American dream'. My performance won me the Critics' Circle Award for best actor and saw me nominated for the Evening Standard Theatre Award for best actor. By the time we finally closed on 22 March 1997, I was exhausted.

Several potential film projects fell apart around me, but that allowed me to spend the school summer holidays with Sheila, Robert and Katherine, the first time I had managed to do that in what seemed like years, as I had been filming Poirot in the summer so often. Then I was offered the leading role in a drama for Scottish Television, another part of ITV, separate from London Weekend, though it had been commissioned by my old Poirot colleague Nick Elliott. It was a part that could not have been further away from the little man.

In a three-part drama called *Seesaw*, that was to be broadcast in the early spring of 1998, I was to play an affluent and successful north London husband and father, Morris Price, in a contemporary drama which sees his seventeen-year-old daughter kidnapped. Morris had made his money selling security equipment, while his wife Val, to be played by my old friend Geraldine James, who had appeared with me in *Blott on the Landscape*, had been an interior designer. Written by Deborah Moggach, who adapted her own original novel, the story has my character being asked to pay £500,000 in ransom for the return of his daughter, Hannah.

It was as close a role to me in reality as I had played in many years – Morris was about my age, fifty-two, had a wife and two children, as I had, and there was to be no padding, no beard, wig or funny moustache. It was the first time in many years that I had appeared on television without wearing some kind of disguise. It also forced me to confront my own worst fears. What if it had happened to my own daughter, Katherine, who was then just fourteen? I only knew one thing: that I would give up my life for my child. Morris decides not to tell the police and sells his business to pay the ransom.

In fact, I had first been offered the role while I was playing *Who's Afraid of Virginia Woolf?*, but it had taken some time to pull the production together, and so we did not actually film it until six months or so after I had finished in the West End. I was very flattered because I had heard that when Geraldine was offered the role of the wife, she said she would only do it if I played the husband, which, thank goodness, ITV had already decided that I should. It was a delight to work with her again so long after *Blott*, where I played her cook, chauffeur and handyman – although we ended up getting married. This time, we were married from the start, which we both found incredibly easy and straightforward. After all, we had done it before.

Seesaw played on successive Thursday evenings in March 1998 and both the audience and the critics seemed to like it. But I hardly had a moment to notice, as I was whisked off to Los Angeles immediately after the filming had finished, and before it was broadcast, to play the lead detective in a remake of Frederick Knott's famous stage play *Dial M for Murder*, which had been so memorably filmed by Alfred Hitchcock in 1954, starring Grace Kelly and Ray Milland. This time, the stars were to be Michael Douglas and Gwyneth Paltrow, while I was to play the part originally made famous by the great British character actor John Williams. In the original play and film, the plot took place in London, but this time the husband's scheme to commit the perfect crime by killing his wife was to take place in New York. The producers had also decided it should be called *A Perfect Murder*.

The experience of making *Executive Decision* in 1995 and now *A Perfect Murder* convinced me that making movies in Hollywood is not quite like anything else. The new movie's producers invited me to New York, where we had breakfast together.

Without any warning, they announced, almost in unison, 'We're so pleased that you can speak Arabic.'

I was a little puzzled. 'What makes you think that?' I said, as I sipped my orange juice.

'Well, you spoke it so brilliantly in *Executive Decision*.'

When I told them that I was terribly sorry but I did not, in fact, speak any Arabic at all, they paused for a moment.

'You don't? Gee. Well, at least you look Arabic.' I was left pretty much speechless.

The Hollywood reality is that it is the stars that sell the tickets. There famous adage 'Put the money on the screen' means that if the audience pays to see Michael Douglas, then they want to see as much of him in the film as they possibly can, from the very opening scene until the end, because that way, they are getting what they paid for.

It is the perfect reflection of that other old Hollywood adage, 'The thing about show business is that the second word is business.' Stars bring in an audience, and so they are the vital ingredient for moviegoers, wherever they may be in the world. They keep the film business flowing. For a British character actor brought up in the democratic traditions of the Royal Shakespeare Company, that can be a hard lesson to learn, but it is an important one.

Making *A Perfect Murder* proved it to me. Even though my part as the lead detective was vital to the plot – and I shot any number of scenes to prove it – when the final version of the film emerged, I seemed to have disappeared onto the cutting-room floor. But then came an unexpected consolation. When the studio tested a first cut of the film at previews in the United States, they discovered that the audiences there wanted to see rather more of my character. So, four months after shooting was finished, they flew Gwyneth Paltrow and an entire set over from the States, erected it at Pinewood in England, and filmed the final scene in the film as it was eventually released.

After that, it was with some relief that I went back to work in the theatre, to play the family patriarch and gentleman's outfitter Don Peppino Priore in the Italian Eduardo de Filippo's splendid comedy

Saturday, Sunday, Monday at the Chichester Festival Theatre in Sussex, for a six-week season. My wife was to be played by the Irish actress Dearbhla Molloy. Entirely set in my character's house in Naples, and one of the great plays of the Italian theatre in the twentieth century, it was a joy after the darkness of both *Oleanna* and *Who's Afraid of Virginia Woolf?* It put a positive spring in my step throughout the spring and early summer of 1998.

But then, over the horizon, came the faintest sight of the little Belgian who had not been a part of my life for the past three years. Rumours started flying about that London Weekend and ITV were thinking of reviving Poirot for some two-hour specials, to be filmed in 1999. In my heart, I had never buried him, and now he might actually be coming back.

CHAPTER 13

'I HAD FORGOTTEN HOW HARD HE WAS TO FIND IN THE FIRST PLACE'

Before Poirot could make his reappearance in my life, however, the theatre intervened once again. The producer Kim Poster came to me with a proposal that I appear as the Viennese composer Antonio Salieri in a new production of *Amadeus*, Peter Shaffer's masterpiece about the life of Mozart. It tells the story of Salieri's jealousy of Mozart's extraordinary talent when he arrives at the court of Emperor Joseph II of Austria in 1781. Salieri tries everything in his power to thwart the young man's success, and does so from a mixture of pride, envy and greed.

Peter Hall had been the play's first director in 1979, when it had its world premiere at the National Theatre in London, and then transferred to the West End with Paul Scofield as Salieri and Simon Callow as Mozart. After transferring to Broadway, it was then turned into a film in 1984 by the Czech director Milos Forman, which not only won him the Oscar for best film of the year, but also won F. Murray Abraham the Oscar for best actor for playing Salieri.

I did not hesitate. I accepted Kim's offer, not least because Peter Shaffer felt that there was a great deal that could be added to the play now. Before rehearsals began I went to Peter to ask him how he wanted the audience to feel about my character Salieri. He felt that the audience should feel he was cruel to Mozart but also feel sorry for him that he could not control his jealousy towards the young composer, no matter how hard he tried. In the original version, Salieri was a delicious part in a superb play about the beauty of great music and the dark passions that so often lie behind it, but during our rehearsals Peter continued to re-write and added a sense of humour, almost of pathos, to Salieri.

The fiercely Welsh young actor Michael Sheen, then just twenty-nine, who would go on to make an international reputation on film and television playing the British Prime Minister Tony Blair and interviewer Sir David Frost, was to play Mozart opposite me. The idea was that we would do a short tour of the British Isles in September and early October 1998, before bringing the play to London. When *Amadeus* opened at the Old Vic on Wednesday, 21 October 1998, the national critics seemed impressed. Michael Billington, in the *Guardian*, called it 'highly theatrical, superbly directed by Peter Hall'. But some had their reservations about Peter Shaffer's rewrite. Charles Spencer, in the *Daily Telegraph*, said, 'This is a play that takes a profound subject but has very little profound to say about it: a second rate drama, in fact, about what it feels like just to be second rate,' although he added that it was a 'cracking night out'.

Kim Poster wanted to build on our British success by taking the play to Broadway immediately, but by then, Brian Eastman had come back to me with a firm plan to make two two-hour Poirot films, and I had committed to them. Kim kindly agreed that she would wait for me to finish the Poirot filming, and would then take our *Amadeus* to Broadway as soon possible afterwards.

After the run ended in London I went to Spain to play Napoleon in a film, but once that was over I was free to return to England and Poirot, and so, almost five years to the day after the joys of *Dumb Witness*, in the early summer of 1999, I walked back onto the set in my spats and homburg hat, to appear in a new two-hour television version of one of Dame Agatha's most famous Poirot stories, *The Murder of Roger Ackroyd*.

The production team had changed a little. The American Arts & Entertainment network had come in to replace London Weekend as the major production company putting up the money and then selling the programmes to ITV, but Brain Eastman was still there as the producer, and Clive Exton was still writing some of the screen-plays. Hugh Fraser and Pauline Moran were not there, because neither Hastings nor Miss Lemon appeared in the story, but Philip Jackson was there again as the indefatigable Inspector Japp.

No matter how pleased I may have been to return to playing Poirot, I had nevertheless profoundly underestimated how much I needed to remind myself about him after five years away. I had forgotten how hard he was to find in the first place – his walk, his mannerisms, how he thinks, and so on. In the first seven years that I played him, he had gradually become more and more like a comfortable glove that I could slip on and off whenever I wanted to. But now, after a five-year break, the glove had got a bit stiff in the cupboard and did not slip on quite so easily.

To make sure I recaptured him exactly as he had been, I watched several hours from the previous forty-five Poirot films we had made before I set foot on the set of *Roger Ackroyd*. I wanted to make absolutely sure that the audience did not detect any differences. And as I watched them, I was reminded of his vain, pernickety, idiosyncratic – and sometimes infuriating – habits, as well as his natural charm and kindness, particularly to servants and those less capable of defending themselves.

The experience sharpened the feeling that had been growing within me for some time, that I really wanted to complete every single one of the Poirot stories on film, all the way until his final story, *Curtain*, in which he dies.

Wisely, Brian Eastman and Clive Exton had decided to make the most of Poirot's absence from the screen for so long by starting this first film after five years with him growing marrows in the garden of his small cottage in the English village of King's Abbott. He had not been at Whitehaven Mansions for some considerable time, and was, theoretically at least, in retirement. I must say, I had one or two reservations about the pretty silly gardening clothes I had to wear in my first appearance on the screen with the marrows. I was sure Poirot would never have dressed that way, but I kept my own counsel for once – it was only one scene, after all.

The Murder of Roger Ackroyd is a wonderful story, and the one that firmly established Dame Agatha as a best-selling crime writer, while at the same time ensuring that Poirot became one of the leading fictional detectives of the time. She wrote it in 1925, at the age of thirty-five, and it was published in the spring of the following year to considerable acclaim, although some readers felt she had 'not quite played fair' with them in her choice of murderer in the plot. They felt it was a little underhand, but Dame Agatha herself firmly disagreed.

Roger Ackroyd became Dame Agatha's – and Poirot's – first major success, selling more than 5,000 copies in hardcover in Britain alone in its first year. One reason for this, I suspect, is that it assembles one of the most ingenious group of suspects in all her murder-mysteries, and even has the murderer narrate the story, without giving his or her identity away. It was an idea said to have been given to Dame Agatha by Lord Louis Mountbatten, although she also credited her brother-in-law, James Watts, with coming up with the same idea – of a murderer describing the crime.

The story also allows Poirot to reveal his dislike of the countryside, in spite of his retiring there from London. 'There are more jealousies and rivalries than Ancient Rome,' Clive Exton has him say at one point in the film, describing country life, before adding, 'I thought I could escape the wickedness of the city.' Japp is only too pleased to see him, however, confiding solemnly, with his hang-dog expression and sad eyes, 'Bit like old times eh?'

One of the things that has always fascinated me about Dame Agatha's original story is that one of the characters, the busybody Caroline, is said to have been the inspiration for her other principal detective, Miss Marple, who would appear in 1930 in her very first mystery, *Murder at the Vicarage.*

Directed by Andrew Grieve, I had the highest hopes for our new *Roger Ackroyd* – the story was terrific, the location was excellent, the sets were good, the cast strong. And yet, somehow, after we had finished, I felt it lacked something. I am not sure exactly why; perhaps it had something to do with my expectations being too high. The denouement was exciting and unexpected – it should have been marvellous, but somehow, there was something missing.

Interestingly, there had been several other attempts to make *The Murder of Roger Ackroyd* work – on film and on stage – and they too had struggled a little, somehow never quite matching the supreme moments of Dame Agatha's novel itself.

A stage version, adapted from the novel by Michael Morton and called *Alibi*, was produced on the West End stage in May 1928 by the actor-manager Gerald du Maurier and starred Charles Laughton as Poirot. It was a decent, but not overwhelming, success and was certainly nothing to rival the phenomenal success of Dame Agatha's *The Mousetrap* a quarter of a century later. A film version, also called *Alibi*, appeared in 1931, with Austin Trevor as Poirot, but it too failed to set the box office alight, and when Laughton took the London stage production to New York in 1932, once again playing Poirot, it closed after just twenty-four performances.

Publication of *The Murder of Roger Ackroyd* coincided with a painful period of Agatha Christie's life, as her marriage to Colonel Archie Christie was coming to an end. They eventually divorced in 1928, and within two years, she had found real happiness in her second marriage, to the archaeologist Max Mallowan, who was fourteen years younger than she. In the wake of her divorce, she had decided to take a holiday by herself in the autumn of 1929, with a journey on the Orient Express train from Calais to Istanbul. From there, she had then gone on to visit an archaeological dig not far from Baghdad. She eventually went home, but the following March, she made the journey to the site again, this time mainly by sea, where she met Mallowan, who had been away with appendicitis on her first visit. The couple travelled back to England together on the Orient Express and, shortly afterwards, he proposed to her.

I find it very romantic that Max Mallowan and Agatha Christie married on 11 September 1930, in a small church in Edinburgh, and then took off on the Orient Express once again for their honeymoon.

Her new husband's occupation was to form part of the central inspiration for her work in the years to come. Within a year, they were back on an archaeological dig, once again not far from Baghdad, at a place called Nineveh. It was there, in the autumn of 1931, that she began writing the Poirot story *Lord Edgware Dies*, which was published in the spring of 1933 in Britain and shortly afterwards in the United States, where it was called *Thirteen at Dinner*. The story was dedicated to one of Max Mallowan's archaeologist colleagues at Nineveh and his wife.

It was this story that was the second of the two-hour films that Brian Eastman and I went on to make in the summer of 1999, and it was a very strange experience. As you may remember, I had appeared in a film version of it before, a made-for-television movie in 1985, which starred Peter Ustinov as Poirot. I had played Inspector Japp, in one of the worst performances I think I have ever given in my life, although Peter kindly suggested to me that I might make a good Poirot myself. Peter was such a nice, entertaining man; I remember him with enormous affection.

When we started filming *Lord Edgware Dies* at Twickenham, memories of playing Japp came flooding back, even though our two films were quite different. Another old Poirot hand, Anthony Horowitz, had written a script that continued the theme of Poirot's return from retirement that Clive Exton had set up in *The Murder of Roger Ackroyd*. There was even a celebratory supper for him at Whitehaven Mansions, attended by Japp, Hastings and Miss Lemon – after Hastings' sudden return from the Argentine, leaving his new wife there alone. As Anthony has Japp say at the reunion, with just a hint of irony, 'Here we are, the four of us together again. There is only one thing missing – the body.' It takes almost no time for one to appear: Lord Edgware's.

Part of Dame Agatha's inspiration for the story came from seeing an American entertainer called Ruth Draper in London in the 1920s. 'I thought how clever she was and how good her impersonations were,' she wrote in her autobiography, and our television version of the story unfolds around Miss Lemon persuading Poirot and Hastings to go and see a similar act. But when it came to the denouement of the story, and Poirot's revelation of the murderer, I found it very difficult indeed not to think of how Peter Ustinov had done it in our American film together. He had made it very funny, and I could not quite get that out of my mind, even though I was determined to stick to my own version of the little man, which I eventually managed to do. What made the difference finally, and allowed me to keep the memory of Peter at bay, was that as the years had passed, I had grown steadily more confident in playing Poirot, and now rediscovering him gave me the courage to play him with a little more gravitas. Unlike Peter's version, my Poirot was a man to be taken seriously, no matter how idiosyncratic he may have appeared.

No sooner had I finished filming than I was back in Peter Hall's hands for the American production of *Amadeus*, once again opposite Michael Sheen as Mozart. We were due to open at the Ahmanson Theatre in Los Angeles on 5 October 1999 and then at the Music Box Theatre on Broadway on 16 December. It meant that I would be spending the end of the Millennium away from home, but the play was so special, it made up for it.

The Los Angeles opening went well, though *Variety* wondered whether the film version had rather sated the appetite for it among theatregoers in California, concluding, 'Shaffer's stage play seems, well, superfluous.' Not everyone agreed. The *Hollywood Reporter* suggested Peter Shaffer had made a 'very good play . . . even better' and kindly described my performance as 'thrilling', although the *Los Angeles Times* also wondered whether there was really an appetite for *Amadeus* again in the wake of the Oscar-winning film.

In New York, the reviews were equally mixed. Some wondered whether the play no longer really held up in the wake of the film.

Ben Brantley, in the *New York Times*, was unimpressed by my Salieri, preferring Michael Sheen's Mozart, but many others seemed to like us both, with *Newsday* calling it 'extravagantly enjoyable, even more satisfying than the original'. The legendary New York critic Clive Barnes described it as 'a thoughtful yet immensely enjoyable play'.

The audiences seemed to agree, and I was nominated for a Critics' Circle Award in Los Angeles, as well as an Outer Critics' Circle Award in New York and a 'Tony' nomination. Every bit as thrilling, however, was the fact that I also received a handwritten letter from Milos Forman – the Czech director who had turned *Amadeus* into an eight-Oscar, four-BAFTA and four-Golden Globe-winning masterpiece of the cinema – congratulating me on my performance.

At the end of May 2000, I packed my bags for London to become Poirot once again, but before I went anywhere near a television studio, Sheila and I were whisked off to Japan as guests of the country's biggest broadcaster, NHK, with its one hundred million viewers. *Agatha Christie's Poirot* was one of their most successful series and Sheila and I found ourselves treated like visiting diplomats when we arrived in Tokyo. There were limousines everywhere and a great many red carpets.

Even out of costume, everyone in Japan seemed to know who I was, and I was interviewed on all the main news bulletins. It was then that I started to explain in public that one of my great ambitions was to film every one of Dame Agatha's Poirot stories, in a body of work that would be unique for television. I told several of the Japanese interviewers that Poirot's life had a definite beginning, middle and end, which I very much wanted to portray on the screen. I wanted to bring Dame Agatha's canon of work about him to a close with Poirot's last case, *Curtain*.

The trip to Japan brought home to me that *Agatha Christie's Poirot* had become one of Britain biggest television exports, overtaking even previous record-holders like *Inspector Morse*. Some experts claimed that more than one billion viewers had watched the series around the world, in countries as diverse as Estonia, Lithuania, Korea, Egypt, Brazil, Angola, Iceland, Mauritius, Iran, Singapore, China, and, of course, Japan; though I should say at once that I do not believe that Sheila and I had quite realised that until we were ushered regally around Japan that summer.

It was something of a shock to come back to reality in England, and then be shipped off to Tunisia in the heat of summer to make the first of a second set of two two-hour specials for the Arts & Entertainments network, this time Dame Agatha's *Murder in Mesopotamia*. The original novel was published in 1936, and was partly written while she was there with her new husband. Given her second marriage to Max Mallowan, it was hardly surprising that Dame Agatha had begun to set some of her stories around archaeological digs in the desert of the Middle East, in what was to become Iraq and Syria. Her novel was dedicated to 'my many archaeological friends'.

Directed by the Lancashire-born director Tom Clegg, who was in his sixties and had never worked on *Agatha Christie's Poirot* before, but was a veteran of the British television series *Sharpe*, it was written by Clive Exton, and once again he made one or two changes to Dame Agatha's original story. In particular, he made Hastings a part of the mystery, even though he never appeared in the original novel, and he also made Poirot rather less enamoured of the desert than he had been in the book itself, where the events were said to have taken place after he had been 'disentangling some military scandal in Syria'. In our film, Clive took another liberty with the original in making Poirot's reason for being in Baghdad an invitation from none other than the exotic and mysterious Countess Rossakoff, who had played no part whatever in Dame Agatha's original story.

One other interesting point struck me as we began filming. At the end of the original novel, Poirot leaves for Syria again, only to find himself 'mixed up' in another murder, this time on the Orient Express on his way home. Dame Agatha's famous mystery about those events was actually published two years before *Murder in Mesopotamia*, in 1934, but the link between the two is unmistakable.

Our location in Tunisia was a real archaeological dig, and the cast of extras working on the site seemed positively enormous. The murder victim is the wife of the expedition's leader, Dr Eric Leidner, who is surrounded by Dame Agatha's customary collection of idiosyncratic characters, all of whom may have had a motive for the killing his wife. Once again, there is a locked-room element to the mystery, as well as elements of 'time-shifting', one of Dame Agatha's favourite plot devices. The denouement is also one of the longest in the whole series, and may have added to the slightly slow pace of the film, but the location added a very particular glamour.

Back in London, we started on the second of the two-hour films in this eighth series, *Evil Under the Sun*. Written when Dame Agatha was working two days a week in the dispensary at University College Hospital in London, in the early days of the war, where she was known as Mrs Mallowan rather than Mrs Christie, it was published in 1941 to great acclaim. The *Times Literary Supplement* in particular applauded it, saying that 'It will take a lot of beating . . . she springs her secret like a landmine,' while the *Daily Telegraph* was even more complimentary, suggesting that Dame Agatha has 'never written anything better' and calling it 'detective story writing at its best'.

It is certainly a fine story and it did bring our film one great advantage – it was to be shot at the extraordinary Burgh Island Hotel, built by an eccentric millionaire called Archibald Nettlefold on a tiny island just off the south Devon coast, not far from Kingsbridge. It is one of the finest Art Deco hotels in England, complete with its own motorised sea-tractor to take its guests to and from the mainland. That meant that I spent a very happy few days there in September 2000, in the midst of some of the most beautiful seaside scenery in the country.

The screenwriter, Anthony Horowitz, once again took the occasional small liberty with Dame Agatha's original story. In the novel, Poirot is just taking a few days' rest from Whitehaven Mansions, but in our version, he is taken ill at a new restaurant that Captain Hastings has backed in London, partly on the basis of his experiences in Argentina, called El Ranchero. But when he and Hastings arrive at the Sandy Cove Health Resort, as we renamed the Burgh Island Hotel, the original story and our new version came together again.

The story is about a famous actress called Arlena Stuart, who is also a guest on the island. Poirot immediately fears that a murder may be committed, not least because so many of the other guests seem to dislike her intensely. 'There is evil everywhere under the sun,' Poirot says carefully when one guest remarks what a beautiful day it is on the coast, and he tries to prevent the murder, but without success. The actress's body is discovered on the beach and the denouement reveals a supremely complex plot that allows every single suspect a fine alibi.

The story had been filmed before, in 1981, by the director Guy Hamilton, and with a script by the playwright Anthony Shaffer (incidentally, the brother of Peter, writer of *Amadeus*). Peter Ustinov had played Poirot, leading a cast that included James Mason and Dame Maggie Smith, but the critics felt it was a little bland by comparison with Dame Agatha's very finest work.

I was a little uneasy. I felt that both the new films we made that summer had seen our Poirot series marking time, neither moving him on as a character. It was as if we were standing still, resting on our laurels, not trying to make each and every new film more interesting and more challenging, which had been my ambition from the very beginning. These two new films were certainly watchable, and they clearly delighted around the world, but I wondered privately if there was an element or two lacking, in particular a sense of excitement and imagination.

Perhaps that was reflected in the reception they got when they were finally broadcast by ITV in Britain. It was to be July and December 2002 before *Murder in Mesopotamia* and *Evil Under the Sun* were aired, and by then, the intensity of the initial wave of Poirot fever seemed to have ebbed. There was none of the buzz that had surrounded the arrival of the first and second series a few years earlier. Their popularity around the world may have been growing, but at home, they seemed to be gently on the wane.

CHAPTER 14

'ONE OF THE TURNING POINTS ...
A LEGACY TO DAME AGATHA'

As 2000 came to an end, I put the slight sense of unease I felt about 'treading water' as Poirot behind me, and turned in a quite different direction – to a radically different character. I made a two-hour crime drama for the BBC called *NCS: Manhunt*, in which I could hardly have been further from Poirot. I was playing a very contemporary British detective inspector in a distinctly gritty drama, complete with a poorly fitting trench coat, a bad-tempered expression, awful manners and no moustache whatever. Even worse, I always seemed to be shouting at everyone around me.

I could hardly have come further from the delicate manners of the little Belgian, but there were consolations. I was playing alongside Samantha Bond, who had played in *The Adventure of the Cheap Flat*, but who was now detective sergeant to my detective inspector in the National Crime Squad, with Kenneth Cranham as our team's target – a sociopathic murderer and kidnapper – in a two-hour film played on two consecutive nights on BBC1. In fact, I ended up playing the same part in another two-hour film a few months later, but that was just the first part of my journey away from Poirot in the new Millennium.

Not long after the first *NCS*, I found myself playing an apparently respectable headmaster who makes a terrible mistake in *Murder in Mind: Teacher*, once again for the BBC. This time, my character killed a gay man in self-defence, only to find himself encouraged to murder again by his daughter, to cover up the original killing. Interestingly, the young man who was killed was played by none other than the Scottish actor James McAvoy, who became a television star in *State of Play* and *Shameless* in Britain, and then conquered Hollywood with films like *The Last King of Scotland* and *X-Men*.

I cannot really explain why, but in the absence of Poirot, darker and darker roles seemed to be finding their way towards me, and none was darker than that of Augustus Melmotte in a four-part adaptation of Anthony Trollope's 1875 masterpiece *The Way We Live Now* for the BBC.

With a magnificent screenplay by Andrew Davies, this was costume drama at its very finest: a wonderful cast, beautiful locations, costumes and props, and memorable characters, not least the villain, my character, Melmotte. He was a sinister Jewish financier from a mysterious background, who arrived in the London of the 1870s to make his mark and his fortune. High society fell over itself to meet him, and take advantage of his money.

Melmotte was as delicious a part as Salieri had been in *Amadeus*, and I could not wait to play him, not least because he reminded me very strongly of another mysterious foreign financier who had arrived in London to charm society – though this time in the 1970s rather than a century before – the charismatic, Czechoslovakian-born Robert Maxwell.

Just as I had done at the beginning of Poirot, to prepare myself for Melmotte, I read every biography of Maxwell I could find, and I found that reading about him gave me an insight into what Melmotte might have been like and how he might have behaved in nineteenth-century London. Maxwell worked in very similar ways, which I confirmed in a meeting with Maxwell's widow, Elizabeth, who kindly gave me an even greater insight into her late husband and the way he operated.

Strangely, the more I understood about Maxwell – and Melmotte – the more I wondered if, just perhaps, there might be something of both of them in me. After all, as I admitted to one interviewer at the time, 'I'm a mixed grill of Russian, French and Jewish descent,' although I was to find out later that there was, in fact, no French in there at all. And even though some of my ancestry was partly Jewish, I turned to Christianity just two years before I started playing Poirot.

Whatever the truth about our similar origins, however, there was certainly something about them both that fascinated me, and made me all the more determined to inhabit Melmotte just as completely as I had Poirot. That feeling became even stronger when I read Trollope's own description of Melmotte in his autobiography. It reminded me just what a contemporary figure he was.

> Nevertheless, a certain class of dishonesty, dishonesty magnificent in its proportions, and climbing into high places, has become at the same time so rampant and so splendid that there seems to be reason for fearing that men and women will be taught to feel that dishonesty, if it can become splendid, will cease to be abominable.
>
> If dishonesty can live in a gorgeous palace with pictures on all its walls and gems in all its cupboards,

with marble and ivory in all its corners, and can give
Apician dinners, and get into Parliament, and deal in
millions, then dishonesty is not disgraceful, and the
man dishonest after such a fashion is not a low
scoundrel.

That was what I wanted to bring to the screen: a man who made
dishonesty acceptable, even fashionable, a man who loved to act
as the spider in a web of his own creation, to capture unsuspecting flies, render them helpless by his charm, and then devour
them. It was the most perfect challenge for a character actor. As
Christopher Howse put it in the *Daily Telegraph*, 'Melmotte is
as powerful a character as Fagin,' and I knew I could bring him
to life.

No expense was spared on the production. The budget was
rumoured to be more than £7 million, and the cast included
Matthew Macfadyen and Paloma Baeza, as well as Cheryl Campbell,
Tony Britton, Rob Brydon and Cillian Murphy, and it was largely
shot in the splendid stately home Luton Hoo, in Bedfordshire.

Then, in an extraordinary coincidence – or was it? – the first of
the four 75-minute episodes was broadcast on 11 November 2001,
the tenth anniversary of Robert Maxwell's death.

The critics certainly seemed to like it. Peter Paterson, in the *Daily
Mail*, captured that exactly when he said, '*The Way We Live Now*
looks as though it will be a big success, not only because it is well-
acted and lavishly produced. For both the title and the subject
matter parallel our own well-remembered Eighties.' In a separate
feature, the same paper called the drama 'an oasis in the desert of
today's television'. *The Times* added that it was 'pacy and funny and
beautifully acted and we should enjoy it while it is there', while the

Guardian concluded, 'This is one of the winter's first must-see dramas,' and called it 'a delicious dollop of Trollope'.

With the American television station WGBH in Boston involved in the production, it was inevitable that *The Way We Live Now* would quickly appear in the United States, and it did so on 22 April 2002, to equally good reviews. The *Boston Globe* called it 'a classic that feels current', while the *San Francisco Chronicle* described it as 'melodrama with uncommon intelligence and depth', and the *Los Angeles Daily News* added that it was 'witty, filled with intrigue and richly detailed . . . a scabrous commentary on the way it seems we will always live'.

By the time those reviews appeared, however, I had already finished another role for the BBC – a drama-documentary about the British barrister George Carman, a man arguably just as conflicted as Melmotte, with a history of alcoholism, domestic violence and gambling, as well as a glittering career in the law. *Get Carman* was broadcast in April 2002 and featured extended interviews with Carman's son, Dominic, who had recently written a book about his complex father.

What was most fascinating for me, however, was that it reconstructed some of the barrister's greatest courtroom moments, including his defence of the Liberal politician Jeremy Thorpe against a charge of conspiracy to murder, and his defence of the comedian Ken Dodd for tax fraud, which included Carman's wonderful phrase in court, 'Some accountants are comedians, but comedians are never accountants.'

Once again, I was lucky enough to have the advice of some of his family, including his third wife, Frances, who kindly wrote to me afterwards to tell me how odd it had been for her, having known him so well, to see him so well characterised.

Even without Poirot, I was suddenly in demand everywhere. No sooner was the Carman documentary broadcast, than I was on my way to play another real figure, this time the Iraqi Information Minister in 1991, in a film for the Home Box Office cable network in the United States, about the effect news can have on the prospect of war, called *Live from Baghdad*. This made-for-television film was shot just a few months before the American and British invasion of Iraq in March 2003, and could hardly have been more controversial. Directed by an Englishman living in Los Angeles, Mick Jackson, the film examined the complexities of 24-hour broadcast news in the days leading up to the first Gulf War, and asked whether news could ever help to avert a conflict.

I was appearing alongside three established film stars, Michael Keaton, who played the senior CNN producer in Iraq at the time, Robert Wiener, and Helena Bonham Carter, as another producer he meets on his arrival, while I was playing Naji al-Hadithi, a man who was by turns cynical and sinister, sharp-witted and seductive. I enjoyed it enormously. It became one of my happiest experiences filming in America, made even more memorable by the fact that during the filming, I was awarded the OBE by the Queen in her Birthday Honours list. I had not told anyone on the set about this, but on the morning of the announcement, I found my canvas chair on the set had the words 'David Suchet OBE' painted on the back. It was very sweet of them.

The next film I made was also in the United States, in the autumn of 2002, and it was my second alongside Michael Douglas, a comedy called *The In-Laws*. The film offered me a chance to get away from playing villains – well, almost. I played an emotionally insecure arms dealer who tries to sell Michael Douglas – who is an undercover CIA agent – all sorts of weapons, including a Russian submarine. I seemed to spend a lot of time wearing white trousers with matching sweaters and looking decidedly camp, not something I suspect Poirot would have approved of entirely.

Shortly after I returned to England, I was invited to Buckingham Palace for the investiture of my OBE by the Queen, which reminded me so much of the mango incident and how I had learned later that Poirot had always been one of her mother's favourite television programmes. Nine years later, I was lucky enough to be awarded a CBE, which was given to me by the Prince of Wales. By then, it had been two years since I had last played the little Belgian, and I was honestly beginning to wonder whether he would ever see the light of day again when a bombshell struck. I was on holiday back in England with Sheila, on our new narrow boat, when I got a call from Brian Eastman to tell me that something was going on about Poirot.

Brian was reticent on the phone. 'I'm not sure what's happening,' he told me. I asked if there was anything I could do, and he said no, but that he would keep in touch.

Not long afterwards, he called me again and told me that the powers that be at Chorion, who represented the Agatha Christie estate and had been partners with the Arts & Entertainment network for the last four films, wanted to make some dramatic changes to the Poirot format, changes that he feared would not involve him, in spite of all he had done to create and foster the show's success. I promised that I would do everything I could to help, but I knew in my heart that I was an actor for hire and had no real control over the direction of the series.

I was at a crossroads. I owed Brian an enormous amount for giving me the opportunity to play Poirot, and for supporting me when I insisted that I alone really understood all his foibles and idiosyncrasies. It was Agatha Christie's family, and in particular her daughter Rosalind, who had first thought of me to play the role and suggested it to Brian, who had then helped to make the series a triumph in so many countries around the world, but now I had to decide whether I wanted to go on without him at my side. It was a tremendously difficult decision, because there was also a part of me that could not bear the thought of never playing Poirot again, never fulfilling my dream of playing him in every single story that Dame Agatha wrote for him.

After a series of meetings, it transpired that Granada Television, part of ITV, wanted to go ahead with four new Poirot films, but they also wanted a far greater input into how they looked and felt than London Weekend had done in the past, when Brian had been the producer. Significantly, they were also prepared to spend many millions of pounds to make them.

There were to be two new executive producers on behalf of Granada and ITV, Michelle Buck and Damien Timmer, who had distinct ideas about how Poirot should evolve. In particular, they wanted each new Poirot to be a two-hour television special, with all the production qualities and cast of a feature film.

They did not want the almost 'family' feel of the original one-hour versions, with Hastings and Miss Lemon fussing over Poirot at Whitehaven Mansions. In fact, they did not want to force either character artificially into any of Dame Agatha's stories in future (as we had sometimes done in the past). Instead, they wanted to be as faithful as they could to the originals. Out would go the opening titles of the train and Christopher Gunning's music. Instead, each film would be a standalone drama, titled *Agatha Christie: Poirot*, and would claim its place in the television schedules on its own merit, rather than as part of a series. To put it simply, the new team, led by Michelle and Damien, wanted to make each of their Poirot films a special event on ITV.

Exactly why Brian was not to be involved is a mystery that I have never been able to solve; all I know is that Michelle and Damien invited me to tea at the Ritz Hotel in London to explain their plans. They were incredibly welcoming and extremely enthusiastic, telling me that they wanted to give Poirot a new atmosphere, as they sensed the series had become a bit formulaic, but that their brief from the estate was also to remain true to Dame Agatha's original stories and character. I was charmed, and excited, but there was still the issue of Brian at the back of my mind.

What should I do? Could I go on without him?

In the end, Sheila asked me the most sensible question of all, 'Do you want to go on playing Poirot?'

The answer, of course, was yes.

'Well then, I think you have to do it,' she said gently. 'Brian will understand.'

And he did. When I telephoned him to say that I was going ahead with the new series and the new team, he was incredibly under-standing.

'Of course you want to continue,' he told me. 'It has nothing to do with our friendship. You must do it.'

It was incredibly generous of him, but I was very upset to lose him, because we had spent fourteen years together, some of the most dramatic years of my professional life. But there were still four new films to be made. What I did not know at the time was that they would turn out to be the turning point in the relationship between Poirot and me.

In the years that have passed since then, Brian has always been very friendly whenever we have met. He and his wife, Christabel, come and see me whenever I am in a West End play, and even took me out to dinner when I was filming in Los Angeles. I am still enormously grateful to him for giving me the chance to play Poirot.

ITV officially announced the new films in November 2002, focusing on their decision to make a new version of Dame Agatha's famous Poirot mystery *Death on the Nile*, while at the same revealing that they had also taken over her Miss Marple series from the BBC.

We started work on the first of the new Poirots early in 2003, as ITV had decided that they would like to broadcast two of them at Christmas that year. The first of the films was to be *Five Little Pigs*, directed by Paul Unwin, who had directed me in *NCS: Manhunt* for the BBC. The screenplay was by a newcomer to Poirot, Kevin Elyot, who would go on to write the last Poirot film *Curtain*.

Five Little Pigs was a very different Poirot from those early days at Twickenham. The new film had a distinctly feature-film feel to it, and that was clear from the moment that we started shooting. Now there were far more shots using hand-held cameras, more elaborate exteriors, even grander props; we were certainly in the world of cinema now – even if the film was being made for television.

That was also reflected in the casting. Michelle and Damien had decided to fill each new story with well-known actors that the audience would recognise and identify with, to underline their determination to make it a television 'event'. This meant that, on *Five Little Pigs*, I found myself surrounded by Gemma Jones, famous at the BBC for playing *The Duchess of Duke Street*; Dame Diana Rigg's daughter, Rachael Stirling; Dame Maggie Smith's son, Toby Stephens; the talented Sophie Winkleman; and the hard-working and much-admired Patrick Malahide, even if only for a comparatively brief appearance as a barrister. There was no Hugh Fraser as Hastings, no Philip Jackson as Japp, nor Pauline Moran as Miss Lemon, as their characters did not appear in Dame Agatha's original. The soap-opera element of the Poirot family was definitely over.

Written in 1942 and published the following year, shortly before her daughter Rosalind gave birth to Dame Agatha's first grandchild, Mathew, *Five Little Pigs* was retitled *Murder in Retrospect* in the United States, and was the first of the Poirot stories in which he is called upon to investigate a cold case – the murder of a famous, and not always likeable, English painter named Amyas Crane, years earlier. Amyas was killed with Poison, and sixteen years after his wife Caroline was hanged for the murder, his daughter Lucy asks Poirot to reconsider the case and clear her mother's name. The British title refers to a well-known children's nursery rhyme which begins, 'This little piggy went to market, this little piggy stayed at home . . .' a passion for which Dame Agatha attributes to Poirot rather than herself, although he makes no reference to it whatever during the mystery.

Brilliantly told in a series of flashbacks, *Five Little Pigs* allows Poirot to visit the five principal suspects in the murder and to interview each of them in his own distinctive style. As Kevin Elyot has him say in the screenplay, 'My success is founded in psychology – the why of human behaviour,' and he demonstrates this superbly in one of Dame Agatha's finest and most complex mysteries. As Poirot confesses, 'Human nature has an infinite capacity to surprise.'

The strength of the cast forced me to raise my game as an actor even further, for not only was I working with some of the finest members of my profession, but the budgets had been raised once again. ITV were reported to be spending more than £2 million on each of the new films. But beyond that, my responsibility as the leading actor had expanded even further, as I had also been given a new role as the unpaid associate producer of the new films, which meant that I had more influence.

This was one of the defining moments in the history of Poirot and me, because now I was entrusted with the role of protector and guardian of my character – and was no longer simply an actor for hire playing a part. In fact, I was the only person among the cast and crew of the new series – apart from Sean, my driver – who had been in the team that had gathered at Twickenham in the summer of 1988.

This really was a whole new world, because suddenly I was involved in almost every decision that was taken about the films. Just to prove it, I was invited to a make-up meeting about my moustache. The new production team wanted to make Poirot's moustaches look more real – and if you look at my moustache in *Five Little Pigs*, you will see that it was quite different from the ones from only four years before. It is thinner, a little wider and it does not curl up towards my nostrils as it had in the past, instead it points straight out.

I was also given a whole new set of padding, which I called my 'armadillo suit', because it had layers that folded up beneath one another, which allowed me – for the first time – to wear shirt sleeves rather than a jacket all the time, and, more important, allowed me to walk with my head carried a little more forward, just like the blackbird that Dame Agatha had once briefly described in her depiction of Poirot's posture.

Now, with the added responsibility of being the associate producer of the series, I really felt as though Poirot and I were joined at the hip. I was even allowed to change Poirot's words, if I believed that he would have said something different. I was invited to 'tone meetings' before we started filming and to view see the early edited versions of all the films and offer my opinions on the way they looked to the audience. In fact, I had a creative say in almost everything we did. Even though I had no direct influence on the choice of director and cast, the team would listen to me if I had a particular idea.

I was no longer simply playing Poirot. That rapidly became clear on the set itself when we were filming, as more and more members of the crew would seek out my advice. It brought me a voice and influence that I had never had before, and I relished it, because it provoked me into committing myself more and more in front of the camera, particularly as I was now working with such fine actors. I was thrilled, for example, by the way that Toby Stephens played the scene of his breakdown towards the end of *Five Little Pigs*.

These changes were confirmed in the second two-hour film we did as part of this ninth series, *Sad Cypress*. Once again, we had a terrific cast, led by the Liverpool-born Paul McGann, part of an acting dynasty and famous for his roles in the cult film *Withnail and I* and the BBC's controversial series *The Monocled Mutineer*. There was also Diana Quick, the first female president of the Oxford Union Dramatic Society and famous for her role as Lady Julia Flyte in the 1980s television version of *Brideshead Revisited*, and Rupert Penry-Jones, who went on to make his reputation in the BBC spy series *Spooks* almost immediately after he finished filming with us.

Originally published in 1940, *Sad Cypress* took its title from Shakespeare's *Twelfth Night*: 'Come away, come away, death, and in sad cypress let me be laid . . .' Indeed, much of its focus is on the indignities of old age, but it also contains one of the few courtroom dramas in a Poirot story – one which rotates around a miscarriage of justice which Poirot tries to avert. Directed by David Moore and with a script by David Pirie, both of whom were new to Poirot, it was darker and more brooding than many of our other Poirot films, and was distinguished by another brilliant performance, this time by Elisabeth Dermot Walsh as Elinor Carlisle, the woman accused, and convicted, of murder.

Dame Agatha had reservations about the story, saying, in 1965, that it 'could have been good, but it was quite ruined by having Poirot in it. I always thought something was wrong with it, but didn't discover what until I read it again sometime after.' Fortunately, many people disagreed with her, and I felt our version of the story – though a touch gloomy at times – worked extremely well.

We filmed many of the exteriors at a Sue Ryder hospice in Surrey, which was filled with elderly ladies and gentlemen, most of whom turned out to be fans of Poirot, which meant that I was invited to visit them on the wards dressed in my costume. It was the first time I remember realising how much pleasure people got from meeting him.

I was very aware, as I went round, that most of the ladies and gentlemen living there related to me only through Poirot, so I made sure to remain in character, answering their questions as Poirot would, and keeping his walk and all his mannerisms. I was also aware that most of the residents would not be going home again, and I could not help but be reminded, as I went from bed to bed, of my own dear father's final days in a home, when he did not always remember exactly who I was when I went to visit him.

Meeting the hospice residents in full costume was a great deal easier for me then being recognised as Poirot when we were not filming – although that had its extraordinary moments. There was one particular moment that happened around this time which I will never forgot.

I was coming into London on the Tube from our house in Pinner one morning for a meeting, quietly reading and minding my own business as the Tube wound its way through Metroland and into town, when all of a sudden – quite out of the blue – someone in the carriage yelled at the top of their voice, 'It's Poirot!'

I looked up to discover that the shout had come from a nun, dressed in full habit, who was now running down the carriage towards me. She proceeded to sit down directly opposite me, squeezing herself between two other unsuspecting passengers, and then reached out, grabbed my hand and shook it vigorously, saying how pleased she was to meet me. I smiled as best I could, and nodded politely.

Things did not end there, however. The nun explained to me that she had just 'come out of silence' and could not wait to express her joy at seeing me. She then went on to tell the entire carriage, pretty much at the top of her voice, that she and the other nuns at her convent liked to watch Poirot after dark on Sunday evenings, even though the rules of the convent did not really allow them to do so.

'It is one of our forbidden secrets,' she chortled, with a broad smile on her face. 'It is quite wonderful.'

By now I was as red in the face as a beetroot, and wanted nothing more than for the carriage floor to open up and deposit me on the track beneath – anything to escape – not least because I began to feel rather as though I had become a star in a blue movie which showed every Sunday evening at the convent.

I managed to wish the nun a cheery goodbye as I stepped off the train at Baker Street and disappeared into the crowd, with my cap pulled firmly down over my eyes. But, looking back, it serves to remind me just how lucky I am to have so many different kinds of fans around the world, all of whom seemed thrilled by Poirot. I learnt recently that the series was almost the only English-language programme that was allowed on East German television before the fall of the Berlin Wall – all the others were censored. What is it that makes him so loved? It is a question that came to absorb me more and more.

Back on the set, things were rather calmer. The third film in the new series, *The Hollow*, was written at the end of the Second World War and published in 1946, becoming one of Dame Agatha's great successes, selling more than 40,000 copies in hardback in its first year, even in those times of austerity. She herself called it 'rather more of a novel than a detective story', and there is no doubt that she peopled her book with some of her most engaging characters – not least Sir Henry and Lady Angkatell, whose country house is called The Hollow.

In fact, Dame Agatha partly took the title from Alfred, Lord Tennyson's poem 'Maud', which talks about 'the dreadful hollow behind the little wood' which lies beneath a field whose 'red-ribb'd ledges drip with a silent horror of blood'. But she was also inspired by the Surrey home of the formidably double-chinned, London-born actor Francis L. Sullivan, who had played Poirot for her in the 1930s, but is probably now best remembered for playing Mr Bumble in David Lean's 1948 film of Dickens' *Oliver Twist*. Sullivan and his wife had a house in Haslemere called The Hollow and Dame Agatha's book is dedicated to them, 'with apologies for using their swimming pool as the scene of a murder'.

Once again, the new production team were determined to provide the film with actors of the highest quality, and so, to play Sir Henry Angkatell, we were lucky enough to have my dear friend from Stratford Edward Hardwicke, son of the famous English film star

Sir Cedric Hardwicke, and probably best known for playing Doctor Watson to Jeremy Brett's Sherlock Holmes for eight years in ITV's series about the famous detective.

Lady Angkatell, the catalyst in Dame Agatha's story, who invites the guests to her house party at The Hollow for the weekend, was to be played by the legendary film actress Sarah Miles, who had made her name in *Term of Trial* in 1962, alongside Laurence Olivier, and had then gone on to appear in David Lean's *Ryan's Daughter*, for which she was nominated for an Oscar. Famously unconventional, Sarah does very little television, but had been tempted to do a Poirot with me.

The Angkatells' butler, Gudgeon, was played by another film star, Edward Fox, forever remembered by me as the assassin in Fred Zinnemann's film *The Day of the Jackal*. The appearance of not one but two iconic movie stars alongside me was almost overwhelming, and I talked to Edward about filming *Jackal* whenever I could.

Meanwhile, Sarah enjoyed herself more and more as the shooting progressed, and would arrive on the set in the morning and say to me – rather embarrassingly – 'You're him. You're him reborn.' I was not quite sure what she meant until I realised that she was comparing me with Laurence Olivier.

I thought to myself, 'I should be so lucky.'

I also loved being with my old friend Edward Hardwicke. We had both been at the Royal Shakespeare Company, although at different times, and he had appeared beside me in my first major television role, in *Oppenheimer*. Between takes on the set, we would tell each other stories about the wonderful times we had had together all those years ago. It all helped to make *The Hollow* one of the most memorable Poirots for me.

Sadly, the film itself did not quite live up to the cast. Even though Nick Dear wrote a terrific script, it could not quite save it. As with *Sad Cypress*, Dame Agatha herself admitted that the story was not really a case for Poirot – and it shows. No matter how you look at it, he seems a little out of place. In her autobiography, she admitted, '*The Hollow* was a book I always thought I had ruined by the introduction of Poirot. I had got used to having Poirot in my books, and so naturally he had come into this one, but he is all wrong there. He did his stuff all right, but how much better, I kept thinking, would the book have been without him.'

In fact, when Dame Agatha came to turn her book into a play in 1951, just six years after it was first published, 'out went Poirot', as she put it herself, and in came Detective Inspector Colquhoun from Scotland Yard. She believed that Poirot would have drawn the audience's attention away from the other characters, whereas a blander policeman would focus attention on them. It would also be fair to say that she had not always enjoyed the various stage Poirots who had appeared in the first years after she created the character.

Nevertheless, I think our two-hour television version, under Simon Langton's direction, worked pretty well, and I believe it stands up now, looking back. But it certainly does not bear comparison with the fourth and final film in our new series, a reworking of one of Dame Agatha's classic stories, *Death on the Nile*. That was in a rather different class.

But the honest truth is that all four of these new films are very dear to me, and I am exceptionally proud to leave them behind as a legacy to Dame Agatha. I only wish that she had been there to see them, because I think she would have enjoyed them all, and especially our new version of *Death on the Nile*, which we shot mostly on location in Egypt, from a new script by Kevin Elyot, and directed by

Andy Wilson. She would certainly have enjoyed the fact that, for the SS *Karnak*, we used the same river-steamer that had appeared in Peter Ustinov's all-star film version of the story in 1978, starring Bette Davis, David Niven and Mia Farrow, among many others.

First published in 1937 and written during one of her many trips to Egypt with Max Mallowan in the first years after their marriage, *Death on the Nile* is one of her very finest, and most popular, stories. She herself was to say later, 'I think myself that the book is one of the best of my "foreign travel" ones. I think the central situation is intriguing and has dramatic possibilities, and the three characters, Simon, Linnet, and Jacqueline, seem to me to be real and alive.' In the eight decades that have passed since then, I doubt anyone would disagree.

Mind you, our new version may have startled Dame Agatha just a little, as it opens with a young couple making love, not something ever found in one of her novels – no matter how much that possibility might have been implied. It tells the story of a spoiled, unlikeable, rich young socialite, Linnet Ridgeway, who steals the handsome but broke Simon Doyle from her best friend Jacqueline de Bellefort, and then marries him. The couple go to Egypt for their honeymoon, only to be followed there by Jacqueline, but when they try to escape on a cruise down the Nile by boat, she follows them again. It is on the steamer that Linnet is killed and the mystery begins.

The other passengers on the cruise are among some of Dame Agatha's finest characters, including an American grande dame and her mousy companion, a lady novelist and her daughter, a fierce young socialist (who turns out to be an English peer), Linnet's shady American attorney, and a senior officer in the British Secret Service, Colonel Race, who arrives, in our version, riding a camel out of the desert, in a suitably mysterious manner.

While no match for Ustinov's cast, ours boasted some exceptional actors, including James Fox, brother of Edward, whom I had just played alongside in *The Hollow*, as Colonel Race. There was also the English actress Frances de la Tour, the American David Soul, best known for his role in the television series *Starsky and Hutch*, and the beautiful Emily Blunt as Linnet. Our new version, which we finished in the early autumn of 2003, is one of my favourites of all my Poirots. I remember the experiences as though they were yesterday, and I am very proud of it indeed.

One memory that sticks in my mind, however, is that every single member of the cast and crew were struck down at some point during the shoot with a rather severe stomach upset – everyone, that is, except Sheila and me. Sheila had come on the trip with me, as the children were no longer even teenagers. Perhaps our good health had something to do with the fact that we never ate anything that had not been cooked, not even salad or fruit, throughout our time there. But I did not escape entirely. No sooner had I finished filming and flown back to London, than I was struck with the worst form of 'Montezuma's revenge'. Unwisely, after my abstinence, I had eaten some fresh fruit salad on the plane, and that had taken its toll. Thankfully, it was my only bad memory of the shoot.

Death on the Nile also gave me an opportunity to deepen my portrait of Poirot, and underline his particular sense of vulnerability and loneliness. There is one scene, in particular, where he is standing at the stern of the steamer, looking into the falling dusk. I believe that it conveys something of the sadness and loneliness that Poirot feels because he has never had a domestic life, nor had ever been able to love a woman with such intensity.

Looking back, I think these four films were one of the turning points in the years of Poirot and me, for somehow they helped us to grow even closer, with me as his protector and guardian, and he relishing the chance to reveal more and more of himself to the watching audience. They were very important to both of us.

There is one other rather remarkable thing that occurred to me as we finished shooting that tenth series, and it is this. At home in Pinner, I discovered a picture of my grandfather on my father's side, who was always known as the best-dressed man in Cape Town, in South Africa, where he lived. Taken in about 1895, he is dressed in a brimmed hat, a three-piece suit, and he is carrying a cane. It is uncanny – you really would think it was Poirot.

CHAPTER 15

'EASILY THE WORST BOOK I EVER WROTE'

The British critics certainly seemed to like the new-style Poirot, and, true to their word, ITV made a considerable splash with the four new films, not least by broadcasting the first two in the peak viewing days of December: *Five Little Pigs* went out on Sunday, 14 December 2003, and *Sad Cypress* on Boxing Day Sunday 2003 at the prime time of nine in the evening.

The critics noticed at once that the whole series had been renewed in a very particular way. Peter Paterson captured it exactly, in the *Daily Mail*, when he commented, 'This first of a new series of four Poirot stories was slick and expensive enough to quieten those who think that ITV has been performing under par for far too long,' and he described *Five Little Pigs* as 'entertaining and classy'. It was a view that Sheila and I shared, as she was particularly impressed by it when we watched it together on that Sunday evening.

In *The Times*, Paul Hoggart was equally complimentary, and he too had caught on to the stronger production values, commenting on the strong cast and 'the intriguingly edgy quality of Kevin Elyot's script. It was visually adventurous too.'

In the *Daily Express*, Robert Gore-Langton added, 'The thing with Poirot is you can watch it with the whole family and have a sweepstake on whodunit' and went on to give me 'a lot of credit' for the show's success – kindly adding that I was 'perfect' as the detective.

Sad Cypress was every bit as well received, though I felt personally that it was not quite appropriate viewing for Boxing Day. It is a fine story, but it is also hardly a festive Christmas television treat. I worried that this might affect the audience's enjoyment, but I was in no position to do anything about the scheduling, as that was a matter for ITV. In the end, the viewing figures were very good indeed, and so I clearly need not have been concerned.

The network then gave our new version of *Death on the Nile* every bit as glamorous a scheduling, screening it on Easter Monday, 12 April 2004, again at nine in the evening. The *Daily Mail* called it 'Murder most pleasing', with Peter Paterson praising its 'excellent cast' and concluding that he thoroughly enjoyed 'this skittish production which half-guyed the Christie formula while remaining faithful to it'.

By coincidence, another British broadcaster, Channel 4, had screened the Ustinov version on the Saturday evening before ours went out on the Monday, and this caught the eye of some of the reviewers. Charlie Catchpole, in the *Daily Express*, pointed out the contrast, saying that while Channel 4 had 'wheeled out the 1978 film of Agatha Christie's classic whodunit for what seemed like the one hundredth time', ours – by comparison – was a 'sumptuous treat, which made the movie look stagey and laborious'.

To underline the three main production companies' confidence in *Death on the Nile*, they had arranged a special screening of the film at the Marché International des Films et des Programmes Pour la Télévision festival (always known as MIP in the trade) in Cannes the month after its British broadcast at Easter. The aim was to introduce the new-style Poirot to television buyers around the world, and there were very good reasons to do so.

By then, the Poirot series had sold to eighty-three countries around the world, and had been one of the bestselling British programmes internationally for nearly a decade. Granada International, which was responsible for selling the film to other countries, seized the opportunity to demonstrate to 4,000 television buyers exactly how what was now known as *Agatha Christie: Poirot* had improved, and become a television event in the process. I was only too happy to go along to support them in doing so.

The Hollow, the final film of the new series of four, was given just as good a send-off by ITV, being broadcast on Bank Holiday Monday, 30 August 2004, at nine in the evening. Yet, in spite of the excellent cast, the reviews were less overwhelming. *The Times* commented rather sadly, 'Poirot is becoming like a game of charades after dinner – you're either in the mood or you just can't be bothered to play along,' while James Watson, in the *Daily Telegraph*, added, 'Unfortunately, for all the fun along the way, nobody involved could disguise the obvious flaw: that, as Christie plots go, yesterday's was rather routine.'

That was not the view of the film's actors, however. After the filming, both Sarah Miles and Edward Fox wrote to me to say how much they had enjoyed making *The Hollow*. I was very touched, just as I was proud of the film.

But the critics' muted reaction did nothing to stem the enthusiasm for the programmes around the world, as the new series sold even more successfully than its predecessors. Suddenly everyone involved with Poirot seemed rejuvenated, and ITV rapidly decided to make another four films, which we shot during 2005.

The success of the first of the new-style series had reinvigorated me too. It now seemed possible, if not entirely certain, that I might actually be able to play in all of Dame Agatha's Poirot stories, as I had wanted for so long. I told one interviewer at the time that I would like to do it before I reached the age of sixty-five, which would be in 2011. I did not know then that it would take a couple more years before I would finally make my dream come true.

The first of the second series of Poirot under the new production team was *The Mystery of the Blue Train*, another of Dame Agatha's great set-piece mysteries, although she herself did not care for it, calling it 'easily the worst book I ever wrote', in a newspaper interview in 1966, and adding, 'I hate it.' She was being far too hard on herself and her story.

There can be no denying, however, that Dame Agatha wrote it during one of the least happy periods of her life, when she was on holiday with her daughter Rosalind in February 1927 on the Canary Islands – and that may well have coloured her opinion of her story. She was writing it in the wake of her separation from Archie and her eleven-day disappearance. Heartache must have taken its toll on her attitude. What is certain is that she did not enjoy writing it for one moment, and only did so because she had an obligation to her publisher.

But it marked a turning point in her career. As she was to explain many years later in her autobiography, 'That was the moment when I changed from an amateur to a professional. I assumed the burden of a profession, which is to write even when you don't want to, don't much like what you are writing, and aren't writing particularly well.' In fact, the book was to sell 7,000 copies in hardback in its first edition in Britain, doing just as well as her previous book had done. It was published in March 1928 in Britain, and later that same year in the United States.

The following month, Dame Agatha was granted a divorce, and almost immediately afterwards Archie married long-term mistress Nancy Neele. The two were to remain married until 1958, when Nancy died of cancer, and Archie himself died just four years later. In the wake of her divorce, Dame Agatha wanted to stop using her husband's name for her books, but her publishers in both Britain and the United States were firmly against any change, as she was already so well established. As a result, she remained Agatha Christie to her readers for the rest of her life.

For our new version of *The Mystery of the Blue Train*, Guy Andrews, the screenwriter, took a number of liberties with the details of Dame Agatha's original story, not least in adding characters that were never there in the first place, to expand the story, and moving it from the 1920s to the 1930s. Hettie Macdonald, who was new to the series, took charge of the project, to bring it a sharper, more contemporary feel.

Once again, there was to be no Hastings, Japp or Miss Lemon, but the producers gave me a spectacular cast, including Lindsay Duncan, Roger Lloyd-Pack and Nicholas Farrell from Britain, as well as a real movie star, Elliott Gould, from the United States. I was thrilled to have Elliott with us, and I discovered later that he had been dying to be in a Poirot and was delighted to be asked. The cast was so good that I had to pinch myself. Here I was, appearing with an iconic movie star, a man who was a cult in Hollywood, in a Poirot. What's more, he seemed to be enjoying himself hugely.

We filmed in Menton in the south of France, which stood in for Nice, the train's destination, as well as on a set at Shepperton in

England, which was built to the precise dimensions of the train itself, so that we could feel the claustrophobia of the carriages and the corridors. But for the exteriors of the train, we spent some time in Peterborough in England, which had some of the original carriages from the Blue Train itself, though it didn't have quite the climate of the Côte d'Azur.

In spite of Dame Agatha's dislike for the story, our version certainly remains one of my favourites. It is a little dark, but it nevertheless contains some wonderful performances, not just by Elliott Gould, but also by Lindsay Duncan and British actor Trevor Eve's talented daughter Alice. There was also a haunting musical score by Stephen McKeon to add to the atmosphere. It is one of the films I look back on today with real pleasure.

The second in the new series that we filmed in 2005 was *After the Funeral*, which had been published in the British Coronation year of 1953, and the following year in the United States – where it was called *Funerals Are Fatal*. It is another of Dame Agatha's portraits of a dysfunctional family, where everyone seems to be at each other's throats. Indeed, in this story, the relationships between the family members are so complicated that Dame Agatha thought it wise to include a complete family tree in her book, to help the reader sort out exactly who was who.

Once again, Poirot is acting alone, called in to investigate a change to the will of the wealthy Richard Abernethie, whose surviving sister remarks to her relatives at the official reading of the will, 'But he was murdered, wasn't he?' Until then, it had been assumed by everyone that he had died of natural causes. The family solicitor calls Poirot.

And, once again, the cast was wonderful. Geraldine James, who had played my character's wife in *Blott on the Landscape* and had also done the ITV thriller *Seesaw* with me, Anna Calder-Marshall, Anthony Valentine, and – perhaps the most exciting of all – a young Michael Fassbender, who was to go on to have a tremendous career in Hollywood as one of the new generation of dashing leading men, in films like *Inglourious Basterds* and Ridley Scott's *Prometheus*. Michael had also appeared with me in the BBC crime drama *NCS*.

Once again, there were a number of substantial changes from Dame Agatha's original story, and our new screenwriter, Philomena McDonagh, also took some trouble to delve even deeper into Poirot's psyche, giving me a line of dialogue which reveals his intense sense of loneliness, which we had gradually been revealing in the last series. She has Poirot say, 'The journey of life, it can be hard for those who travel alone.'

Mind you, in the original book, Dame Agatha also reveals a little more of Poirot's complex character when she has him say, 'Women are never kind, though they can sometimes be tender.' That is not the remark of a misogynist, but rather the view of a man who does not experience sexual attraction. Poirot, for me, was never in the least interested in sex, although he could recognise the symptoms of desire in others. He was sceptical about romance, with the exception, perhaps, of Countess Rossakoff and Virginie Mesnard, and a touch sentimental when it came to motherly affection, but from the waist down, he did not really exist. His life remained firmly based on his logic and his 'little grey cells', which brought him his unique powers of deduction and his acute perception of character in other people.

That is part of Dame Agatha's genius. She writes wonderful characters, and it is they who sustain the readers' or viewers' interest as the plot develops. She has total understanding for the minds of the people she writes about, and she endows Poirot with her understanding, and then allows him to demonstrate it – particularly in the denouements to her stories.

You see, I think, and it is only my view, that she started her stories from the end and worked backwards towards the beginning as she developed them. She thought of a plot, and who might have committed the crime, but then travelled back with the idea, which she worked into a story, peopling every member of her cast with individual qualities, including a motive for murder. That is why, so often, it seems as though every single character in her story could have committed the crime.

For my part, I certainly find that it helps me to work from the denouement backwards when I first read a new Poirot script. To look at it that way round establishes each individual character in my mind, and allows me to check, as we go along, that all the relevant facts that are necessary for the conclusion really do appear in the story itself. It is one reason why the denouements in the films have grown slightly longer. These are Poirot's moment of theatre, the culmination of all that has gone before, and the time when he commands the story and its characters completely. It is there that he resolves the puzzle that is the crime itself.

Since the arrival of Michele Buck and Damien Timmer, we had started filming with two cameras running simultaneously. That meant that I could deliver my explanation at the end of the film in one long speech – sometimes taking twenty minutes to do so – without ever stopping filming. The denouement was my opportunity to bring my own theatre experience to the film, because I did not need to take a break.

Not that I find learning the denouements easy. In fact, it has grown steadily harder as the years have passed, but there is no other way that I can do it except by learning it all in detail. I rely on my discipline as a stage actor – which is what I am, above and beyond even Poirot. I learn the lines myself, but there are also two people who have heard every single line of my Poirot – my driver Sean and Sheila. Just as I had for the very first series, I still practised my lines with Sean in the car on the way to the set, and Sheila and I always worked together on learning the script, and especially the denouements. She would play all the other characters for me, as I rehearsed my lines with her.

It was hard work, and sometimes we found ourselves getting up at four or five in the morning, learning lines for an hour until the car came to take me to the set. When I'd come back, at eight that evening, I would have a bowl of soup and then we would spend another hour and a half or so going over my lines again, before going to bed at ten, so that we could get up at four or five the next morning to start the process all over again.

Interestingly, in *After the Funeral*, which was directed by a newcomer to the series, Maurice Phillips, and shot in the summer of 2005, partly at Shepperton Studios and partly at Rotherfield Park in Hampshire, there were even some backstage moments in a theatre, which I thought made the story even better, because they played to Poirot's sense of the theatrical and brought into focus everything I was trying to do as an actor in the denouement.

There were also a series of other delights for me in the film. Sean, my driver, got his first ever appearance on the screen, playing the part of Poirot's driver in an echo of what we did every single morning, though he was not hearing my lines and he did not make any comment whatever – in real life he certainly does! Plus, Geraldine James was terrific to work with – again – and the cast were incredibly supportive, with Anthony Valentine giving a superb cameo performance as an Italian.

I enjoyed *After the Funeral*, but it was not as significant to me as the third film in the new series, *Cards on the Table*, which brought one of the biggest and most important changes to my life as Poirot on film: the arrival of the idiosyncratic crime writer Mrs Ariadne Oliver, played by the wonderful Zoë Wanamaker.

When Dame Agatha first started *Cards on the Table*, which was published in 1936, she had an idea for a story that would assemble four murderers and four detectives together in a single flat for two games of bridge – one for the murderers, and the other for the detectives. The ninth person in the flat, the host, who does not play bridge with either group, is sitting in a chair in the room in which the four murderers are playing, and becomes the murder victim. The question Dame Agatha posed was simple – which of the murderers committed the crime, and which of the sleuths would solve it?

Worried that her readers might not like such a straightforward plot – with just four apparent suspects – Dame Agatha explained in the foreword to her novel, 'The deduction must, therefore, be entirely psychological, but it is none the less interesting for that, because when all is said and done it is the mind of the murderer that is of supreme interest.' As so often in her stories, it is the psychology of the characters that drives the solution.

One of the four detectives is Mrs Ariadne Oliver, a crime writer who has created a Finnish detective called Sven Hjerson, and is, quite obviously, a fictional self-portrait of Dame Agatha herself. For me, she is one of Dame Agatha's most endearing characters, a view shared by her second husband, Max Mallowan, as he confirms in his memoirs.

Significantly, after twenty years of writing Poirot stories by this time, she gives Mrs Oliver a telling series of explanations about why she has become bored with her Finnish fictional detective. 'I only regret one thing,' Ariadne admits to Superintendant Battle, another of the detectives (who is actually called Wheeler in our film, though I don't know why), 'making my detective a Finn. I really don't know anything about Finns and I'm always getting letters from Finland pointing out something impossible that he's said and done.' There is very little doubt that Dame Agatha was expressing her own growing feelings of dissatisfaction with Poirot.

Dame Agatha must have liked her fictional alter ego, however, for Ariadne Oliver was to turn up regularly in Poirot stories from then on, and, in particular, in the ones that our production team wanted to film in the future. As a result, they were looking for one actress who would play her from now on, and suggested to me that they would like to cast Zoë Wanamaker in the part. I was thrilled by the idea, because Zoë and I had first joined forces on the stage in 1978, in the RSC's season, and later appeared together in the Company's iconic production of *Once in a Lifetime*, Moss Hart and George S. Kaufman's 1930 satirical comedy about the effect of talking pictures on Hollywood. (Ironically, shortly after we finished this series of Poirot, I was to reprise my role of the studio boss for a new production at the National Theatre in London.)

The Hart and Kaufman comedy was one of my happiest memories in the first years of my stage career, and Zoë and I had become very close. Of all the actresses I know, she is the one that feels most like a sister to me. We seem to act together instinctively, and I was delighted when she accepted a contract to play Mrs Oliver in all the remaining Poirot films. I knew it would be a great reunion, and that the sparks would fly whenever we appeared together.

Wonderful though it was be to be back with Zoë, there was a far bigger issue that had come to preoccupy me about the films since the new production team had taken over: the fact that Poirot did not have a home. He was now always somewhere else, never at home, and, as a result, had become far too much like so many other detectives, because he had lost his domestic life. The studio set for his old flat in Whitehaven Mansions had been dismantled, and I was beginning to feel that Poirot was increasingly adrift – especially as he no longer had Hastings, Japp and Miss Lemon.

I wanted him to have a home again, and so I asked for a meeting with Michele Buck and Damien Timmer to discuss it. To my intense relief, they both agreed with me and asked the designer, Jeff Tessler, to create one for us – which was to remain in place until *The Big Four*, in the very final series of Poirot films. When he had finished, Jeff asked me to come to the set early one morning to see it – and he was very nervous indeed, because he knew how particular I was about Poirot and everything he did.

Before Jeff and I walked into the studio to see the new flat, I paused and got into character, so that I could look at it through Poirot's eyes. I am so glad that I did, because when I walked into it, I was almost in tears. It was so perfect for Poirot. Every single tiny detail was right, from the bonsai tree that he trims, to the clock on the mantelpiece; from the square furniture with orange upholstery, in true Art Deco style, to the chrome side tables. It had exactly the precision and symmetry that he would have wanted. It meant that Poirot had his own home again.

It even had one of my own clocks in it. I am a great lover and collector of clocks, and not long after the change in production team, I spotted, in one of my favourite clock shops, a magnificent Art Deco clock, with a marble base and two columns standing beside a diamond-shaped face, and with a chrome dog standing on top of it. I knew that Poirot describes an almost exactly similar clock, though with a fox on top of it, which he would stroke and then polish away his fingerprints with his handkerchief. I bought the clock at once and donated it to the production, and it sat on the mantelpiece of his new flat.

That marvellous Art Deco clock is now in my own flat, but it was not the only similarity between Poirot's home and mine. I love barometers, and insisted that Poirot's new flat should have one – just I have several at home. The bonsai tree that Jeff put into the new flat is also now back in my own flat – and I even have the little set of gardening tools that Poirot used to look after the tiny tree. It all seems to prove that, somehow or other, I have some of the same obsessions he does.

Another part of the domestic life that I wanted to create for Poirot again was a manservant. There was no longer a Miss Lemon to look after him, but *Cards on the Table* called for him to have a valet, a man called George, who attended to his every need.

I knew the actor I wanted to play the part. Just before we had started filming, I had appeared in a revival of Terence Rattigan's 1963 play *Man and Boy*, at the Duchess Theatre in London, which was very well received. One of the other leading actors, who played my assistant Sven in the play, was David Yelland, who is exactly the same age as I am, but looks rather younger, and whose daughter Hannah had already appeared in a Poirot film, *Lord Edgware Dies*. David made his name playing the future King Edward VIII in the film *Chariots of Fire*, and I could think of no one who could play the role of George better than he would. Like Zoë, he was contracted to play the part throughout every remaining Poirot film in which George appeared.

Directed by another newcomer, Sarah Harding, and with a screenplay by Nick Dear, who had written *The Hollow*, *Cards on the*

Table also starred Honeysuckle Weeks, from the television series *Foyle's War*, and the marvellous actor Alex Jennings, who I believe could become a theatrical star to rival the late Sir John Gielgud. But it was my relationship with Zoë, and Poirot's with Ariadne, that seemed to overshadow almost everything else. We were on the screen together even before the titles appeared, and never looked back.

Cards on the Table is one of Dame Agatha's most original crimes, which our script reflected, with a denouement that is beautifully devised – even though, as she explains at the start of her novel, the murderer is one of only four suspects.

Deepening the audience's understanding of Poirot's character took another step forward in the fourth and last of this tenth series of films, *Taken at the Flood*, which was published in both Britain and the United States in 1948. Originally set in post-war Britain, where the delight of victory in Europe has been overshadowed by austerity, we decided to set it in the 1930s. But it would be fair to say that it still reflects its origins in those difficult years after the Second World War. There is a sense of sadness in it, and it takes its title from Shakespeare's *Julius Caesar*, from Brutus's speech in Act IV: 'There is a tide in the affairs of men, / Which, taken at the flood, leads on to fortune.'

The story, and our film version of it, reveals yet another of Poirot's psychological qualities: his moral beliefs, and, in particular, his Catholicism, which the screenwriter Guy Andrews brought out in his script. I had always known that Poirot's religious convictions were intensely strong, and, indeed, had added this to my list of notes on his character so many years before. He read from his prayer book and Bible every night before he went to bed with his hot chocolate, and held his rosary while he was doing so.

For me, an essential part of what made Poirot the man he was lay in his conviction that God had put him on this earth so that he could rid the world of evil. That was the raison d'être at the heart of every single one of his actions. As the films had developed, so my conviction that this was the case had grown even stronger. It was to reach its height in *Murder on the Orient Express*, in which Poirot is faced with a terrible moral dilemma, but it is also very clear in *Taken at the Flood*, where Poirot confronts his attitude to abortion and is seen praying with his rosary in his hand. It is one of the most striking moments in the film.

The production was based at Shepperton Studios, with Andy Wilson as the director, and another great cast, including Jenny Agutter, Celia Imrie and Nicholas Le Prevost. There was also Tim Woodward, son of Edward, and, of course, David Yelland as George, to look after the new Whitehaven Mansions flat. The story once again focuses on a battle over a will carried out in an English country house.

Indeed, the house in Dame Agatha's original story was based on Warmsley Heath, Archie and Dame Agatha's house near Sunningdale golf course, which did not hold the happiest of memories for her, which may help to account for some of the darkness in the story and our film. In a review of the novel, the writer Elizabeth Bowen complimented Dame Agatha by saying, 'Her gift for blending the cosy with the macabre has seldom been more evident than it is here.' It was a quality that was certainly reflected in our film.

During the filming, I was asked to contribute to one of those 'behind the scenes' documentaries, which was to appear on the DVD when it was released. I greatly enjoyed doing that, and I confessed to the interviewer that 2005 had been 'my happiest year of all' on Poirot, and I meant it. The little man and I had revealed to one another a depth and companionship that was very special indeed.

CHAPTER 16

'WHY-WHY-WHY DID I EVER INVENT THIS DETESTABLE, BOMBASTIC, TIRESOME LITTLE CREATURE!'

No sooner had I finished *Taken at the Flood*, in the autumn of 2005, the last of Dame Agatha's Poirot stories in the tenth series, than I was in rehearsals for Moss Hart and George Kaufman's great 1930s comedy *Once in a Lifetime*, at the National Theatre in London. And just as I had done twenty-six years before at the Royal Shakespeare Company, I was playing the grotesque, but hugely funny, movie-mogul Herman Glogauer. It was about as far away from Poirot as it was possible to imagine. There I was, brandishing massive cigars, wearing the loudest and most vulgar suits and swaggering all over the stage. It was tremendous fun.

In fact, the following year, 2006, was to be an interesting year for me. Immediately after I finished at the National, I made a television movie for ITV called *The Flood*, about a storm surge in the Thames that threatened to overwhelm London, alongside Robert Carlyle and Sir Tom Courtenay. Filmed in South Africa, and crammed with special effects, I was playing the Deputy Prime Minister, in charge of the crisis because the Prime Minister was out of the country – just part of a character actor's life, you might say.

But then I went on to participate in a project that truly touched my heart. I was invited to make a documentary about animals facing extinction, and was asked which one I would like to choose. There was not a moment's doubt in my mind – I wanted to make a film about the threat to the existence of giant pandas. As an animal lover, they have always held a special place in my heart, and I have always been horrified by how precarious their existence has always seemed to be. The Chinese emperors of the past considered them so magical that they kept them in their palaces to protect members of their dynasties from evil spirits.

Sadly, those days are gone. Giant pandas are now being hunted and their ability to survive is being eroded. Their black and white markings are no camouflage against hunters – because they stand out like a sore thumb against the green bamboo – and their forest habitat is being decimated, as China's population and economy expands at such a rapid rate. They also sleep for sixteen hours a day, have a terribly troubled love life and have such sorrowful eyes that I cannot resist them. ITV, who were making the documentary, suggested I visit the Wolong research centre in south-west China for a week, to find out more about them.

When I got there, it was extraordinary. The first time I saw a giant panda in China, it stood so still that I thought I was looking at a model. I got a terrible fright when it moved. Yet it looked so vulnerable, as it padded slowly along, and when it turned to look at me with its wonderful black and white clown face – which must surely have been an elaborate practical joked played by God – my heart melted. There are so few giant pandas left in the world, but it is not too late for us to prevent their extinction.

That was the message I wanted to convey in my documentary. But what also struck me while I was there was how, even in China, I could not escape Poirot. At one point, as I was filming the documentary, a group of Japanese tourists arrived to see the pandas. Suddenly, and I really do not know how, one of the group recognised me and a great shout went up: 'It's Hercule Poirot!' The pandas were forgotten, and I was surrounded by smiling Japanese tourists, terribly anxious for me to sign autographs and have my picture taken with them. It was very flattering, but a little embarrassing, as I believed the pandas were far more important – and interesting – than I was. But, yet again, it reminded me of the extraordinary affection Poirot is held in by all kinds of people from around the world.

When I got back from China, there was no sign of another Poirot series, but I was offered what was to become one of the most interesting roles in my television career so far – to play the controversial newspaper and publishing tycoon Robert Maxwell, owner of the *Daily Mirror* and a British MP, who had disappeared from his yacht off the Canary Islands in suspicious circumstances on 5 November 1991, at the age of sixty-eight. His body was later found floating in the Atlantic, an apparent suicide, as there was no evidence of foul play, though rumours abounded as to whether he had been assassinated. He was given what amounted to a state funeral in Israel, and the BBC wanted to make a documentary-drama about the final months of his life.

I had of course used 'Captain Bob' Maxwell's career as part of my inspiration to capture Augustus Melmotte in Anthony Trollope's *The Way We Live Now*, and here I was being asked to play the man himself. It was a wonderful opportunity to convey his extraordinary, serpentine charm, which was always mixed with touches of paranoia, in a script by Craig Warner called simply *Maxwell*. I relished the chance to play a robber-baron: the *real* Robert Maxwell.

There was a problem, however. I was neither as tall nor as broad as the six-foot-three, twenty-two-stone Maxwell. But I decided that I did not want to be padded up to look bigger, or to wear lifts in my shoes; I simply wanted to capture his voice. For me, that was the true entry point into his character, not his size, because his voice came from deep down within him. It was an expression of his power, his self-assurance and his incredible self-confidence – no small feat for a man who had not even owned a pair of shoes until he was nine years old. I had also been lucky enough to meet Maxwell's wife, Betty, when I was playing Melmotte, and had the greatest respect for her and the way she had coped with her husband's excesses with such dignity and grace. It was another reason to portray him as a complicated man, rather than as a caricature.

The critics seemed to like the result. The *Independent* said that 'Maxwell's lethal arbitrariness was beautifully conveyed,' while *The Times* accepted that although it 'took about a minute to forget that the real Bob was twice his weight and size . . . his voice, uncannily near Maxwell's own, occupied the space that his girth failed to'.

Immediately after filming *Maxwell*, I joined the cast of a British crime movie called *The Bank Job*, loosely based on an event in September 1971, when thieves tunnelled into the vault of a bank in Baker Street, London, and stole millions of pounds' worth of jewellery and cash from a string of safety-deposit boxes. The robbers were never caught, and the film suggested that the reason for this may have been that the boxes also contained details of police corruption, as well as evidence that a female member of the royal family had been caught up in a sex scandal. Written by Dick Clement and Ian La Frenais, creators of the unforgettable comedy *Porridge* starring Ronnie Barker for BBC television, and directed by the Australian Roger Donaldson, it was a caper from beginning to end. But it gave me the chance to play a sleazy porn baron called Lew Vogel, with some tremendous dialogue from Dick and Ian. Something must have worked, because it reached number one at the British box office when it was released in February 2008.

By the time filming was over, and just after *Maxwell* was transmitted on BBC2 on 4 May 2007, there was still no sign of any further Poirots, and so I went back to the theatre and rehearsals for a new play at the Chichester Festival Theatre in Sussex. Written by an American lawyer, Roger Crane, and called *The Last Confession*, it was a thriller about the election of Pope John Paul I in 1978, and I was playing the power-broking, though God-doubting, Cardinal Giovanni Benelli, who engineers the election of the Cardinal of Venice, Albino Luciani, to his short-lived papacy as John Paul I. He died just thirty-three days after his election, among rumours that he may have been murdered.

The company took this portrait of Vatican politics at their most Machiavellian on tour in England, visiting Plymouth, Bath, Malvern and Milton Keynes, before arriving at the Theatre Royal in London for a limited run between 28 June and 15 September 2007. Most of the national theatre critics liked David Jones's production, with *The Times* capturing precisely what I had in mind for the part. 'Suchet's Benelli is a darkly silky creature,' their critic wrote, 'rent by a mounting crisis of faith and by his guilt over his unwitting complicity in Luciani's destruction.' Meanwhile, the *Daily Telegraph* suggested that I had managed to give 'another compelling portrait of power' in the wake of my performance as Robert Maxwell.

In November 2008, I was lucky enough to win the International

Emmy Award for best performance by an actor for my portrait of Maxwell, at the thirty-sixth annual awards ceremony of the International Academy of Television Arts and Sciences in New York.

During the run of *The Last Confession*, ITV finally decided that they did indeed want to do another four Poirot films, ending with one of her best 'foreign' stories, *Appointment with Death*, set on an archaeological dig in Egypt. And so, in the early autumn of 2007, Sean and I found ourselves driving to the Poirot set again, though no longer from the house in Pinner. In March 2006, Sheila and I had decided to move back to London, to a flat by the Thames, after nearly twenty years in the suburbs. The children had grown up, and we did not need the same amount of space and quiet that we had enjoyed when they were young. Besides, we wanted to go to the theatre again, and being in London made that a lot easier.

The first of the eleventh series of Poirot films was to be Dame Agatha's *Mrs McGinty's Dead*, which was first published in America as *Blood Will Tell*. She had written the novel in 1952, the year in which her record-breaking play, *The Mousetrap*, first appeared in the West End of London, where it is running still. Indeed, she dedicated the book to Peter Saunders, who had produced her play, 'in gratitude for his kindness to authors'. Originally set in post-war Britain, describing some of the hardships that the now impoverished middle-classes had to contend with, it re-introduced Dame Agatha's fictional alter ego, the crime novelist Ariadne Oliver, who had first appeared in *Cards on the Table*.

By now, Ariadne is as fed up with her Finnish detective, Sven Hjerson, as Dame Agatha had privately become with Hercule Poirot. In her novel, she even has her fictional novelist explain, 'Fond of him? If I met that bony, gangling, vegetable-eating Finn in real life, I'd do a better murder than any I've ever invented.' I am sure that there were moments when Dame Agatha felt exactly the same way about Hercule Poirot.

In the introduction to the serialisation of *Appointment with Death* in the *Daily Mail* in 1938, for example, she had memorably remarked, 'There are moments when I have felt: "Why-why-why did I ever invent this detestable, bombastic, tiresome little creature!" . . . eternally straightening things, eternally boasting, eternally twisting his moustache and tilting his egg-shaped head . . . In moments of irritation, I point out that by a few strokes of the pen . . . I could destroy him utterly. He replies, grandiloquently: "Impossible to get rid of Poirot like that! He is much too clever."'

Dame Agatha knew only too well that she was 'beholden to him financially' – as she put it – but that did nothing to prevent her, just two years later, from writing the novel that depicted the end of Poirot's life, *Curtain*. Reportedly, Collins became aware of the story's existence but did not want Poirot killed off, and certainly she went on writing stories about him for another thirty years. Indeed, the story of his death was not published until 1975, shortly before her own death.

Given Dame Agatha's annoyance with Poirot at that time, it could be significant that when *Mrs McGinty's Dead* was turned into a film, it was renamed *Murder Most Foul*, by Metro-Goldwyn-Mayer in 1964, Hercule Poirot was eliminated completely and replaced by Miss Marple, played by Margaret Rutherford.

With Zoë Wanamaker back as Ariadne, and directed by Ashley Pearce, from a script by Nick Dear, who had written *The Hollow*, the start of filming was like returning to the Poirot family. I knew so many of the crew, from the make-up ladies to the sound men, the runners to the wardrobe mistresses. But I was determined not to allow that sense of family to prevent me from deepening still further my portrait of Poirot, as I had been doing in the past two series. As I told one interviewer at the time, 'I've discovered quite a cruel side to him, which you'll see at the end of *Mrs McGinty's Dead*.'

The brutal story of the murder of an elderly cleaning lady in the fictional village of Broadhinny, a crime for which her lodger is convicted and sentenced to death, it calls for Poirot to race against time to prove the man's innocence. It is also one of the few stories in which the little Belgian is all but killed, when someone tries to push him under a train in order to prevent him discovering the truth. The attempt provokes a fierce reaction from Poirot, and sees him lose his temper spectacularly, though without losing his natural poise.

With a splendid cast, including Sian Philips and Paul Rhys, *Mrs McGinty's Dead* also revealed something that I had not quite grasped before. I noticed that more and more of the actors appearing with me came up and talked to me about my interpretation of Poirot. They were interested in the way I playing him. I think some of that had to do with my profile in the theatre, which had grown steadily since *Oleanna* in 1994, and had been cemented since the last Poirot series.

The second film in the series, which we also filmed in the autumn of 2007, was based on what is considered by many to be one of Dame Agatha's 'finest' of the later Poirot novels. Published in 1959 in Britain and the following year in the United States, *Cat Among the Pigeons* is set in 'the best girls' boarding school in England', where Poirot is asked to present the prizes at Speech Day. The school, known as Meadowbank in the story, is said to have been based on the school that Dame Agatha's daughter Rosalind attended as a young girl, Caledonia in Bexhill, East Sussex.

The novel was set in the 1950s, but the screenwriter – actor and writer Mark Gatiss, a member of the comedy writing and performing group The League of Gentlemen, and writer for the BBC's *Doctor Who* – moved it back to the 1930s. That was always our practice in the films. From the very earliest days of the series, when Brian Eastman was the producer, it had been agreed that we would always locate the stories in the mid 1930s, to give the audience a sense of time and place which would never change.

It was one of the many reasons why the titles would always point out that our films were 'based on' Dame Agatha's original stories. That also allowed us to alter the characters in some instances, and even – though rarely – to alter the motives of one or two of the suspects. In this case, it allowed us to have Poirot there from the very beginning of the story, rather than appearing almost halfway through, as he does in the original.

Directed by James Kent, and with another great cast, led by Harriet Walter as the school's headmistress, Miss Gloria Bulstrode, it reminded me again of the status that the Poirot films had reached in the film and television industry in Britain. All the actors seemed to have a tremendous respect for the series – and reinforced the point that Michele Buck and Damien Timmer had made to me when they took over: 'We want to make films.' That was exactly what they had done.

The story of *Cat Among the Pigeons* is a touch gory – one mistress is killed with a javelin, for example. But the lasting impression that I took away from the shoot was that I was almost the only man in it. Anton Lesser did appear as Inspector Kelsey, the lead policeman, but otherwise the cast was almost entirely women. That meant that I was almost the only man in the summing up, speaking to a room crammed with ladies. It was a rather an odd experience, and not one that I had ever encountered before. The plot itself, however, was quite familiar territory for Dame Agatha, including jewels stolen from an Arab prince ousted in a revolution, a kidnapping that might not have been a kidnapping, and a possible impersonation – hence 'cat among the pigeons' – in a school in which nothing was what it seemed, and everyone had a secret.

There was then a gap in the filming, between November 2007 and the following spring, which I must say I was grateful for, as I had been so busy throughout the year. We did not start filming Poirot again until the following April, when we made *The Third Girl*, one of Dame Agatha's very last Poirot stories, published in 1966. She had designed it to be a commentary on the 'modern youth' of the 'swinging sixties', but, as ever, our screenwriter, Peter Flannery, transposed the story back to the 1930s, and it lost none of its charm or ability to captivate with its complexity.

The film brought the return of the indefatigable Ariadne Oliver, whom Dame Agatha always allowed to reflect her own views on the 'trade' of being a crime novelist. In the original story, she even has her fictional alter ego complain about publishers. 'I don't believe you know whether anything I write is good or bad,' she says, though neither lady would ever have dreamt of stopping writing for a single moment.

Directed by Dan Reed, and with a cast that included Peter Bowles, star of the famous BBC sitcom *To the Manor Born*, James Wilby and Haydn Gwynne, it was further evidence of the series' power to attract the most talented actors. The cast were absolutely terrific, but Jemima Rooper, the young actress playing the leading lady, Norma Restarick, particularly caught the eye. Her character arrives at the flat in Whitehaven Mansions and confesses that she thinks she 'might have murdered someone' to George, Poirot's manservant, and then to Poirot himself. Two years later, I was delighted to find her playing alongside me on the West End stage, in Arthur Miller's great play *All My Sons*.

The jewel in the crown of the four films in this series, however, was the one that we filmed last, *Appointment with Death*, one of Dame Agatha's most popular Poirot stories, and one which, to my great delight, was to be filmed abroad. It was always wonderful for me to go on location outside Britain; it brought me a sense of freedom, even though I knew only too well that it makes Poirot himself feel more than a little uncomfortable. He is always uncomfortable in the heat, hates getting dust on his suit, and is less than enthusiastic about sleeping in a tent. I suspect that he is never quite as much at home in foreign parts as he is in Britain, even though I knew that he travels regularly in Dame Agatha's stories, particularly to the Middle East.

Dame Agatha set her original story, published in 1938, in Petra in Jordan, but because of the political uncertainty in the Middle East, we actually filmed our archaeological dig near a ruined eighteenth-century French fortress, located in the dusty countryside about an hour's drive from the Moroccan port of El Jadida, and two hours from Casablanca. Once again, it was inspired by an expedition that she made with Max Mallowan. And this time, Dame Agatha added a splendid set of characters, led by the flamboyant Lord Boynton, who is determined to locate the head of John the Baptist, which he is convinced is to be found somewhere in the area, and has spent years trying to locate it. He has invited Poirot, who is, of course, a Catholic, to witness what he thinks will be his great triumph.

Written by Guy Andrews and directed by Ashley Pearce, who had done *Mrs McGinty's Dead* the previous year, it boasted another superb cast, including Tim Curry as the ever-emotional Lord

Boynton, Cheryl Campbell as his wife, John Hannah as a psychiatrist, Mark Gatiss, who had written *Cat Among the Pigeons* for us, and the lovely American actress Elizabeth McGovern as Dame Celia Westholme, who, according to Dame Agatha, is 'much respected and almost universally disliked', and who is often said to be based on the first British female MP, Lady Astor.

Filming was a joy. Sheila came with me, and so many of the cast seemed to enjoy themselves, in spite of the heat of the desert in May. John Hannah, who is as keen an amateur photographer as I am, tried to persuade me to switch from my Leica to a modern digital camera – without much success, I should add, as I am still using my Leica. Tim Curry also seemed to be having a wonderful time, and there was also an emotional reunion for me with another member of the cast, Paul Freeman. I remembered only too well arriving at the Gateway Theatre in Chester in England in 1969 as a young actor and being in the cast when Paul played Becket in T. S. Eliot's *Murder in the Cathedral*. I was so happy to be with him again.

Once again, Guy Andrews had gone deeper into Poirot's character, and strengthened his commitment to his faith, with a scene in which he reads his Bible, holding his rosary, and confirming his stern moral compass when he describes one character as 'an evil woman'. These essential elements had become ever more central in my own portrayal of Poirot, which had developed over the previous three series. They meant that I now played Poirot with considerably more seriousness than I had done twenty years before. There was humour in him still, but now there was an added and deeper sense of faith and conviction.

But there was also a sense, during the filming, that this might, just might, be the very last of my Poirots. I do not know where the rumours came from, but people suddenly kept asking me whether it would be, and I kept on saying that I really did not know. I did realise that this was a very expensive film to shoot, with so many characters and so many extras in the desert, and that there was some feeling within ITV that perhaps it was all costing too much to be justified in a world of much cheaper 'reality' shows. Certainly, there seemed to be a huge question mark hanging over the future – and one which was echoed at the end of the film.

The final scene of *Appointment with Death* has Poirot present a crucifix to the lovely Zoe Boyle, playing the orphaned young woman Jinny, reminding her, as he does so, that 'nothing cannot be repaired' providing one trusts in the hand of 'Almighty God'. With that, Poirot walks across the garden towards the exit of the hotel, where he is captured in silhouette. Jinny looks down at the crucifix in her hand, and when she looks up, a moment later, Poirot has disappeared.

There were many people among the cast and crew who thought they might well have seen Poirot's final moments on film at that moment, and I confess that I thought so too.

CHAPTER 17

'YOU'RE NOT GOING TO WEAR THOSE HORRIBLE HAIRNET OR MOUSTACHE-NET THINGS, ARE YOU?'

Part of me was still convinced that my Poirot had disappeared forever as the first of our latest films, *Mrs McGinty's Dead*, was broadcast by ITV on 14 September 2008. After all, I was sixty-two. It had been twenty years since we had started back at Twickenham Studios, in the summer of 1988, and this was the sixty-second film. Why should it go on?

Looking back, I could hardly believe the years of uncertainty and yet of extraordinary delight. There was no question that the British and American television audiences still seemed to be enjoying them. They had grown familiar with my little Belgian, and they seemed happy to see him again. But it was not only Britain and America. As the years had passed, many other countries had joined his fan club, with the series playing across Europe, Russia, India, Japan, China, Australia and New Zealand, not to mention Brazil, Argentina and South Africa.

One of the things that made the series so successful was that the audience seemed to love Poirot and me by now. As one of the press previews in England put it, when *Mrs McGinty's Dead* was shown, 'The great delight with Poirot is that you always know what you are going to get – a cast jammed with well-known names, high production values, and of course the inimitable Suchet as the possessor of those astonishingly efficient little grey cells.'

Not that everyone was quite so complimentary, however. One reviewer described it as 'blissful, high-camp, settle-down-on-the-sofa-with-a-bottle-of-wine-and-turn-your-brain-off-stuff', with a 'Vaseliney glow' on the lens and 'silly accents'.

I still liked Poirot a great deal, even though I was prepared to admit to one interviewer, when *Mrs McGinty* was screened, that he could be a bit of a pain. 'I find him irritating sometimes, with his unforgiving view of life and pernickety attitudes, but there you are; that's him!' I explained.

But I still desperately wanted to film the last stories and complete the entire canon. It was my greatest ambition, even though I knew that not everyone at ITV agreed with me. We had completed sixty-five of Dame Agatha's stories about him, but there were still five to go, including the story of his death. If I could reach that landmark, it would mean that I had filmed every single Poirot story. There was nothing that I wanted to do more. It would allow me to say goodbye to him properly.

Cat Among the Pigeons was transmitted on the following Sunday, and *The Third Girl* the Sunday after that, and once again, the critics were nothing if not kind, while the audiences had grown again. It was so nice to see Zoë Wanamaker, Harriet Walter and Jemima Rooper grace these three films, just as it was a joy to see David Yelland enjoying himself playing George and serving Poirot crème de menthe in the new Whitehaven Mansions flat.

But it was to be fifteen months before *Appointment with Death*, the fourth film in that eleventh series, would eventually be broadcast. ITV were very proud of it, and wanted to give it the best possible transmission date, on Christmas Day 2009, but I wondered if there was a subliminal message in their delay. Were they quietly implying that this might indeed be Poirot's final bow?

I certainly had no idea of what their intentions were, but neither was I going to sit at home worrying about it. Just before Christmas 2008, I got a telephone call out of the blue from the American actor Kevin Spacey, who had been acting as artistic director of the Old Vic for the past six years. He wanted to ask a favour – would I be prepared to step in at the very last moment to play an American lawyer called Roger Cowan in a new play called *Complicit*, by the Pulitzer-prize-winning author Joe Sutton. It explored the question of press ethics and whether reporters were prepared to cooperate with the authorities to overlook the torture of terrorist suspects.

Kevin Spacey was going to direct the play himself, and it would not be a long run, about five weeks between late January and late February 2009. There were to be only two other actors in the cast, Elizabeth McGovern, who had appeared with me in *Appointment with Death*, and the Hollywood legend Richard Dreyfuss, star of *Jaws, Close Encounters of the Third Kind* and *The Goodbye Girl*, which won him an Oscar as best actor. My part as Dreyfuss's lawyer was going to be played by another actor, but he had been forced to pull out at the last moment.

I could not resist the challenge. I wanted to work with Kevin Spacey, whom I much admired, and the play was about an interesting and important moral issue – whether investigative journalists should be forced by law to reveal their private sources. The play's hero, played by Dreyfuss, had written – in the wake of the 9/11 attacks on New York – a powerful opinion piece advocating the use of torture in the 'war on terror', but had then undergone a change of heart, in the wake of the American government's apparent disregard for international law and alleged military brutality. A government source had provided him with documents that apparently supported his new opinion, but as a result, he is summoned before an American grand jury, who want him to reveal his source. If he refuses, he risks a prison sentence.

It was a strong subject, and I enjoyed playing it, but sadly it did not seem to capture the imagination of the London audience at the Old Vic. To my delight, however, shortly after the run of *Complicit* was finished, ITV confirmed that *Appointment with Death* was certainly not going to be the last Poirot. They announced that they intended to make another four films, culminating in a new version of Dame Agatha's classic, *Murder on the Orient Express*. When Damien Timmer rang me to tell me, I had a sense of thrill and panic mixed together. The thrill was in making that wonderful story again – which I had very strong views about – but at the same time, I was worried that I would never be able to match Albert Finney's masterful performance in the 1974 film, directed by Sidney Lumet, with its glittering all-star cast. Albert was nominated for an Oscar as best actor for his performance and Ingrid Bergman won one as best supporting actress. It was a worldwide success, and spawned a further five cinema versions of Poirot stories, including *Death on the Nile*, *Evil Under the Sun* and *Appointment with Death*, although Peter Ustinov replaced Albert Finney as Poirot in all the others.

But we were not going to start with *Orient Express*; the first in what would become the twelfth series would be one of Dame

Agatha's later stories, *The Clocks*, published in Britain in 1963 and the following year in the United States. When it was first published, Maurice Richardson noted in his review in the *Observer* that it was 'Not as zestful as usual. Plenty of ingenuity about the timing, though.' Our version was going to be a little different.

Directed by Charlie Palmer, the screenplay was written by Stewart Harcourt, who made a string of changes to the original novel. In particular, in the novel, Poirot never visits the scene of the crime and never interviews any witnesses, to defend his often-made boast that a crime can be solved by use of the intellect alone. In our film, however, he interviews every suspect and witness and visits every crime scene, particularly the house in a town on the Sussex coast in which a young secretary has found a body.

Our ambition was to make it a good deal more 'zestful', and I am glad to say that I think it worked, not least because we had another terrific cast, led by Anna Massey, in what would be her very last role on television, as the elderly spinster Miss Plebmarsh. What was just as exciting for me, however, was that we also gathered together a group of excellent young actors, two of whom were the son and daughter of old colleagues in the profession.

Tom Burke, who played the leading young man, I had known since he was a baby as I knew his father David and his mother Anna Calder-Marshall. David and I had worked together in Shakespeare's *Measure for Measure* at the Edinburgh Festival, before Sheila and I had married. Jaime Winston, who played the young typist who discovers the first body, was the daughter of London-born actor Ray Winstone, whom I had worked with in a BBC production of Shakespeare's *Henry VIII*. Add the fact that the director was working with his father, Geoffrey Palmer, another old friend, and it gave me a tremendous sense of pride that the

Poirot films were attracting so many of the next generation of actors.

The Clocks underlines Piorot's patriotism in his wish to defend his new home in England against spies, and also allows him to say something which lies at the heart of what he believes: 'The world is full of good people who do bad things.' In fact, that sentiment lay behind much of what we were trying to say in these four films, and culminated in the intense moral dilemma that Poirot faces in *Murder on the Orient Express*. Significantly, Stewart Harcourt was to go on to write that screenplay after he finished *The Clocks*.

The second film we made that summer in 2009 was *Three Act Tragedy*, which had been published almost thirty years before *The Clocks*, in 1935, and had appeared as *Murder in Three Acts* in the United States the following year. When it first appeared, the critics had been generous, suggesting it led its readers a merry dance before Poirot revealed the true identity of the murderer. Originally, Dame Agatha had divided her novel into three acts: Suspicion, Certainty and Discovery, but our screenwriter, Nick Dear, did not stick to that formula for his television version. There had been a previous film version of the story in 1986, starring Peter Ustinov and Tony Curtis, and set in Acapulco, but that had no impact on anything we were trying to do now.

It was a fine script, but what I found most interesting was that I had begun to realise the effect the entire Poirot series was having on young actors. That became even clearer to me when I arrived for the first read-through of Nick's script with the cast. One young actress was so shocked to suddenly hear me speaking in Poirot's voice that she screamed out loud. She could not believe she was actually appearing in a Poirot, and it made me think that the series must have become something of a cult among the younger members of my profession. That view was confirmed by the female lead, a lovely young actress called Kimberley Nixon, whom, I quickly learnt, had been a fan of the series since she was a child, and she could hardly believe she was about to appear in one. She was almost overwhelmed by the whole experience, and turned out to be as much of an aficionado of Poirot and all his works as I was. After we had finished, I gave her a present of one of Poirot's stiff white collars with one of his bow ties around it.

Not that the senior members were not slightly affected by it as well. The producers had been lucky enough to get Martin Shaw to play the leading man, who is famous for a string of television series, starting with *The Professionals* in the 1970s, and then progressing by way of *Judge John Deed* and *Inspector George Gently*. Martin is just a year older than I am, and the irony was that – as a much younger man – I had even appeared in an episode of *The Professionals* alongside him, when he was a star and I most certainly was not. This was the first time we had acted together since then, and it was a pleasure to have him, not least because he gave a bravura performance as the stage actor and matinee idol Sir George Cartwright, who was said to have been modelled by Dame Agatha on the great 1920s actor Sir Gerald du Maurier, the first man to play Captain Hook in J. M. Barrie's *Peter Pan*. It was entirely fitting that our denouement should be filmed on the stage of a theatre.

I had been so lucky to have had such good casts, but the really important thing for me was that the writers we were using were now determined to reveal the strength of Poirot's religious faith and his moral convictions in each of our new films. In *Three Act Tragedy*, they revealed his dislike of divorce, because of his Catholicism, and yet also allowed him to accept the complexities of life, leading him to say at one point, 'I investigate, I do not judge.'

The third of the new films, *Hallowe'en Party*, was one of Dame Agatha's very last Poirot stories, published both in Britain and the United States in her eightieth year, 1969. By that time, she had begun to describe herself as a 'sausage machine', adding, 'As soon as one is made and cut off the string, I have to think of the next one.' Interestingly, she dedicated the novel to the comic writer P. G. Wodehouse, 'whose books and stories have brightened my life for so many years'. She then added, 'Also, to show my pleasure in his having been kind enough to tell me that he enjoys *my* books.'

The story was the fourth of our films to include Dame Agatha's alter ego, Ariadne Oliver, and she even allowed Poirot to pronounce his verdict on her, which might also have been a comment on the vision she had of herself. 'It is a pity she is so scatty,' he proclaims in the novel. 'And yet, she had originality of mind,' as Zoë Wanamaker amply demonstrated during the film. It begins with the death of a thirteen-year-old girl who has been telling the other guests at a Hallowe'en party that she once witnessed a murder, only to be drowned in a tub of floating apples. With an expectedly large number of deaths, it is one of Dame Agatha's darkest stories, the depth of which was brought out by Mark Gatiss. An expert in dark material, it is no surprise that he added an even darker side to Dame Agatha's original.

Directed again by Charlie Palmer, it attracted another strong cast, led by Timothy West as the local vicar and Deborah Findlay as Rowena Drake, the host of the party, as well as Amelia Bullmore and Julian Rhind-Tutt. But the actor who gave me the greatest pleasure was the extraordinary comedian and comic writer Eric Sykes, who was there to play a local solicitor. Eric and I had met several years before, when I made a documentary about the comedian Sid Field, in the wake of the play I did about him in the West End, and I was thrilled to be with him again. At this point, he was eighty-six years old, and was greeted with the most tremendous respect by his fellow members of the cast, as well as the crew. He gave a simply wonderful performance, and very generously presented me with a copy of his autobiography at the end of filming. Typically self-effacing, his inscription said, 'It's been a privilege and indeed an honour to work with a giant in the theatre, with love Eric.' In fact, the privilege and honour was entirely mine.

Yet the seriousness which had increasingly come to inhabit Poirot and me in recent years was all too apparent, in spite of Eric's insatiable appetite for comedy and good humour. This was a story about the murder of children, and there was no way Poirot could ignore or dilute that terrible fact. The denouement reflects that exactly, when he loses his temper at the group of suspects for their attitude to the crimes that have 'led this village to become a slaughterhouse'. It is an anger that positively boils within Poirot throughout the end of the story, and one which I was certainly not going to ignore.

There was another trait, however, that was also part of Poirot's make-up, the concept of 'an eye for an eye'. The theme of capital punishment runs through many of the Poirot stories, because it underlines Poirot's, attitude to murder. Throughout the novels, and the television series, there are regular hangings – as a man, or woman, pays the ultimate price for their crime. It is not something that Dame Agatha shies away from, and certainly Poirot does not either. Remember the ending of *Death on the Nile*, when it is clear that Poirot knows that the guilty parties will kill themselves rather than face the hangman – he both knows and accepts it.

To allow a killer, or killers, to go free, or at least not to face the possibility of the death penalty, is an alien concept to Poirot. Evil is there to be eradicated, and there can be no escape from the absolute necessity of retribution for a crime that sees a man, woman or child lose their life to a murderer – no matter how disgusting, avaricious, selfish or uncaring the victim may have been. Taking a life demanded that a life be taken in return, that a murderer should face the ultimate price.

The moral dilemma of whether murder can ever be justified, and whether a killer or killers should ever be allowed to go free, lies at the heart of the final film in the series that I started in the summer and autumn of 2009, arguably Dame Agatha's best-known Poirot story, *Murder on the Orient Express*. Filming began in January 2010. The notion of retribution is at the heart of what – to my mind – was one of her most disturbing stories, though that had never truly surfaced in the 1974 film. No one could ever gainsay that movie. It was simply wonderful film-making, though Dame Agatha herself had never been utterly certain about it. Most important of all, however, was the fact that there were very significant elements of her original story which were simply never covered in the film. In particular, it had never addressed Poirot's deeply held conviction that murder can never be justified, and should always be punished.

When I first heard that we were going to do a new version of the story, I read and re-read the book, to remind myself how just serious it was, and how directly it addressed the core of Poirot's faith and beliefs. After I had finished, I was more determined than ever that we should be true to the tone of the novel in our new version and bring that conviction into the script, and therefore into my performance. There are no jokes in *Murder on the Orient Express*. It is an essay in brutal murder, and I wanted to reveal that fact. It is not about a Poirot who is famous for his pernickety behaviour, or his funny hair- and moustache-net; it is a story about evil, and whether it can ever be justified.

In the original novel Dame Agatha never wrote about Poirot wearing a hairnet or a moustache-net, as he did in the original film, never gave him little sly asides, never once made him funny. Instead, she portrayed him as a man confronted by a murder most foul, but who then, in solving it, presents himself with a dilemma that racks his conscience. I remembered clearly her daughter Rosalind's words to me before I started our very first film: 'We must never, ever, laugh at him,' and she then went on, 'You're not going to wear those horrible hairnet or moustache-net things, are you? My mother never wrote about them.'

There was nothing whatever to laugh about in Dame Agatha's magnificent story, for it confronts Poirot, a committed Catholic, with a desperate dilemma, by solving a premeditated murder based in revenge, which some might be tempted to justify on the grounds that it dispensed with the life of a man who took pleasure in destroying other people for his own selfish satisfaction.

That dilemma is what I wanted to bring out, and I was delighted when the director, Philip Martin, and the screenwriter, Stewart Harcourt, who had just written *The Clocks*, arrived at my flat in London and told me that they wanted to do exactly that – to reveal Poirot's anger at the murder and his agony at what his conscience would allow him to do once he had uncovered the truth.

That is why Stewart's screenplay started by demonstrating to the audience Poirot's dark mood, with a scene in which a young British officer shoots himself in front of him, spattering his face with spots of blood, and then a brutal scene of a woman being stoned to death. This was not a comfortable country house murder-mystery, where Miss Scarlet may have committed the crime with the candlestick in the billiard room. This was a story about murder most foul, set at a time when killing led to the hangman's noose.

Written by Dame Agatha while on an archaeological dig with Max Mallowan in what is now Iraq in 1933, *Murder on the Orient Express* was published the following year. It was dedicated to her second husband, who is said to have suggested the solution. The book was retitled *Murder in the Calais Coach* for the United States, because it appeared just two years after Graham Greene's first major success, his novel *Stamboul Train*, which had been renamed *Orient Express* in the United States. The publishers were afraid there might be confusion between the two.

Dame Agatha had travelled on the Orient Express several times on her way back from archaeological sites before she wrote the novel, and when she came back in 1933, with the story all but completed, she used the opportunity to check some of the details on the train, to be sure they matched her novel. The train was part of her inspiration. In 1929, just a year after she had first travelled on it, the Orient Express was caught in a snowdrift following a blizzard in Turkey and was unable to move for six days. Two years later, in December 1931, she herself was trapped on the train for twenty-four hours, following flooding and a landslide that washed part of the track away.

The other part of Dame Agatha's inspiration was, of course, the Lindbergh kidnapping in the United States in 1932. The American aviator Charles Lindbergh, who had made the first solo crossing of the Atlantic in 1927, had his infant son kidnapped and killed just five years later, in 1932. A maid was suspected of involvement in the crime, and after being harshly interrogated by the police, committed suicide. Some of the elements of that crime lie at the very heart of *Murder on the Orient Express*.

The book was certainly well received after its publication. In the *Daily Mail*, the novelist Compton Mackenzie called it 'a capital example of its class', while Dorothy L. Sayers, no mean hand at crime fiction herself, described it as 'a murder mystery conceived and carried out on the finest classical lines' in the *Sunday Times*. Meanwhile, the *New York Times* commented, 'The great Belgian detective's guesses are more than shrewd; they are positively miraculous,' and *Time* magazine added, 'Clues abound. Alibis are frequent and unassailable. But nothing confounds the great Hercule ...'

It is another closed-room mystery, though this time one set on a stationary train trapped in a snowdrift, rather than a country house. We chose to recreate the train itself in a studio at Pinewood, to give the cast the same feeling of claustrophobia that the characters would have felt on the train itself, and I think that worked tremendously well. We also benefitted from an extraordinarily good script, and the director, Philip Martin, made the whole piece far darker and moodier than perhaps the audience had been expecting.

In particular, Philip decided to use a lot of close-ups of my face to underline the nature of the dilemma Poirot was facing, and how perturbed he was by it. Philip shot me in a way that I had never been shot before as Poirot, with so much emphasis on my face, and repeatedly told me not to rush and to go inside the character in search of how Poirot was truly feeling. As a result, it became one of the most exciting experiences with a director that I have ever had. It was challenging every single day, and it was very brave of him to do it, because from it emerged the face of a Poirot trapped in a personal agony, and that was what Philip wanted to shoot. I do not believe I smile once in the entire film; to do so would have been inappropriate to the story, to me, and I was desperate, as I always was, to serve Dame Agatha's vision in her original novel.

Once again, ITV had provided a simply wonderful cast, including Toby Jones as the victim of the crime, Dame Eileen Atkins, David

Morrissey, Sam West, Hugh Bonneville, the American actress Barbara Hershey and the recently twice-Oscar-nominated (for *The Help* and *Zero Dark Thirty*) Jessica Chastain. They all gave tremendous performances.

The miracle was that we got it done in just twenty-three shooting days, and, to this day, I am not sure quite how we did it, because there is such a lot of dialogue. Poirot's summing-up speech in the dining car is one of the longest and most difficult that I have ever had to learn and deliver, not least because he rages at those who would seek to overturn the 'rule of law' by taking matters into their own hands. It was so testing that Sheila came down with me to help me get through it, and even sat in an adjoining railway carriage during the denouement, to help me get the lines right and make sure I did not lose my way.

For me, Poirot is fighting both his Catholic faith and his moral reasoning as he confronts what should be done at the end of the story. His faith tells him firmly that man should not kill, but he also knows that the Bible instructs that man should love his neighbour and forgive their sins. He wants to please God and stay true to his belief that part of his role in life is to defeat evil wherever it may be, but that faith contradicts what his moral reasoning suggests: that sometimes people deserve to be forgiven.

The contradiction finds him trapped in confusion and anger, a most unusual place for him to find himself, and helps to account for the torment that he seems to find himself in throughout the story. I am convinced that when he returns to his compartment after the denouement, to consider exactly what he should do, he spends his time alone there not only praying for God's guidance, but also painfully aware that he may not be able to follow it.

In the end, Poirot reaches his decision, but it does not sit easily with him, and I made sure that the last time we see him in the film, he is walking away with his back to the camera, but with his rosary clearly to be seen in his hand. He is carrying the pain of going against his Catholic faith, but at the same time is conscious that sometimes there is no alternative other than to do so.

Now, I realise that the darkness of this choice means that some people who had only seen the 1974 film, and had never read Dame Agatha's original novel, might not be quite as enthusiastic about our version. Indeed, I suspect it may never be quite as popular as the earlier film, but the director, the writer and I were trying as hard as we could to stay true to the tone and depth of Dame Agatha's original, and I think it shows exactly what I always mean when I say that my role as an actor is to serve my writer.

I did not know it at the time, but it was to be more than two years before Poirot and I would be together again. In fact, I again feared, as we finished shooting, that I might never finish the entire canon of Dame Agatha's Poirot stories for television. Yet, by a strange turn of events, the next time I climbed back into his waistcoat, spats and gloves, I was to play his death in her final story of his life, *Curtain*.

CHAPTER 18

'IT IS NEVER FINISHED WITH A MURDER. JAMAIS!'

The shoot for *Murder on the Orient Express* ended in February 2010, but it was not broadcast in Britain until Christmas Day the following year, rather confirming my suspicion that I might never actually complete the last five stories Dame Agatha had written for Poirot. There was no doubt in my mind that the very best ones had been done already, and although there were four gentle and engaging stories left, there was only one jewel in the crown of what remained: *Curtain*, Poirot's final case, which had never been filmed.

In fact, most of her fans did not even know that she had written a story about Poirot's death. When I talked to people about it, they were almost all taken by surprise that she had ever allowed him to die. It was as if it were a secret that no one quite wanted to tell. The little man was so loved by almost everyone that it seemed blasphemous to suggest that he might be mortal, even though he was in his sixties when he first appeared in *The Mysterious Affair at Styles* in 1920, which meant that he would have been, at the very least, 112 when he appeared in his last full-length story, *Elephants Can Remember*, in 1972.

Our films had always kept him ageless, setting each story between 1936 and 1938, to preserve the period flavour that was so important to him and his stories, while also ensuring that his strict moral code did not seem out of place in the constantly changing world of Britain, moving from the years of austerity into the 'swinging sixties', and then on into the recession-plagued 1970s. For us, and the television audience, Poirot was stuck in his time, and all the better for it.

But I still wanted to serve Dame Agatha, complete the canon of the Poirot stories, and then portray his death. I thought that would give both the audience and me an opportunity to say goodbye to him properly, and allow me to complete a project that had been so close to my heart. So few actors ever get the chance to do that with a character that they have inhabited for so many years – any relationship you have is usually cut off without a moment's thought or hesitation.

To complete the canon of seventy films was, however, a big decision for ITV. The shoots had grown more and more expensive, with *Murder on the Orient Express* costing almost as much as a small-scale feature film, at approaching £2 million, and to commit to another five stories – including *Curtain* – could comfortably cost them more than £9 million. I knew that it was going to be a hard decision for them to make – especially as they had spent so much already over the years – but I still very much hoped that they would take it.

There was nothing I could do to influence them, however, and so I went back to work, accepting an offer to play the leading role of Joe

Keller in the American Arthur Miller's great play, set during the Second World War, about greed and the effect it can have on a family, *All My Sons*. It was a tremendously challenging part, which ended with my character committing suicide off stage at the end of every performance, which meant eight times a week, hardly the cheeriest of experiences for an actor. But I was lucky enough to have not one but two dear friends from Poirot with me, Zoë Wanamaker, who was to play my wife Kate, and Jemima Rooper, who had been with us in *The Third Girl*.

Even though *All My Sons* was one of the more gruelling nights in the theatre, a dark portrait of my character's utter lack of conscience, it turned out to be a wonderful experience. Directed by the experienced Howard Davies, just a year older than me, it seemed to work from the very beginning of rehearsals, and just got better and better after we opened in the West End at the end of May 2010.

Thankfully, the critics seemed to agree, because the opening night was greeted with a standing ovation, and the critic from the *New York Times* even reported hearing the sound of weeping coming from the audience, and when he turned to see where it was coming from, 'I saw a business-suited man the size of a line-backer, his head buried in his hands, being comforted by a petite blonde woman.'

I was lucky enough to win the What's On Stage award as best actor for my performance, while Zoë won the award for best actress.

On Boxing Day 2011, ITV finally showed *The Clocks*, which we had filmed no less than two and a half years earlier, which suggested to me that they still saw the films as television special events, and encouraged me to think that, perhaps, just perhaps, they really would commit to filming the final five stories in 2012, and finish them in 2013, twenty-five years after we had filmed *The Adventure of the Clapham Cook* at Twickenham, way back in 1988.

But still no one was quite certain, and so I accepted all sorts of offers, including playing the lawyer Jaggers in a new BBC version of Charles Dickens' *Great Expectations*. Finally, however, I went back to the theatre again, to play another of the great parts in the history of contemporary American theatre, the drunken, tight-fisted actor James Tyrone in Eugene O'Neill's masterpiece *Long Day's Journey into Night*. We started rehearsals just after Christmas 2011, and did a five-week tour of the provinces, before bringing the show into London on 2 April, for a five-month run. Like Joe Keller, Tyrone is no saint. He is a man who has driven his wife to drug abuse and his sons to alcoholism, but he represented a tremendous challenge, as the part was one of the great peaks of modern American drama.

Nothing could ever quite match the joy of my experience in *All My Sons*, and O'Neill's play is a brutal examination of a truly dysfunctional family, but I revelled in the opportunity to explore Tyrone. As the critic Michael Billington was kind enough to say, in the *Guardian*, he thought I brought out 'James's forlorn passion for his wife: when he tells her "it is you who are leaving us", his voice is filled with a sorrowful resignation that stops the heart.'

The audiences were enormously enthusiastic, but I slowly began to realise that they were certainly not all there to see Eugene O'Neill's work. After the show was over, group after group of fans from all over the world would come round to the stage door of the Apollo Theatre on Shaftesbury Avenue to see me, most of them fascinated to meet both Poirot and me.

Some of them could not speak any English at all – even though they had just sat through almost three hours of the O'Neill play.

The Russians were particularly enthusiastic. One group came over from Moscow for the weekend to see the play, even though they could not understand a single word of it, because – as they told me, in faltering English – 'We come to see Hercule Poirot.' A Japanese group said exactly the same thing, and so did a Chinese group.

In the end, we put a map of the world up on the wall inside the stage door in the theatre and started to stick pins in it to represent the countries that all the Poirot lovers had come from to see the play. By the time I finished the run, in August 2012, there were pins everywhere around the world. It was an extraordinary commentary on Poirot's success at touching the hearts of so many people.

But now, Poirot really did come back into my life again – even if it was to be for the final time. During the latter part of the run of *Long Day's Journey into Night*, ITV decided that they would indeed make the final five films, and they wanted to make them in one sequence, ending with *Curtain*, but I knew that would be utterly beyond me, and Poirot.

If you read Dame Agatha's original novel of Poirot's demise, you will see that in it, he has lost a considerable amount of weight, not just from his body but also from his face, and I wanted to show that to the audience. I needed time to lose a little weight from my face myself, and – even more important – to adjust to the idea that I was saying my final goodbye to him. That meant that I wanted to film *Curtain* first, and then leave a gap between that shoot and the filming of the final four, more conventional, stories, so that I could recover the weight. That would also give me a chance to recover my emotional equilibrium after the pain of losing him.

I was delighted when ITV agreed. They accepted that we could film *Curtain* in October and November 2012, and then go on to finish the other four stories after a break, between January and June

2013. And so it was that, in September 2012, I went for my final costume-fitting for Poirot, first for his clothes for his final *Curtain*, and then for the four films that were to follow.

My dresser helped me into the clothes I would be wearing for my final scenes. I had been living and breathing with Poirot for a quarter of a century, and I now realised that our relationship was actually coming to an end. It was bound to have an effect on me, because I had already decided that I would never make a film which was not based on Dame Agatha's work. I had no wish to play the part in Poirot films that were not based on her stories.

When I arrived at Shirburn Castle near Wallingford in Oxfordshire for the first day of shooting, driven there by Sean, it was an extraordinary, almost out-of-body, experience. The crew treated me with kid gloves, though they were almost as much in mourning for Poirot as I was. But we were in good hands. ITV had suggested that Hettie Macdonald, who had worked with me on *The Mystery of the Blue Train* back at Shepperton in the summer of 2005, might direct *Curtain*, and I was delighted with the choice. I thought she had exactly the right sort of empathy for this delicate but strong story, which sees Poirot confront one of the most evil, and audacious, murderers in his career.

The original novel was, almost certainly, written in 1940, when Dame Agatha had become truly fed up with her most famous detective, but her publishers had insisted she continue to write about him because he was so popular. By 1975, however, just a year before her death, they accepted that she was no longer capable of completing another novel, and agreed that it was time for *Curtain* to see the light of day. It was published just a few months before her death in January 1976, as if the fictional detective and his creator could not really live without one another.

It was an instant bestseller on both sides of the Atlantic, with the first hardback edition selling 120,000 copies, and the American paperback rights selling for $1 million. In the *Observer*, Dame Agatha's long-time admirer, but also stern critic, Maurice Richardson, described it as, 'One of her most highly contrived jobs, artificial as a mechanical birdcage, but an unputdownable swansong.' The *Guardian*'s critic, Matthew Coady, nominated it as his 'Book of the Year', saying, 'No crime story . . . has given me more undiluted pleasure,' and adding, paying another tribute to Dame Agatha, 'As a critic, I welcome it, as a reminder that sheer ingenuity can still amaze.'

To be honest, it may not have been her finest Poirot story, but it was certainly her most deeply felt. and the whole world seemed to be affected. No other fictional detective, for example has ever been honoured with a report of his death on the front page of the *New York Times*, written as an obituary, without the slightest sign of its tongue in its cheek, concluding: '"Nothing in his life became him quite like the leaving of it," to quote Shakespeare, whom Poirot frequently misquoted.'

In *Curtain*, Hastings goes to visit Poirot in Styles, the scene of their first encounter, and now a country guest house, where he is being looked after. Our screenwriter, Kevin Elyot, who had written the excellent script for *Death on the Nile*, carefully brought out the poignancy of their reunion. But Hastings' return also meant my final reunion with Hugh Fraser, so long my most stalwart friend throughout the early series, but who had disappeared from the films in the years after Brian Eastman had left. It was such a joy to see him back again, and there was no one that either Poirot or I would rather have spent our dying moments beside.

When we finished filming, at the end of November 2012, I

made a brief speech to the crew on the set at Pinewood, and then retired to my trailer. To see someone you have loved for so long disappear from your life is one of the most difficult things for any actor to cope with. The sense of grief and loss almost overwhelmed me for a while, but I was lucky enough to have Sheila beside me on the set in the final moments of Poirot's life, and after we had quietly packed up my things, Sean drove us home to our flat. A part of my life had gone, even though, ironically, I still had four films to finish.

It was not until the middle of January 2013 that I went back to Pinewood to film *Elephants Can Remember,* the very last Poirot novel that Dame Agatha wrote, which was published in 1972, fifty-two years after her first, *The Mysterious Affair at Styles.* It held one great consolation for me – it marked the return of Ariadne Oliver, and my dear friend Zoë Wanamaker. She, and Sheila, made the return to the 'armadillo' costume, the moustaches, the spats and the waistcoats, bearable in the wake of his death. It seemed strange to resurrect him, but that is part of an actor's life. You can find yourself doing the oddest things.

But I did wonder to myself, as I walked back onto the sound stage at Pinewood, 'Where am I?' The answer was simple: 'Right back where you started, and where you and Dame Agatha have been for the past twenty-five years.'

I also knew that this was the beginning of the final act, the last stage of my journey with Poirot. The cast which had assembled around me made it easier to deal with the knowledge that our voyage together was coming to its end. Not only was Zoë back, but there was also Iain Glen, whom I much admired, Vincent Regan and a beautiful young actress called Elsa Mollien. The script by Nick Dear was excellent, and the whole thing was beautifully shot

– very much keeping up the production standards the series had always displayed.

The story was strong, with Poirot re-examining the case of what may or may not have been a murder, committed more than twenty years earlier, after being asked to do so by the daughter of the dead couple found on a cliff-top overlooking the English Channel. It was a good film, but nothing like as challenging for me as *Curtain*.

By now, however, ITV had realised that the worldwide interest in the thirteenth and final Poirot series was growing at an extra-ordinary pace, and so they decided to respond by scheduling *Elephants Can Remember* for its first transmission on Sunday, 9 June 2013, barely three months after we had finished shooting it. There was no doubt that they were well aware – and I have to say, so was I – just how much interest there was around the world in the final five films of the series, and, most of all, in *Curtain*.

That became abundantly clear in early April 2013, when, during a break in the filming, Sheila and I were invited to the MIP television festival in Cannes for a gala in honour of the series. It turned out to be the most extraordinary event we have ever attended. There were 400 television buyers from around the world, all of them – apparently – huge fans of Poirot and the series, and all there not only to honour the sixty-five films that we had already made and had been broadcast, but also to express their enthusiasm for the final five, and especially *Curtain*.

There was a tremendous promotional video, and then a private dinner, which ended with a set of speeches, including one from me. I thanked everyone for their kindness and support for the series, and did my best to try and stay calm, which was not exactly easy, because, as Sheila and I said to each other as we left, the whole event was almost overwhelming, with all those industry professionals at the party and the dinner standing and applauding something that we had been making for twenty-five years, and which had all begun with me walking round and round my garden in Acton, trying to capture Poirot's mincing strides.

It was almost an anti-climax to find myself back at Pinewood again, to film the next in the last series, *The Big Four*, published in 1927, the year after Dame Agatha's disappearance and the collapse of her marriage to Archie Christie. She had hardly written anything since those twin dramas in her life, but she had also realised that she needed to keep up the flow of novels to satisfy her ever more enthusiastic readers. It is said to have been Archie's brother, Campbell, who came up with the idea that she did not need to write a new book until she was ready to, and suggested that she could adapt the twelve short stories that she had written for the weekly magazine the *Sketch* in the months before her disappearance. He thought, and she agreed, that they could be reassembled into one long story, and thereby transformed into a novel. Dame Agatha was only too well aware that, with Archie pressing for a divorce, and without a recognisable source of income of her own except from her writing, she needed to ensure that she made a living.

Hardly surprisingly, the novel was not among Dame Agatha's finest. It felt like something that had been cobbled together in a rush, and the four central characters were reminiscent of something her contemporary, the English thriller writer Edgar Wallace, might have come up with. After all, he had published his own thriller series, *The Four Just Men*, starting in 1905. That too had grown out of newspaper serialisations, although Wallace's four main characters were acting for good, while Dame Agatha's were certainly set upon evil.

The four were a shadowy Chinaman called Li Chang Yen, a

French femme fatale called Madame Olivier, a vulgar American multimillionaire called Abe Ryland, and a mysterious Englishman known only as 'The Destroyer'. I cannot help thinking that another part of Dame Agatha's inspiration came from the fictional Chinese villain Fu Manchu, created by the Birmingham-born novelist Arthur Henry Sarsfield Ward, always known by his pen name of Sax Rohmer, in a set of novels beginning in 1915.

In Dame Agatha's original novel, Poirot's brother, Achille, made a brief appearance, to help his only sibling, rather as Mycroft Holmes would sometimes come to the rescue of his brother Sherlock. Meanwhile, the one woman Poirot truly admired, the flamboyant Russian Countess Vera Rossakoff, also appeared in the original story, but neither she nor Achille appeared in Mark Gattis and Ian Hallard's version for our new film.

In fact, both screenwriters took a number of liberties with her original story to make the film work for a television audience in the twenty-first century. But Dame Agatha's original novel did see the return of Hastings, Miss Lemon and Chief Inspector Japp, and they did indeed feature in our version. It was a delight for us all to be back together again.

Almost as a foretaste of *Curtain*, our new version of *The Big Four* opens with Poirot's funeral, as if to prepare the audience for the fact that he would be taking his leave of them at some point in the not too distant future. Hastings, Miss Lemon and Japp are at the graveside, and then assemble back at Whitehaven Mansions, with Poirot's manservant George, to pay tribute to the man George calls 'the best of masters' and Hastings calls 'the best of men' as they raise their sherry glasses.

In fact, Poirot's 'death' is simply a device in the story, which then goes into flashback to reveal the ambitions of the so-called 'Big Four' to control the world, a desire that Poirot thwarts in Dame Agatha's original novel. In our version, their desire is rather more for 'world peace', in the face of the prospect of an impending war in Europe, but there is also a domestic element to our film. In spite of his apparent death, Poirot is not ready to leave the stage quite yet, and takes some pleasure in conducting the denouement, once again in a theatre, with the principals assembled around him, including Madame Olivier, played by my old friend Patricia Hodge, who had appeared as my wife in the BBC film about Robert Maxwell.

For *The Labours of Hercules*, which we started filming in the middle of April 2013, it was all but impossible to remain loyal to Dame Agatha's original collection of twelve delightful short stories, published in 1947, in which an old academic friend insists that Poirot will never retire, even though he is discussing his desire to give it all up and grow marrows.

In the original stories, Poirot then asks Miss Lemon to provide him with the background to the Greek myth of Hercules' twelve labours, which were imposed upon him by the King of Tiryns. As a result of her research, Poirot decides that he will complete just twelve more cases himself and then retire – although, of course, neither Dame Agatha nor her publishers ever allowed him to, no matter what she may have said in her stories.

When the collection was first published, Dame Agatha's fellow crime novelist Margery Allingham described it as every bit 'as satisfactory as its title', adding that she 'often thought that Mrs Christie was not so much the best as the only living writer of the true or classic detective story'.

The twelve 'labours' Poirot chooses in Dame Agatha's original are so diverse that Guy Andrews, who was writing the new screenplay and who had adapted so many of her stories for the television series over the years, decided to create an almost entirely new story, though using some of her characters. He based his new version around a jewel thief and murderer called Marrascaud – 'the most vicious maniac in the history of crime' – who kills a young woman whom Poirot has promised to protect, before fleeing to a hotel in the Swiss Alps, only to be trapped there in a snowstorm. To add to the mystery and stay close to the title, the whole affair pivots around the theft of a series of paintings known as 'The Labours of Hercules', by an entirely fictional Dutch painter named Hugo van Druys.

Guy's new version is enlivened by the return of the Countess Rossakoff, who had captured a portion of Poirot's heart before abandoning him to continue her career as a jewel thief in the United States, at the end of Dame Agatha's story *The Double Clue*. In fact, the Countess appears in the last of the twelve original stories, called *The Capture of Cerberus*, where she is running a London nightclub called Hell, guarded by an enormous dog. But in this new version, she is simply staying in the hotel in the Alps with her daughter Alice. Orla Brady took over the part of the Countess from Kika Markham, who had played her in *The Double Clue*, which had been broadcast no less than twenty-two years earlier. Orla was joined in the cast by actor and writer Simon Callow, now rightly famous for his one-man shows portraying the life and works of Charles Dickens.

In the best Poirot tradition, Guy gave everyone in the Swiss hotel some kind of guilty secret, which they are protecting when Poirot arrives, and the denouement is distinctly more dramatic than in some of the earlier stories. It even includes a struggle with a gun, but Andy Wilson, who directed the film and had done both *Death on the Nile* and *Taken at the Flood* in the past, made sure to keep the touch primarily light throughout, in spite of the drama of the ending. After we had finished it, I found I had enjoyed it more than

I had expected to, being so aware how very different our version was to Dame Agatha's original. Somehow, I do not think she would have objected too much to what we had done, as we had included so many of her trademark twists and turns. Indeed, it was almost as if we were now following in her footsteps, aware of her looking over our shoulders.

Then, towards the end of May 2013, came the moment that I had been preparing myself for quietly since the filming of *Curtain* at the end of 2012. We started to film our very last Poirot film, and the reality of what life might be like after the little Belgian and I finally parted became a stark reality. Not that I had much time to think about that as we began; there was so much to do, and so little time to do it in. The shooting schedule demanded that we were finished by the end of June, so that the programmes could be broadcast later in the year, and so I did not have much time to reflect as we gathered together at Pinewood again to make *Dead Man's Folly*.

Not one of Dame Agatha's Poirot masterpieces, it was published in 1956, the year she was awarded a CBE in the New Year's Honours by the new young Queen Elizabeth II – it was not until 1971 that she became a dame. *Dead Man's Folly* has many typical Poirot characteristics. There is a country house, an aristocratic family intent on bickering, some dysfunctional friends from the 'county set', and a former owner who may bear a grudge, while, to add a little piquancy, there is also the reappearance of her favourite fictional crime writer Ariadne Oliver. When it first appeared, the critic Maurice Richardson, in the *Observer*, called it 'Nowhere near a vintage Christie, but a pleasing table read.'

The story opens with Mrs Oliver invited to a country house to help organise a 'murder hunt' (instead of a 'treasure hunt') at the village fete, held in the grounds of the fictional Nasse House on the banks of the fictional River Helm in Devon. It is owned by Sir George Stubbs and his young wife, Lady Hattie. Part of Mrs Oliver's idea is to have the 'body' found in the boathouse on the edge of the river, but as she is planning what to do, she senses that something is dreadfully wrong and sends a telegram to Poirot, urging him to come down at once.

Our new version – there had been a television film made from the story in 1986, with Peter Ustinov as Poirot – was written by Nick Dear and remained absolutely true to Dame Agatha's original story. To my delight, Zoë Wanamaker was back again, to play Ariadne Oliver; it was such a treat to have her with me for this last film in the series. It was the seventieth Poirot television film I had made since that summer morning in Twickenham a quarter of a century earlier.

As we started shooting, I was not quite sure what to expect. Would the memories of the past twenty-five years ambush me every day, the ghosts of so many stories and so many characters stalk me as I climbed back into my padding and spats for the final time? I really did not know, but one thing I was certain of: I was determined to make this last film a true celebration of the whole experience of being Poirot. I knew I would mourn him when he was gone – I thought millions of other people would too – but I was not going to allow him to depart without the most joyful experience I could bring to him. This was my final chance to show just how much I loved and admired the little man.

There would even be one last chance for Poirot to reveal something of his firm moral compass. At one point, he tells the former owner of Nasse House, Mrs Folliatt, played by the Irish-born actress Sinéad Cusack – wife of actor Jeremy Irons – that she knows who the killer is but is not prepared to say so, because she thinks that would be 'wrong – even wicked'. At that point, Poirot struggles to keep his temper: 'As wicked as the killing of a fourteen-year-old girl?' he demands. When she replies that the matter is 'over and done', Poirot attacks her as fiercely as he did the passengers trapped in the Orient Express. 'It is never finished with a murder. *Jamais*!'

That was the voice of the Poirot who had grown in depth and complexity with me over the years of filming, that was the Poirot who could rage at the foolishness of people who thought they were above the law, and who thought that they could – literally – get away with murder, because they had every right to do so. That was the man whom I had always fought to protect, the man who wanted to save the world, and the innocent, from evil, the man who had grown to be so much a part of me.

The filming was particularly personal and poignant for another reason – far beyond even Poirot's character. The second most significant thing about *Dead Man's Folly*, beyond the fact that it was the last film in the series, was that the fictional Nasse House was so clearly inspired by Dame Agatha's own magnificent Georgian house, Greenway, on the banks of the River Dart in Devon, which she and Max Mallowan had bought in 1939 for £6,000. They remained there after the outbreak of war, but then it was requisitioned to be used first as a nursery for children evacuated from London, and then as accommodation for men from the United States Navy.

After they left Greenway, the Mallowans moved to London, where they remained for the remainder of the war, only returning to Greenway for the summers after the war was over. It was to become one of three houses they had, along with one in Chelsea in London – where Dame Agatha always insisted she felt it was 'easier to write' – and another in Wallingford in Berkshire. But the one she loved the most was Greenway.

So, in some strange twist of fate for Poirot and for me, we were to shoot the final sequences of *Dead Man's Folly* at Greenway itself in the last days of June 2013, sending Hercule Poirot to Dame Agatha's own home. It would be the first time that the fictional character of Poirot arrived at the home of his creator. What would it be like? How would he feel? How would I feel? I could not get the thought out of my mind.

CHAPTER 19

'BUT MOST OF ALL, TO YOU ALL, AU REVOIR AND MERCI BEAUCOUP!'

The afternoon's summer sun is glinting off the River Dart below me as I am sitting in the back of a vintage car driving towards the square white front of Greenway, Dame Agatha's three-storey Georgian house on the banks of the river in Devon. I am in full Poirot costume – black patent leather shoes, spats, three-piece suit complete with waistcoat and watch chain, light overcoat, Homburg hat, moustache and, of course, carrying Poirot's favourite silver-handled cane – when I climb out of the car and walk towards the front door.

It feels distinctly strange. For this is the first time that Poirot has ever visited the home of the woman who created him, the first time that her fictional detective has set foot in the house that she bought with her second husband Max Mallowan in 1938. Greenway is now very much the spiritual home of the woman who went on to become the biggest-selling novelist the world has ever known, with two billion books to her name.

As I put my hand out to reach for the handle, there is a moment, a single, piercing moment, when I am not truly sure who I am. Am I an actor, who has played the role of Poirot for a quarter of a century in seventy television films, or have I actually become this little man that the world, and I, love so much? Where do I stop, and where does he begin? It feels as if I am in a dream, watching me being me, and yet playing Poirot.

It is only when Tom Vaughan, the director of this very last film in the thirteenth and final series of Poirot films, shouts, 'Cut' at the top of his voice that I snap out of my reverie and back into the reality of the final five days of shooting of *Dead Man's Folly*, the last Poirot that I will ever make.

But apart from a kind of strange confusion, there also a sense of achievement, because I know how fortunate I am to have had the opportunity to play such an astonishing character over all these years, and to see him blossom so dramatically around me, to see his exploits dubbed into more than fifty languages and broadcast in almost every country around the world. It is amazing, humbling, and the greatest present that I could ever have been given.

Yet on this summer Sunday afternoon in June 2013, I also know only too well that it is the beginning of the very end. In four days' time, I will take off my armadillo padding for the final time, take the pocket watch from my waistcoat, the little silver vase from my lapel, and the moustache from my face for the last time.

But even though a part of me is sad at the thought or letting go of Poirot, there is another part of me that is enormously elated that he has finally been done justice on the screen – I have brought every one of his stories, with the exception of a tiny short story called *The Lemesurier Inheritance*, to the television audience.

I never expected it, never – certainly not when we started

shooting the first films at Twickenham Studios on 1 July 1988. By a strange coincidence, we will finish shooting the final film on 28 June 2013, almost exactly twenty-five years later to the day. It has been the most extraordinary journey, but it feels entirely appropriate to finish it by filming in the grounds of Greenway, haunting the gardens and grounds where Dame Agatha imagined Poirot for so many of her stories.

Certainly she was fascinated by him. Indeed, I have been told, though I cannot say whether it is true, that she twice reported actually having seen him alive during her life – so real was he in her imagination. He is the extraordinary gift that she passed on to me, one which I can never thank her for, because she died a dozen years before I first played him on television.

Looking out across the River Dart outside Dame Agatha's house now, I am so grateful for the opportunity, and for the assistance I have received from our team of writers over the years. Each and every one has helped me to give Poirot depth and complexity for the television audience, which has made a difference to the way in which the world views the little Belgian.

I think we have expanded on Poirot's moral faith, which takes him beyond a secular society; explored his particular sense of isolation, which sets him apart from others around him; allowed him to look wistfully at lovers, aware that they have something which has been missing from his life; brought his passion to control the world as a way of controlling his own life to the fore; and – perhaps most of important of all – allowed his intuition to reveal itself. His 'little grey cells' are important to him, of course, but his ability to intuit exceeds even their importance, for, as Poirot puts it himself, 'I listen to what you say, but I hear what you mean.'

What no one can ignore in this most beautiful part of the Devon countryside is that this is the end of an era. That feeling grows stronger and stronger among the crew on these last days of shooting. There is wistfulness in the air, even though no one else here at Greenway this week has been there since the beginning in 1988 – except for my driver Sean and me. But there is also happiness, and a sense of achievement in helping Poirot through some of his most difficult moments.

Now, finishing the final film, I know I was right to film *Dead Man's Folly* last. It is infinitely better that he should remain alive in my memory as we shoot the final scenes in the summer sunshine outside Dame Agatha's house. Filming with Poirot alive as we finish brings a feeling of exultation at his memory. That is what Poirot would have wanted, what Dame Agatha would have wanted, and that is what we have managed to do. He is alive in all our minds at the end: a man that can never truly die.

There are so many moments that stick in my mind. On the Wednesday after we arrive, for example, I speak my very last words as Poirot on film: and they are incredibly mundane.

Poirot asks Ariadne Oliver whose idea it was to hold a 'murder hunt' at the fete that is the centre of the story.

'The Warburtons', I think,' she replies.

There is no great, dramatic monologue to mark my end as Poirot. He simply says, 'The owners of this property?'

Those are my very last lines to camera.

Early that evening, I celebrate that moment privately with every member of the crew of seventy or so, from the assistant directors to the designers, from the costume and make-up ladies to the camera department, from the props boys to the sound team. I buy some bottles of Champagne and we sit in the dining tent that we have erected in the garden of Dame Agatha's house, toasting her memory and the final series.

There are strong emotions among each and every one of us as I stand beside Sean and look across at the many friends I have made over the years, not least my stand-in, Peter Hale, who has been there with me for the past fourteen years. Any series of films makes a family of the crew who help to make them, but this series has been particularly special because it marks the end for an exceptional character.

After the small party for the crew, I go inside Greenway itself for dinner in Dame Agatha's own dining room, with her grandson, Mathew Prichard, and he is kind and generous. It brings back memories for me of the lunch I had all those years ago – before I had even made my first film as Poirot – with his mother Rosalind and her husband Anthony Hicks, where they warned me that the audience must never laugh at Poirot, only with him. I think I have managed to do that. I truly hope so.

Later that night, Sheila arrives from London to spend the final day's filming with me, and we say to each other what an extraordinary journey it has been for us both. It was one which we never knew, from year to year, whether it would ever continue. We were always on tenterhooks. But when this episode finishes, it will be the first time in my life when I won't have to wait to be told whether or not we are going to be filming Poirot again. We will have finished, and I am sixty-seven. We started when I was forty-two. It is half my adult lifetime.

To say that this is going to be a relief is an understatement, because Sheila knows only too well just how much the uncertainty about whether or not there would ever be a new series cost me year after year. This final film means that the stress has slipped quietly away. There never will be another series with me playing Poirot, not after tomorrow.

Sitting quietly alone together, Sheila and I also ask each other what exactly it is that makes Poirot so special to so many millions of people around the world. After a little thought, we agree that our son-in-law, Elliott, Katherine's husband, summed it up beautifully when he explained to us not long ago that what makes Poirot so appealing, enduring and timeless as a man is that he possesses one of the finest and clearest moral compasses of any fictional character. Somehow, Elliott explains, we would all like to be him, to have his clarity and moral strength. Sheila and I agree: that lies at the very heart of his appeal.

The final day dawns bright and sunny, but with barely a breath of wind, and the still air brings a kind of languor to Greenway and its gardens. The crew have no need of me in the morning, because they are filming on the river, and so I am free to do some press interviews to support the final series. That means that Sean does not collect Sheila and me from our hotel until after eleven, and we do not get to my trailer at Greenway until just before noon. I don't have to change into my costume yet – that can wait until lunch. We just have to film two scenes of my walking down to the boathouse and then up to the house again.

In the middle of the afternoon, the camera crew come back up from the river, while I am in make-up, and begin to set up outside Greenway. They know, and so does everyone there, that this really is the end, and everyone seems intent to shake my hand and hug me to mark the occasion.

By the time I am getting into my costume late that afternoon, however, the weather has changed. There are now rain clouds in the air as I watch Sian Turner Miller, my make-up lady, stick on my moustache in the trailer, hidden away behind the walls of Greenway's great vegetable garden, complete with its own greenhouse, one that Poirot would have been proud to use for his marrows.

Then, as I walk out in front of Greenway for the final scenes, a large crowd has gathered, mostly made up of the crew, but there are also visitors and tourists who have come to admire Dame Agatha's house. Most of them had no idea that filming was going on, nor that this was Poirot's final day. They just happened upon the unit, and me.

Once again, I find myself wondering – just before the director shouts, 'Action' – whether I am Poirot or David Suchet in this most unreal of moments. But there are no tears in my eyes as I walk down towards the boathouse, nor are there any when I walk back up, open the front door of Greenway and go inside.

It is just before five o'clock on Thursday 28 June 2013 when Tom Vaughan, the director, shouts, 'Cut.'

Then, when I step outside Greenway again, there is a huge round of applause as Marcus Catlin, the first assistant director on the shoot, announces, 'Ladies and Gentlemen, that is a wrap for Poirot.' He pauses: 'After twenty-five years.'

People are clapping and crying as I walk across the front porch of the house and raise my arms aloft to thank them. Then my tears come. I cannot stop them. This is the end of something that I have lived with for half my life, the culmination of a dream that has lasted years, the pinnacle of what I had worked towards for so long.

The rain drizzles down on us, but no one minds or moves. Mathew Prichard, in a brief speech, calls it 'an historic moment' and then generously explains how sure he is that his grandmother would have approved of my Poirot. Then Michelle Buck, one of the executive producers who helped to transform the films, makes a brief speech of her own, in which she admits, 'We've pulled off something that we did not think was possible.'

Now it is my turn. But I do not speak as me. I speak in Poirot's own unmistakeable Belgian accent and thank everyone for their support, even 'David Suchet, who zinks he knows me.'

I tell the crew that Poirot is always there to help if they need him. 'You know ze telephone number. It is Trafalgar 8137.'

Then I pause: 'But most of all, to you all, *au revoir* and *merci beaucoup!*'

My mind went back to Poirot's last moments of life in *Curtain*, which we filmed all those months ago, because here I am again saying farewell to a *cher ami* for the last time.

POIROT

CHARACTER NOTES.

1. Belgian! NOT French.
2. Drinks TISANE(s) — hardly ever Tea which he calls "The English Poison." Will drink coffee — black only.
3. Has 4 lumps of sugar in tea and coffee — sometimes 3. Once or twice 5!
4. Wears pointed, tight very shiny patent leather shoes.
5. Bows a great deal — even when shaking hands.
6. Hates to fly. Makes him feel sick.
7. Hates travelling by water. Uses the "so excellent Laverguier method" to prevent sea-sickness.
8. Regards his Moustaches as a thing of perfect beauty. Uses a scented Pomade.
9. Order and method are his "Gods".
10. A man of faith and morals. Always reads his Bible. Regards himself as "Un bon Catholique."
11. A great thinker who says he has "undoubtedly the finest brain in Europe."
12. Likes neatness — can't tolerate a mess or anything disorderly. Even untidy trays.
13. Conceited professionally — but not as a person.
14. Loves his work and genuinely believes he is the best in the world and expects everyone to know him.
15. Dislikes Publicity.
16. A real "Towny." Dislikes the country and is grateful to artists who paint the countryside. "It avoids the necessity to venture therein." He feels uneasy in the country.
17. A great "Twinkler." Has very "twinkly eyes." (green !!)
18. Likes people.
19. Always wears a hat when going out into the evening air.
20. Does not like the English aristocracy or the inheritance of riches. He thinks the English are unnecessarily romantic. He is definitely NOT a romantic — or so he would like to think!
21. Will always take his Moustache grooming solid silver set with him when travelling.
22. Very particular over his appearance.

23½ Carries a "Turnip-face" pocket watch (silver).

24½ Always wears a separate collar — wing collar.

25½ Lives in London. Telephone number is TRA 8137 (Trafalgar no.)

26½ Will always stand when a lady enters or leaves a room — similarly when a lady sits down to table or gets up from table.

27½ An excellent listener. Often disconcertingly silent. Lets other people do the talking.

28½ Dislikes Marmalade — takes only Jam (confiture) for breakfast on small squares of toast. Each square being perfect.

29½ Wishes that he had married.

30½ Sometimes uses a pocket notebook.

● 31½ A PASSION for tidiness and will always straighten objects if crooked or unsymmetrical.

32½ He likes furniture, rooms, fireplaces to be square. He does not like living with rounde objects.

33½ His appearance (including hair) is always immaculate. His nails groomed and shined.

34½ Garish silk dressing gown — very resplendent.

35½ His slippers are embroidered.

36½ Will always tidy and clean his room before his valet or cleaner arrives.

37½ Will always tidy a room before anyone or guest enters.

● 38½ Smokes tiny black russian cigarettes from a cigarette case (silver).

39½ Relies on his "little grey cells."

40½ Relies on the truth within not on the senses without.

41½ Will often sit quietly — shut his eyes and just think.

42½ Will often have Boiled eggs for breakfast. If more than one then they must be the same size or he really can't eat them!

43½ Enjoys and is grateful for Hastings's inability to grasp true facts.

44½ Thinks Hastings to be a good judge of character except where women are concerned. "As I always tell to you Hastings — I see nothing."

45½ Uses and is very proud of his walking stick / cane.

46½ Will always brush his hat "tenderly" before leaving his flat.

47½ When dissatisfied, restless, frustrated or angry will make the sound of cat sneezing "Tchat."

48. Can't abide being or feeling untidy. A speck of dirt on his clothes is "as painful as a bullet wound."

49. HATES to be overdrawn at the bank.

50. He desperately tries to keep his bank balance at £ 444 – 4 s. – 4 d. Simply because of the perfect symmetry of the numbers.

51. Dislikes gambling – Thinks it is a human evil.

52. Likes inspector Japp.

53. Doesn't like hardly any other British Police or detectives.

54. Dislikes "ill manners."

55. Doesn't like the English "reserve." Thinks the English are mad.

56. After putting a log on the fire – will always wipe his hands on a small duster placed on a nail next to the fireplace. Prefers to use old gloves, though, for the purpose.

57. Used to head the Belgian detective force.

58. Will occasionally though not often use disguise. But only if necessary.

59. Has a most charming geniality but can also be as cold as ice.

60. His piercing eyes sees right into the heart of a person. No one can lie to him and get away with it. A wonderful listener.

61. Very good with servants and working classes. Never patronises them.

62. HATES the English Class system.

63. Always carries his professional card.

64. Sees himself as a "specialist" professional detective. Likens himself to a Harley Street specialist.

65. Will usually wear a morning suit when working at home – like a Harley Street specialist.

66. A kind man – not stingy at all. Very wealthy.

67. Once fell in love with an English girl who used to cook him fluffy omelettes.

68. Nearly always will drink "Sirop de cassis" as an aperitif or an after dinner drink.

69. Loves good food and wine.

70. In the short story "The Dream" p.146 – he replaced his pocket watch for his wrist watch.

71. His taste in art is somewhat bourgeois. Likes the opulent and the florid.

72. Always brushes his coat before venturing outside. A clothes brush is nearby.

the coatstand.

73. He will never explain until the end. "It is not my habit to explain until the end — it is reached."

74. Meticulous and very concentrated with everything he does.

75. Women find him very sympathetic — "A dear little Man" says Cynthia in "Mysterious affair at Styles."

76. If he sees a matchstick on a flower bed — he will bury it !!

77. Rarely shows his emotions and yet dislikes the English reserve. Sometimes though with his arms raised he will utter "Oh là là.".

78. Often shrugs and emits the sound "Porph."

79. Never or very rarely says "Non Dieu!" But often will exclaim "Sacré." "Milles Tonnerres!"

80. Will utter "CHUT!" instead of "Sst."

81. Has little regard for imagination. — "Imagination is a good servant and a bad master. The 'Facts Hastings — the facts."

82. Hastings says of him "For about ten minutes he would sit in deadly silence, perfectly still except for several expressive motions of his eyebrows. His eyes closed. Suddenly a heave, a sigh of relief — his eyes would open glowing a bright green — he would then smile and then it was over."

83. He enjoys his "little ideas." — this became a catchword.

84. He often often straightens Hastings tie. He will remove a ladies brooch and replace it because it was put in crooked (M. Affair at Styles —Cynthia p.130).

85. When he hasn't got his lighter, will light his small Russian cigarettes with a match which he will then place in a small pottery pot.

86. Cynthia from M. Affair at Styles says. "He's such a dear little man! But he is funny!

87. Hastings: "Sometimes I feel sure he is as mad as a hatter; and then just as he is at his maddest, I find there is method in his madness.

88. Likes to build Houses of cards.
    "Non, mon ami, I am not in my second childhood. I steady my nerves that is all. This employment requires precision of the fingers. With precision of the fingers goes precision of the brain.

89. Genuinely believes that the happiness of one man and one woman is the greatest thing in all the world.

90. "In the little grey cells of the brain lies the solution of every mystery."
91. Always drinks a hot chocolate before going to sleep.
92. Dislikes Golf.
93. Will wipe dirty seats or benches with his handkerchief before sitting down. Similarly when

kneeling on floor

Then, of course there is the definitive self-description in his letter

to M. Dodd. in which there are other characteristics.

ACKNOWLEDGEMENTS

Playing Hercule Poirot for a quarter of a century would not have been possible for me without the help of many, many people, all of whom I owe my most grateful thanks. The television executives, directors, producers, writers, production teams all helped to make it an unforgettable experience. To all the teams over all the shows, to the costume designers, costumiers, tailors, dressers, personal make-up artists, set designers and the art directors, who made the production values of Poirot so special, let me say at once, I could not have done it without you, thank you all so much.

I must also thank all the extraordinary and talented actors and actresses who have appeared alongside me and supported me throughout the years, especially Hugh Fraser, Philip Jackson and Pauline Moran – the central members of the Poirot family at the very beginning and for so many episodes thereafter. I cannot thank them enough.

But there are another special group whom I really must thank individually for their contribution to making the programmes with me. The first among those are the late Rosalind Hicks, Dame Agatha's daughter, and her husband, the late Anthony Hicks, who believed that I was capable of bringing Poirot to life for an audience around the world, a view that was reinforced by their son Mathew Prichard. I could not have created and sustained Poirot without their help.

Then there is Brian Eastman, who first approached me about playing the role in 1988 and produced the series through its formative years with the greatest skill and determination. I owe a similar debt to Michelle Buck, Damien Timmer and Karen Thrussell, the executive producers who took over the series and saw it to its conclusion in 2013. *Poirot* would not have become the worldwide phenomenon that it has without them.

My final word of thanks to the television executives, however, must go the Peter Fincham, the director of programmes at ITV, who promised me that all the Poirot stories would indeed be filmed, and he was true to his word. I cannot thank him enough.

As for this book, there are a host of people who have contributed to it, not least my dear friend Geoffrey Wansell who help me to write it. Also Michael Alcock at the literary agency Johnson and Alcock, who believed in it and introduced me to the team at Headline, led by editor Emma Tait. There was also Siobhan Hooper, who designed the jacket, James Eckersley, who took the cover photographs, Holly Harris, Laura Esslemont in production, Juliana Foster, the indefatigable copy editor, and Fiona Andreanelli who designed the picture sections. Last, but by no means least, I also have to thank Samantha Eades for her publicity guidance and Jo Liddiard for her marketing skill.

No one of them should be held accountable for my opinions, however, those are mine alone, but, most of all, I am grateful to the thousands of fans from around the world who have written to me over the years telling me how much Poirot has come to mean to them. Each and every one of their letters has warmed my heart, and I hope this book explains how much he meant to me as well.

David Suchet, London, August 2013

INDEX